QUESTIONS &
ANSWERS

Criminal Law

QUESTIONS & ANSWERS SERIES

Company Law

Constitutional and Administrative Law

Conveyancing

Criminal Law

EC Law

Employment Law

English Legal System

Equity and Trusts

Evidence

Family Law

Land Law

Landlord and Tenant

Law of Contract

Law of Torts

Other titles in preparation

QUESTIONS & ANSWERS

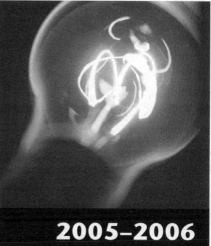

2005–2006

Criminal Law

FOURTH EDITION

Geoff Douglas

LLM, Solicitor
Previously Lecturer in Law, University of the West of England, Bristol

Mike Molan

Professor of Legal Education, Pro Dean, Faculty of Arts and Human Sciences,
London South Bank University

OXFORD
UNIVERSITY PRESS

OXFORD
UNIVERSITY PRESS

Great Clarendon Street, Oxford OX2 6DP

Oxford University Press is a department of the University of Oxford.
It furthers the University's objective of excellence in research, scholarship,
and education by publishing worldwide in

Oxford New York

Auckland Cape Town Dar es Salaam Hong Kong Karachi
Kuala Lumpur Madrid Melbourne Mexico City Nairobi
New Delhi Shanghai Taipei Toronto

With offices in

Argentina Austria Brazil Chile Czech Republic France Greece
Guatemala Hungary Italy Japan South Korea Poland Portugal
Singapore Switzerland Thailand Turkey Ukraine Vietnam

Oxford is a registered trade mark of Oxford University Press
in the UK and in certain other countries

Published in the United States
by Oxford University Press Inc., New York

A Blackstone Press book

© Geoff Douglas, Mike Molan 2005

The moral rights of the author have been asserted
Database right Oxford University Press (maker)

First published 1999
Second edition 2001
Third edition 2003
Fourth edition 2005

British Library Cataloguing in Publication Data
Data available

Library of Congress Cataloging in Publication Data
Data available

ISBN-13: 978–0–19–927802–2
ISBN-10: 0–19–927802–4

3 5 7 9 10 8 6 4 2

Typeset by Re neCatch Limited, Bungay, Suffolk
Printed in Great Britain by
Ashford Colour Press, Gosport, Hampshire

Contents

The Q&A Series

Key features

The Q&A series provides full coverage of key subjects in a clear and logical way. This new edition contains the following features:

- Question
- Commentary
- Bullet point list
- Suggested answer
- Further reading
- Diagrams

Preface

In preparing this fourth edition of the Q & A in Criminal Law I have been fortunate to be able to build upon the firm foundations laid in previous editions by the late Geoff Douglas, who died in October 2002. The new edition strives to retain the strengths found in his earlier editions, particularly the clear and logical exposition of difficult issues, and the selection of materials that provide students with a sound preparation for criminal law assessments.

Although there are substantial revisions to many chapters, not least to reflect recent changes in the law relating to sexual offences, and the abandonment of '*Caldwell* recklessness', the principal aim of the book remains unchanged. It is designed to help students who have a good basic knowledge of the criminal law to maximise their potential by adopting appropriate styles and structures for their answers.

There is, of course, no such thing as a model answer. What this text provides is examples of suggested solutions. So often good candidates fare badly simply because they have not mastered the techniques of adopting a logical structure and providing a concise analysis of the legal issues arising.

Whilst the answers in the text are meant to provide the reader with a framework that can be used to tackle criminal law assessments, it must be borne in mind that any answer submitted for assessment on a criminal law course must be the student's own work. In short, emulate the style, but make the content your own!

In preparing this edition I would like to acknowledge the contribution made by students I have taught over the years to my understanding of their difficulties in dealing with criminal law assessments, and the comments of colleagues on drafts of the questions used.

As ever my thanks and love to Alison, Grace, Joy and Miles for their forbearance whilst I was busy with this text.

Mike Molan
London South Bank University
June 2004

Table of Cases

Table of Statutes

Introduction: exam technique

Many students mistakenly believe that techniques required to succeed in examinations are totally distinct from what they have learnt throughout the year-long course. This is not the case; although certain techniques may need to be modified for exam purposes, a student will be well served by following the skills and disciplines that have been acquired during the course.

It is therefore very important to acquire good habits as early in the course as possible. When a problem or essay question is set for discussion in lectures or seminars, you should treat it as a possible exam question, but with the luxury that you are not under the pressure of the examination room. You will therefore have much longer to prepare, research and consider your answer; but when this has been done, you will obtain the maximum future benefit if you tackle it in the same way as an examination question. In this way you will acquire good habits, which may need only minor modification in the examination.

The plan

Stage 1 is to plan your answer. For problem questions, identify the issues raised and make a list of all the offences you must consider, writing down the *actus reus* and *mens rea* of each offence. Then briefly note the relevant defences that may be available, and add the case names that you may be using as authority or discussing in detail. Then re-read the question and check your list to ensure that you have not missed anything. You are now in a position to put your list into logical order — in other words an organised plan — in which you can identify those issues which need to be discussed in detail and those which can be referred to briefly; which cases should be used to illustrate your points and which ones you will briefly quote as authority for a principle.

Lastly, still at the planning stage, you should consider your conclusion. More is said regarding the conclusion later, but the advantage of considering a conclusion at this stage is that it helps to crystallise your thoughts and identify any errors in your plan; and, possibly more importantly, it does give you confidence when you start to write your answer, because you know what conclusion you are working towards.

Answer the problem

Give more space to the more important points. If the problem raises various possibilities, start with the most serious or the most obvious.

It generally makes sense to deal with the *actus reus* of an offence before dealing with the *mens rea*. When these issues have been dealt with consider any defences.

Is there doubt about liability? If so, may a lesser offence be proved? Here again, deal with the relevant considerations for liability.

The basic point is to answer the question set — apply the law to the facts given. Take the facts as stated in the problem as conclusive — you must examine the facts as proved. Sometimes the facts are deliberately vague, e.g., what exactly was D's state of mind when he killed V? If this is the case, you may have to discuss murder, manslaughter and accident. Do not be afraid in some circumstances to fail to reach a rock solid conclusion. It may be perfectly acceptable — indeed highly appropriate — to say, for instance: 'If . . . then he may be liable for murder, if . . . then he may be liable for manslaughter'. Identifying unclear areas is a skill in itself, where either the facts or the law itself are unclear. What you are effectively required to do in many problem questions is argue in the alternative. For example, if the harm done to the victim amounts to a wound, then the answer is . . .

On the other hand if the harm is held not to amount to a wound the alternative lesser offences may be . . .

You may have a problem which involves the potential liability of several parties. If this is the case, there is no need, for instance, to reiterate the ingredients of say, murder. There may, however, be differences which must be noted e.g., one party being under 10, one being an accomplice rather than a principal offender. It often helps to discuss the parties in order of their appearance in the problem.

Your statements of law should be backed up by reference to authorities, statute or case law. You may also refer to relevant articles and textbook theories, and draw an analogy or use hypothetical examples.

The question may say 'discuss'. This will require discussion of all the possibilities raised by the facts, all offences, all parties and any possible defences. Alternatively, you may be asked to 'advise A' or 'discuss the criminal liability of D'. Your answer clearly will have to be tailored to suit. Often the rubric will provide gateways — e.g., it will ask you to advise on the liability of A for theft and the liability of B for criminal damage. It is never wise to ignore these pointers and provide advice on other offences. Irrelevant material, however well researched or presented, will gain no marks but will waste time and space.

Be prepared to see both sides of the question. For instance, give proper weight to defences which may be applicable. There is no need to discuss potential defences not raised by the facts, e.g., if the problem says 'A kills Y' you need not go into the question of whether perhaps A was nine years old. If you were required to discuss infancy, the problem should involve facts to lead you to do so. The permutations otherwise would be endless! Do not forget to deal with the burden of proof, where appropriate.

Some identifiable pitfalls

A cardinal fault is irrelevance. Even if a question seems squarely on a certain area of law, it should not be a case of 'writing all you know' on such a topic. Instead, your answer should demonstrate your ability to recognise what is in issue and apply legal principles to it, backed up by authorities. Your ability in selecting the relevant areas for in-depth treatment will also be assessed; a problem question may contain minor points as well as central issues. Be selective in the way you answer, giving priority to the main points, dealing briefly with the rest.

Mistakes identified as common include illogical order, inadequate introduction and conclusion, repetition, poor or inappropriate use of authority and a conclusion which does not follow from the evidence. Not only do such mistakes cost you marks, they give the marker a negative view of the rest of your answer or entire paper. So the favourable impression you may have created earlier quickly disappears. It is therefore essential to eliminate sloppy, fundamental errors. Most markers accept that in the heat of the examination certain errors will be made, but they heavily penalise errors that reveal a lack of technique or lawyerly skill.

Examination technique

Two central pieces of advice are these:

(a)   Answer the required number of questions.

(b)   Keep to time.

If you answer, for instance, three questions instead of the four required, you are immediately giving yourself an absolutely total potential maximum of 75 per cent rather than 100 per cent. If one calls 50 per cent an average secure pass, your 'score' (assuming such standard of answer to three questions) would be 50 per cent of 75, i.e., 37 or 38, a *fail*. It cannot be stressed too strongly: it is vital that you attempt the required number of questions. Be careful to read through the 'rubric', the instructions on the examination paper. You may be asked to answer so many questions from part A, part B and so on. One or more questions may be compulsory. Some questions may have particular instructions built into them. Accurate interpretation of such instructions is *very important*. You should be given an indication by the relevant lecturer of what will be required, but do ask in advance if you are not sure. You ought to know when you are revising what exactly it is that you are revising for. If certain aids are allowed in the examination, you should know this — and be familiar enough with the aids to use them.

It is most important that you make the maximum use of time. The duration of the examination will vary according to the amount of material to be covered. For year-long criminal law courses exams will normally be of three hours duration, with additional reading time. On semesterised modular courses examinations may be only 90 minutes plus reading time. Either way, it is rarely the case that a student will run out of time during a criminal law exam. The usual problem for a weak student is that he or she has completed the answers, and there is still some 30 minutes left. Obviously in some cases this is because the student does not possess enough knowledge, but in the vast majority of cases, the problem is that the student has panicked and rushed into the answer without preparing a plan. At the start of an exam, there is a feeling that, as there is so much to do, the answers must be started immediately. This temptation must be resisted, for it is at the start of your exam that you are freshest and best able to plan your answers, and the order in which you tackle them. You do not want to be panicking with 45 minutes to go, and it is therefore worthwhile considering leaving one of your stronger answers to the end, to enable you confidently to cover material you are sure of, rather than dealing with troublesome topics with a tired mind.

In an ideal situation, your four and five answers will all be strong, but unfortunately experience shows that on even the best of scripts, there is often one relatively weak answer.

It is well worth using some calm time at the beginning of the examination to look through the *whole* paper. Read slowly through the questions, deciding which you will choose (or be forced) to answer. To do this at the outset saves a lot of potential 'dithering' time during the course of the examination. You may find as you initially go through the paper that certain issues or cases leap out at you as you read. It is worth making a marginal note of such matters as you go through, because it may be that you may not be able to bring them to mind later on.

Having stressed the importance of *timing*, the need to *read the questions carefully* must also be highlighted. You will be asked questions which are often quite specific in their terms. It is unlikely that you will be asked to write 'all you know about conspiracy, strict liability etc.'. Much more likely would be a question investigating a certain aspect of the topic in question. It is here that you have to be very precise and concentrated in your reading of the question so that you answer the *question posed*, not something like it and not the question you would have liked to have been asked!

If you have worked out the time allocation for each individual question, you can proceed to your first answer. It is strongly recommended that you stick strictly to your time plan, leaving one question and passing on to another when the allotted time is up. You can always return to add the finishing touches. Just leave a gap, start a new page and *press on*. Remember, when you are working out the amount of time you will allow for each question, you have to take into account thinking time, calming time and note-making time.

It is suggested that the making of an answer plan is essential. This should help to get your thoughts in order and promote the feeling of your being in control. Your answer structure will be greatly assisted by the formulation of a plan in advance. The best approach is to prepare plans for all answers before actually writing the first answer. This requires discipline and nerve, but arguably you are doing your most important thinking while your mind is at its freshest.

You will know your own strengths and weaknesses. You should, for instance, know if you are better at answering problems/writing essays; theory/practice; history/ modern angle; broad/detailed questions. You have to choose as far as you can in line with your knowledge of your own abilities generally, and the selection you see before you. (Of course, on the day you may see a wonderful essay question on a topic you have fully revised and decide to answer that instead of the problem you would normally go for.)

Some things should be watched out for, guarded against. Be careful to *answer* the *question*. This may sound daft, but it cannot be emphasised enough. If the question has several parts, make sure you answer *every part*. If there is a quotation to be discussed in an essay question, you have to really pick the quote to pieces so that you discuss every facet of it. Obviously, the angle you take will depend on the wording of the question — does it say 'Evaluate', or 'Contrast' or 'Critically analyse', for instance? Beware latching on to one key word in the question and writing all you can drag up about the subject.

This is a really crucial point. All you write has to be *relevant* in order to gain you marks. Irrelevancies lose you precious time and will gain no marks. You have to aim for balance in your answer, too. Devote most time to the central issues in a problem, for instance, making brief reference only to subsidiary points.

Problem questions

If you have a long problem question involving, say, several parties to a crime and several substantive offences, and you are told at the beginning of the question that 'A and B agree to . . .', then you would not be expected to enter into a lengthy discourse about conspiracy law. The question here calls for the briefest of references to that possible offence. It would be different if the question appeared to hinge largely on the issue of conspiracy. As a general rule it is best to deal with completed substantive offences first. You can then return to inchoate offences towards the end of your answer on the basis that, if the completed offences cannot be made out, there may be residual liability for inchoate offences.

If a problem gives you no indication of the possible relevance of a particular defence then you would not be expected to deal with that issue, otherwise the permutations would be endless. If the problem mentions, for instance, a serious injury to a person but there is no mention of death, there is no need to develop an argument about what the situation would be if the victim died.

What this really means is that you have to interpret what it is the examiner is trying to test. What is the question essentially about? Within that question, you then have to decide what emphasis you think should be accorded to various aspects of the question.

It is very important to include in your answer clear definitions where appropriate. For instance, if you are going to discuss insanity, make sure that you state what amounts to insanity; if you are discussing provocation, say what it is. Clear definitions set the tone of your answer and put the marker in an optimistic frame of mind. The same is true of a good, clear opening paragraph — it bodes well and is worth aiming for.

It is also very important to display your understanding clearly concerning the burden of proof, particularly in relation to defences. Be careful that you do not suggest that there is a burden of proof on the defence when there is not. As you revise, you should be very alert to this point.

While on the question of displaying your knowledge, if you have read a relevant article or have been swayed by a particular writer's approach, make sure that you state this. In the case of essay questions, show the marker that you have read widely. Capitalise on your research. Get the credit.

In answering a problem question, don't feel that you have to come to a rock solid conclusion. Very often it will be impossible to do so. It is perfectly acceptable to say, for example, 'If D is found to have intended grievous bodily harm then. . . .' and so on. As long as you indicate what the issues are, what the relevant principles of liability are, that is sufficient. There is no need to predict the decision of the jury/magistrates, although you do have to indicate, where appropriate, how the jury should be directed, for instance.

Your conclusion may differ from that of another student, and may differ from that of the marker. This does not matter. So long as you can illustrate why you reach your conclusion by reference to authorities, analogy and argument, that is fine. It is quite likely that you cannot, on the facts presented, reach a definite conclusion. It may depend, for instance, on whether the jury believed that A had the necessary intention to kill or cause grievous bodily harm. If they did the verdict could be guilty of murder unless the jury considered that A had used reasonable force in self defence, in which case he would be acquitted of all charges. In situations like this, it would be wrong to conclude that A was definitely guilty or not guilty. What you must do is cover the alternatives — this demonstrates your understanding of the position. In certain questions there may be many alternative outcomes. Remember that the marks allocated for the conclusion are not simply given for arriving at the same result as the examiner (e.g., A guilty of murder) but for analysis and awareness.

Essay questions

In answering essay questions it is necessary to include the traditional introduction, followed by discussion, followed by conclusion. Neither the introduction nor the conclusion need be lengthy. The advantage of the essay question is that you can play to your strengths — so long as what you write is relevant. Beware writing all you know on a topic; it is essential to be discriminating, to tailor your answer to the way the question is worded. Simply ask yourself 'Am I answering the question set?'

Candidates sometimes tend to forget authorities when answering essay-style questions, particularly under examination conditions. You still need reference to case law, statutory definitions and general principles in an essay answer. The onus is more on you, since in a problem the facts will (or should) suggest which authorities you are being asked to discuss.

If the essay question revolves around a particular case, clearly you will need to concentrate on that decision — but the odds are that you will still need plenty of reference to other case law and statutory provisions, to place the case in its historical perspective, or to highlight the way in which the central decision will or may affect existing law.

The major task in essay writing, given that you know the subject matter, is to structure the material. You have to determine for yourself the scope and shape of your answer. It is easy to tell when marking essay answers who has followed a plan — it really shows.

A good answer to an essay question, therefore, will go beyond simply describing or giving an account of those issues to which the question relates. A good answer will have a point to make — a view to express. It will present a polemic of some sort. It will seek to persuade the reader, by means of reasoned and supported argument, to agree with a particular view on the subject.

Conclusion

In an exam your goal must be to obtain the highest mark possible, given your knowledge and ability. Student A may have the same attributes as student B, but student A may obtain 10–20 more marks in the exam because of good exam technique. It is therefore essential that you incorporate into your answer the style and techniques covered in this chapter. So remember to:

- read the instructions thoroughly;
- answer the correct number of questions;
- prepare your answer plan;
- answer the question set;
- deal with one issue fully before going on to the next;
- write a logical conclusion which does not conflict with the rest of your answer;
- read through your answers at the end of the exam.

2 Q&A

The elements of a crime: *actus reus* and *mens rea*

Introduction

The traditional starting point for the study of criminal law is the constituents of a criminal offence: *actus reus* (often referred to as the prohibited conduct, but more accurately described as the external elements of the offence) and *mens rea* (often referred to as the mental element, but more accurately described as the fault element). Commentators and students alike want to find consistency and certainty in the application and development of the criminal law, and most criminal law textbooks dealing with the elements of crimes try to state principles that the student should see consistently applied in later chapters covering specific offences. The main problem is that the offences have developed in a piecemeal fashion, exhibiting no underlying rationale or common approach. Thus in examining *actus reus*, the student might be covering an offence defined in modern terms, e.g., by the Criminal Damage Act 1971, or in obscure outdated language, e.g., in the Offences Against the Person Act 1861 or — the definition of *actus reus* may arise from the common law, perhaps amended or augmented by statute, e.g., murder.

Similarly, when we examine our approach to *mens rea*, we can see little common ground. If the offence requires the prosecution to prove intention, this must generally be left to the jury without detailed guidance from the trial judge (*R* v *Moloney* [1985] 1 All ER 1025); but if recklessness is the issue, a direction spelling out to the jury what they must find may be required. Prior to the decision of the House of Lords in *R* v *G* [2003] 4 All ER 765, a case involving criminal damage would have involved a court in trying to assess whether the defendant was reckless according to the definition laid down in *Metropolitan Police Commissioner* v *Caldwell* [1981] 1 All ER 961. But now, following the abandonment of '*Caldwell* recklessness', the issue has been simplified so that a court now has to concentrate on whether or not the defendant was aware of the risk in question.

If dishonesty is the *mens rea* (see Theft Acts 1968–1996) the jury must consider two specific questions (would ordinary people consider D dishonest?; if so, did D realise that they would?); but these are questions of fact for them to resolve (*R* v *Ghosh* [1982] 2 All ER 689). In other words, there are three different approaches in establishing the *mens rea* for different offences. A search for consistency is therefore a futile exercise!

Students should therefore be aware that studying the chapters on *actus reus* and *mens rea* can produce a distorted impression of the criminal law. One is dealing with concepts in isolation and could form the impression that these general principles are consistently applied.

One particular criticism is that the criminal law is not consistent in applying objective or subjective tests for liability. Objective tests consider what the reasonable person would have foreseen. Subjective tests judge the defendant on the facts as he honestly believed them to be. There appears to be an absence of any underlying rationale and the offences develop independently of each other. One can understand why Sir Henry Brooke (former head of the Law Commission) and many others wish for codification of some, if not all, of the criminal law (see [1995] Crim LR 911 — 'The Law Commission and Criminal Law Reform').

Even established concepts that have been applied by the courts for many years, may suddenly come under attack and be interpreted differently by the judiciary. Thus the House of Lords in *Attorney-General's Reference (No. 3 of 1994)* [1997] 3 All ER 936, reversed the Court of Appeal decision ([1996] 2 WLR 412), holding that the doctrine of transferred malice could not apply to convict an accused of murder when he deliberately injured a pregnant woman in circumstances where the baby was born alive but subsequently died. Lord Mustill criticised the doctrine as having no sound intellectual basis and involving a fiction, although the *Criminal Law Review* disagrees with his view ([1997] Crim LR 830).

In this chapter questions have been chosen to cover all major aspects of this area. There are some problem questions, but you would expect the essay questions in an exam to be selected from these topics. Essays are therefore included on the important aspects of *mens rea*: intention and recklessness.

A question is also included based on the Law Commission's recommendations on corporate killing (Law Com. No. 237). The Law Commission has made many suggestions on most areas of the substantive criminal law, and it is helpful to be aware of their views as they highlight the defects and anomalies in the existing law. However, when answering problem questions, the examiner will want you to cover the existing principles, stating what the law actually is rather than what it should be. You should also be aware that, whilst relatively few of the Law Commission's recommendations are ever implemented, there is considerable pressure for legislation in this area.

Q Question 1

The practice of leaving the issue of intention to the jury without any judicial guidance as to its meaning is unworkable and likely to produce inconsistent decisions.

Discuss this statement with reference to decided cases.

Commentary

There have been so many important decisions on this important aspect of criminal law, that it is always likely to be the subject of an examination question.

Because the facts of *R v Moloney* [1985] 1 All ER 641 are so well known, there is a temptation simply to regurgitate them with the House of Lords' decisions. This must be resisted as there are many ingredients in the answer, which requires careful planning and organisation.

In summary, this is a question where it is quite easy to obtain a pass mark but difficult to obtain a high grade.

- *Mens rea*

- Intention — definition

- *Moloney* [1985] — 'the golden rule'

- *Woollin* [1998] — direction on intention

- Law Commission No. 218

⚙ Suggested answer

Except with strict (or absolute) liability offences, in order for an accused to be found guilty of a criminal offence, the prosecution must prove that the accused committed the *actus reus* of the offence with the appropriate *mens rea*. *Mens rea* generally signifies blameworthiness, although in *R v Kingston* [1994] 3 All ER 353, the House of Lords confirmed that the accused was guilty of an offence requiring the prosecution to prove intention, although he was morally blameless. *Mens rea* is the mental element, which varies from one offence to another; but generally, for the more serious offences, it comprises intention or recklessness, with intention being reserved for the most serious crimes.

One would therefore think that, being of such fundamental importance, intention would be specifically defined and rigidly applied, but this is not the case. There have always been difficulties with the concept of intention within the criminal law. What is it? How should it be defined? How do the prosecution prove it? How does the trial judge direct the jury? These issues have been the subject of much judicial and academic debate in recent years.

Although the word 'intention' implies purpose or even desire, there have been many diverse definitions by the judiciary, and commentators have also identified different types of intention. First, direct intent, where it was the accused's purpose or motive to bring about a result. Thus in *R v Steane* [1947] 1 All ER 813, the accused, who assisted the enemy during the war, had his conviction quashed as the court decided that he did not intend to assist the enemy; he intended to protect his family, who would have been harmed had he not cooperated. Secondly, oblique intent, where the accused does not necessarily desire the result but foresees it as highly probable. Thus in *Hyam* v *DPP* [1974] 2 All ER 41, the House of Lords upheld the conviction for murder of the accused who set fire to the victim's house, as she foresaw that death or grievous bodily harm was highly probable. Thirdly, ulterior intent, where it must be shown that in intentionally doing one act the accused has a related purpose. Thus to be guilty of burglary under s. 9(1)(a) of the Theft Act 1968, it is necessary for the prosecution to prove that the accused, when deliberately entering a building as a trespasser, did so with a specific related purpose in mind, e.g., to steal or commit criminal damage. It would not be sufficient if the accused intentionally broke into the house with the sole purpose of sheltering from the weather. Other forms of intention, specific and basic, are also used to apply the defence of intoxication to certain offences (*DPP* v *Majewski* [1976] 2 All ER 142).

Although there is an overlap between intention on the one hand and motive and foresight on the other, and these latter concepts assist the jury in their deliberations on intention, it is clear that the concepts are not synonymous. Motive is the reason why a person acts, while intention is his or her mental awareness at the time of the act. Foresight can be evidence of intention, but it is not conclusive proof of it. Section 8 of the Criminal Justice Act 1967 states that a court shall not be bound in law to infer that the accused intended or foresaw a result of his actions by reason only of its being a natural and probable consequence of those actions, but 'shall decide whether he did intend or foresee that result by reference to all the evidence, drawing such inferences from the evidence as appear proper in the circumstances'.

The issue of intention was debated by the House of Lords in *R* v *Moloney* [1985] 1 All ER 641 and *R* v *Hancock and Shankland* [1986] 1 All ER 641. In the former case, Moloney shot his stepfather from point blank range and was convicted of murder after the trial judge (following *Archbold Criminal Pleading Evidence and Practice*, 40th edn, para. 17–13, p. 995) directed the jury that:

> In law a man intends the consequence of his voluntary act:
>
> (a) when he desires it to happen, whether or not he foresees that it probably will happen, or
>
> (b) when he foresees that it will probably happen, whether he desires it or not.

The House of Lords quashed the conviction on the basis that this was a misdirection, Lord Bridge stating that:

> the golden rule should be that, when directing a jury on the mental element necessary in a crime of specific intent (i.e., intention), the judge should avoid any elaboration or paraphrase of what is meant by intent, and leave it to the jury's good sense to decide whether the accused

acted with the necessary intent, unless the judge is convinced that, on the facts and having regard to the way the case has been presented to the jury in evidence and argument, some further explanation or elaboration is strictly necessary to avoid misunderstanding.

Although the decision may be criticised on the ground that their Lordships missed a golden opportunity to define intention, it is in keeping with the modern trend of leaving more and more issues to the jury, especially the meaning of words in common use. For example, *Brutus* v *Cozens* [1972] 2 All ER 1297 (insulting); *R* v *Feely* [1973] 1 All ER 341 (dishonestly).

This decision was followed by the House of Lords' ruling in *R* v *Hancock and Shankland*, where Lord Scarman also made the point that if intention required a detailed direction it was best to leave this to the discretion of the trial judge who would have had the benefit of hearing all the witnesses and gauging the ability of the jury. He added that the trial judge could not do as Lord Bridge suggested and simply direct the jury to consider two questions: first, was death or really serious injury in a murder case a natural consequence of the defendant's voluntary act?; secondly, did the defendant foresee that consequence as being a natural consequence of his act? — further instructing them that if they answer 'Yes' to both questions it is a proper inference for them to draw that the accused intended that consequence. Lord Scarman stated that the trial judge must refer to the concept of probability — the more probable the consequence, the more likely the accused foresaw it and intended it.

Despite clear House of Lords' *dicta* to the contrary, the Court of Appeal in *R* v *Nedrick* [1986] 3 All ER 1 did lay down some guidelines to the effect that the jury should not infer intention unless they considered that the accused foresaw the consequence as a virtual certainty. However, this decision has attracted criticism, and the Court of Appeal in *R* v *Walker and Hayles* [1990] 90 Cr App R 226 stated 'we are not persuaded that it is only when death is a virtual certainty that the jury can infer intention to kill'.

Nevertheless, the status of *Nedrick* was confirmed by the House of Lords' discussion in *R* v *Woollin* [1998] 4 All ER 103. The House, stating that where the simple direction was not enough, the jury should be further directed that they were not entitled to find the necessary intention unless they felt sure that death or serious bodily harm was a virtually certain result of D's action (barring some unforeseen intervention) and, that D had appreciated that fact.

This decision also illustrates one of the difficulties of the present approach, i.e., when is the issue of intention so complicated as to warrant a detailed direction? In *R* v *Walker and Hayles*, the Court of Appeal decided that 'the mere fact that a jury calls for a further direction on intention does not of itself make it a rare and exceptional case requiring a foresight direction'. On the other hand, in *R* v *Hancock and Shankland*, the House of Lords confirmed that the trial judge was right to give a detailed direction, even though the content of the direction was wrong.

A further problem is that different juries may have different ideas as to what constitutes intention, some insisting on purpose being necessary, while others are prepared to accept that only foresight of a probable consequence is required. There is clearly the risk of inconsistent decisions and it is therefore not surprising that the Law Commission (Nos 122 and 218) have recommended that the following standard definition of intention be adopted:

a person acts intentionally with respect to a result when

(i)   it is his purpose to cause it; or

(ii)   although it is not his purpose to cause that result, he knows that it would occur in the ordinary course of events if he were to succeed in his purpose of causing some other result.

Q Question 2

'Mens rea is, by definition, the defendant's state of mind.'
   Discuss the accuracy of this statement using case law to support your argument.

Commentary

This question requires examination of some of the assumptions made about *mens rea* and the current trends in judicial thinking. Candidates would be expected to consider the main forms of *mens rea* and the extent to which courts are required to take an objective or subjective view of fault. Although '*Caldwell* recklessness' has now been effectively consigned to legal history (for the time being at least) a good answer will need to show an awareness of that decision and its impact on the *mens rea* debate. Consideration also needs to be given to the issue of mistake and its relationship with *mens rea*. Finally, the answer should encompass some consideration of negligence as a form of *mens rea* and the extent to which its use accords with notions of subjective fault.

- The nature of *mens rea*

- Intention — *R* v *Woollin* — House of Lords' decision

- The recklessness debate *R* v *G* [2003] — abandoning *Caldwell*

- The treatment of mistake and its effect on *mens rea* — *DPP* v *Morgan* [1976]

- Killing by gross negligence — whether objective or subjective

⚙ Suggested answer

Although *mens rea* translates literally as 'guilty mind', relying on this as the meaning given to that term in modern criminal law is likely to lead to error. This is because a defendant may be found to have *mens rea* even though he himself has not acted with the intention of committing an offence, or even with the awareness that this might be the result. The better approach is to regard *mens rea* as denoting the fault element that the prosecution has to prove. In the majority of cases this will involve proof of some positive state of mind on the part of the accused, but in other cases it may be enough to show that the accused failed to advert to something that would have been obvious to the reasonable person.

The two most important fault elements used in modern criminal law are intention and recklessness. It can now be said that, as far as these two forms of *mens rea* are concerned, liability cannot be established without evidence as to what the defendant foresaw when he committed the acts causing the prohibited results.

The modern definition of intention can be derived from a number of House of Lords' decisions, notably *R v Moloney* [1985] 1 All ER 1025 and *R v Woollin* [1998] 4 All ER 103. A defendant cannot be guilty of murder unless he is proved to have acted with intent to kill or do grievous bodily harm. Where a direction on intent is deemed necessary, a jury should be instructed that they should consider the extent to which the defendant foresaw death or grievous bodily harm resulting from his actions. Only where there is evidence that he foresaw either consequence as virtually certain would it be safe for a jury to conclude that a defendant therefore intended either of those consequences. The key here is foresight. Section 8 of the Criminal Justice Act 1967 makes clear that foresight is a subjective concept — i.e., it is based on what the defendant actually foresaw — not on what he ought to have foreseen, or indeed what the reasonable person would have foreseen had he been in the defendant's shoes. Taken together, the definition of foresight in the 1968 Act, and the House of Lords' ruling in *Woollin* ensure that where intention is the necessary *mens rea*, there can be no doubt that it will be based on the defendant's state of mind — i.e., a subjective approach will be adopted.

The rationale for this is fairly obvious — it is hard to describe a defendant as having intended a consequence if there is no evidence of it having occurred to him. Even where there is such evidence, if the possibility of the consequence occurring has only fleetingly crossed his mind it would still be absurd to say he intended it. The law, therefore, requires a very high degree of foresight before a defendant's state of mind is labelled as having been intentional.

Recklessness, by contrast, implies risk taking, as opposed to foresight of certainty. Here there has been great controversy over the past few decades as to the right approach to the determination of fault. The traditional approach to recklessness as a form of *mens rea* very much reflected the view that *mens rea* had to be based on the defendant's state of mind. In *R v Cunningham* [1957] 2 All ER 412, the Court of Appeal held that a defendant was reckless only if he took an unjustifiable risk and was at least aware of the risk materialising. The key point about this approach to recklessness was that there would be no liability if the risk never occurred to the defendant.

However, this settled approach was shattered by the House of Lords' decision in *Metropolitan Police Commissioner* v *Caldwell* [1981] 1 All ER 961. The accused had a grudge against the owner of an old people's home, and while drunk he set fire to it. He was convicted under s. 1(1) of the Criminal Damage Act 1971 of recklessly damaging another's property, and of the more serious offence under s. 1(2) of the Act, destroying or damaging any property:

(a) intending to destroy or damage any property or being reckless as to whether any property would be destroyed or damaged; and

(b) intending by the destruction or damage to endanger the life of another or being reckless as to whether the life of another would be thereby endangered.

The House of Lords, by a majority, held that in relation to criminal damage, a person was reckless if:

(a) he did an act which in fact creates an obvious risk that property would be destroyed or damaged; and

(b) when he did the act he either did not give any thought to the possibility of there being any such risk, or had recognised that there was some risk involved and had nevertheless gone on to do it.

Lord Diplock clearly wanted to introduce liability for failing to think in the guise of this reformulation of recklessness, but this raised a number of issues.

First, what of the defendant who did not think of the risk because it would not have occurred to him even if he had stopped to think? In *Elliot* v *C (A Minor)* [1983] 2 All ER 1005, a 14-year-old schoolgirl of low intelligence, who was tired and hungry, spilt some inflammable spirit and then dropped a lighted match on the wooden floor of a garden shed. She was charged under s. 1(1) of the 1971 Act. It was argued that she did not foresee the risk of fire, nor would she had she addressed her mind to the possible consequences of her action. Although Goff LJ stated that a test for recklessness which allowed the court to take into account the individual characteristics of the accused had much merit, he felt bound by the doctrine of precedent to follow *Caldwell*, and therefore the magistrates should have convicted the accused as the correct test was 'whether this is an obvious risk to a reasonable man'.

Secondly, there was the argument that '*Caldwell* recklessness' was not acceptable as a form of *mens rea* because it was not based on the defendant's state of mind. In *R* v *Reid* [1992] 3 All ER 673, Lord Keith observed by way of response that: 'Absence of something from a person's state of mind is as much part of his state of mind as is its presence. Inadvertence to risk is no less a subjective state of mind than is disregard of a recognised risk.' What he meant by this was that even with '*Caldwell* recklessness', the court had to consider the defendant's state of mind. But, it is submitted, this is a piece of judicial sophistry, as all that was required was for the court to examine the defendant's state of mind and, on finding 'no thought', conclude that he had been reckless provided the risk would have been obvious to the reasonable prudent bystander.

Whilst many might have applauded Lord Diplock's efforts to penalise thoughtlessness in terms of a social policy initiative, the real question was whether he was right to pursue this via a radical judicial reinterpretation of the term 'recklessness'. It is significant that Parliament intervened shortly after *Caldwell* to reform the offence of reckless driving (and therefore causing death by reckless driving) by replacing it with the offence of dangerous driving — see the Road Traffic Act 1991. The effect of this was to make clear that the offence could now be committed without any form of *mens rea* that required reference to the defendant's state of mind. Recklessness was replaced, as a fault element, by the term 'dangerous'. Whilst it could and was argued that recklessness implied some conscious risk-taking by the accused, there was no doubt that 'dangerousness' as a fault element rested entirely upon an objective assessment of the defendant's conduct. In other words a defendant could drive dangerously because he had a badly secured load on the back of his trailer — there was no need for him to be aware of this. In summary this suggests that Parliament liked the idea of criminal liability based on failure to think about risk, but was not comfortable with the idea that 'traditional' *mens rea* terms like 'recklessness' might be used to describe it.

As far as recklessness is concerned the argument has, for the time being at least, been decided in favour of the traditional, subjective, approach. In *R* v *G* [2003] 4 All ER 765, the House of Lords held that a defendant could not be properly convicted under s. 1 of the Criminal Damage Act 1971 on the basis that he was reckless as to whether property was destroyed or damaged when he gave no thought to the risk and, by reason of his age and/or personal characteristics, the risk would not have been obvious to him, even if he had thought about it. Lord Bingham observed that recklessness should at least require a knowing disregard of an appreciated and unacceptable risk of, or a deliberate closing of the mind to such risk. In his view it was not clearly blameworthy to do something involving a risk of injury to another if one genuinely did not perceive the risk.

R v *G* reflects a general judicial trend in favour of subjectivity, as evidenced in decisions such as *B* v *DPP* [2000] 1 All ER WLR 833. Indeed, the high watermark of this approach to fault is the House of Lords' decision in *DPP* v *Morgan* [1976] AC 182, where it was held that if a defendant made a genuine mistake of fact — such as wrongly believing that a woman was consenting to sexual intercourse, he had to be judged on the facts as he believed them to be, not as the reasonable person would have believed them to be. Lord Hailsham made it clear that there was no room either for a 'defence' of honest belief or mistake, or of a defence of honest and reasonable belief or mistake. The reasonableness of the defendant's honest belief was simply a factor relating to its credibility.

As has been noted above in the case of dangerous driving, fault elements that do not require reference to the defendant's state of mind are used. At common law this can be seen in the offence of killing by gross negligence. In *R v Adomako* [1994] 3 WLR 288, Lord Mackay LC explained that liability would be established if the prosecution could prove that the defendant's conduct departed from the proper standard of care incumbent upon him, thereby creating a risk of death, and involved such a departure from acceptable standards of care as to deserve the stigma of criminalisation. As was made clear in *Attorney General's Reference (No. 2 of 1999)* [2000] 3 All ER 182, evidence of the defendant's state of mind might be useful in guiding a jury as to whether or not the negligence was gross, but this fault element can be made out without any direct evidence as to the defendant's state of mind. Whilst this may seem to run counter to the trend in favour of subjectivity it should be remembered that it serves a useful social purpose in making it easier to impose criminal liability on companies that kill.

In summary, therefore, it is undoubtedly true to say that *mens rea* does involve an examination of the defendant's state of mind to ascertain a degree of awareness of the consequences of his actions. The law will, however, allow departures from this where the social utility and fairness of so doing is apparent.

Q Question 3

You are told that the Ancient Book Act 1997 has just received the Royal Assent and that s. 1 provides, 'It shall be an offence to destroy any book printed before 1800'.

Discuss the criminal liability of each party (in relation to the 1997 Act) in the following situation.

Arthur owns 200 books, which he thinks are worthless. He is concerned in case any of the books were printed before 1800 and consults Ben, an expert on old books, who assures him that all the books were printed long after 1800. Arthur destroys the books and is now horrified to discover that three of them were printed in 1750.

Commentary

This is an unusual question which has caused students difficulties, with many writing about the offence of criminal damage. This is a mistake as the question requires a detailed analysis of the *mens rea* requirement of the Ancient Book Act 1997, and in particular analysis of the concept of strict liability.

In a survey by Justice referred to in an article by A. Ashworth and M. Blake, 'The Presumption of Innocence in English Criminal Law' [1996] Crim LR 306, it is estimated that in over one half of criminal offences either strict liability is imposed, or the prosecution have the benefit of a presumption. It is obviously an important topic, and popular with examiners!

A good answer will require a detailed consideration of the possibility of this offence being one of strict liability and the effect of this. You should also consider the position if the courts decide that intention or recklessness is the appropriate mental state.

- **Strict liability** — *Sweet* v *Parsley* [1969]

- **Presumption of** *mens rea* — *B* v *DPP* [2000]

- **The exceptions**

- **Recklessness**

- **Mistake** — *Morgan* [1975]

- **Aiding and abetting** — *Callow* v *Tillstone* [1900]

:Q: Suggested answer

The first point to note is that s. 1 of the Ancient Book Act 1997 is silent as to the *mens rea* requirement of the offence. This could mean that the offence is one of absolute liability (i.e., strict liability in the sense that no *mens rea* whatsoever is required). Alternatively it could be a strict liability offence in the sense that intention, recklessness or negligence is only required as regards one or more elements of the *actus reus*. The imposition of absolute liability may be very harsh on the defendant. For example, in *Pharmaceutical Society of Great Britain* v *Storkwain* [1986] 2 All ER 635, the House of Lords upheld the conviction of a pharmacist who had given drugs to a patient with a forged doctor's prescription, although the court found the pharmacist blameless. Whilst the decision demonstrates the inherent unfairness of strict liability, it can be justified on the basis that the misuse of drugs is a grave social evil and therefore should be prevented at all costs.

The first case of statutory strict liability was *R* v *Woodrow* (1846) 15 M & W 404, where the accused was found guilty of being in possession of adulterated tobacco, even though he did not know that it was adulterated. Many early decisions revealed an inconsistent approach as the courts were trying to interpret old statutes in ascertaining the will of Parliament. However, Lord Reid in the House of Lords' decision in *Sweet* v *Parsley* [1969] 1 All ER 347 laid down the following guidelines:

(a) Wherever a section is silent as to *mens rea* there is a presumption that, in order to give effect to the will of Parliament, words importing *mens rea* must be read into the provision.

(b) It is a universal principle that if a penal provision is reasonably capable of two interpretations, that interpretation which is most favourable to the accused must be adopted.

(c) The fact that other sections of the Act expressly require *mens rea* is not in itself sufficient to justify a decision that a section which is silent as to *mens rea* creates an absolute offence. It is necessary to go outside the Act and examine all relevant circumstances in order to establish that this must have been the intention of Parliament. So in *Cundy* v *Le Coq* (1884) 13 QB 207, a publican was found guilty of selling intoxicating liquor to a drunken person under s. 13 of the Licensing Act 1872, even though the publican did not know and had no reason to know that the customer was drunk; whereas in *Sherras* v *De Rutzen* [1895] 1 QB 918, a publican was not guilty under s. 16(2) of the Licensing Act 1872 of serving alcohol to a police constable while on duty when the accused did not know or have reason to know that the police constable was on duty. The former case was held to be an offence of strict liability, whereas in the latter, in order to obtain a conviction, the prosecution had to prove *mens rea* on behalf of the publican, which they were unable to do.

Despite the fact that there is a presumption in favour of *mens rea* when a statute is silent, the courts have been prepared to rebut this presumption on many occasions. The leading case on this point is *Gammon* v *Attorney-General for Hong Kong* [1985] AC 1, where Lord Scarman set out the applicable principles. If the offence is truly criminal in character the presumption is particularly strong, but it can be displaced where the statute is concerned with an issue of social concern. Thus, in *Gammon*, as the accused's activities involved public safety, the Privy Council were prepared to hold that the legislature intended the offence to be one of strict liability.

On analysis these principles appear inconsistent. It could be argued that all crimes by definition are grave social evils, yet if the offence is truly criminal in character, strict liability does not apply. In practice, the courts have adopted a flexible approach, but it is recognised that certain spheres of activity are always likely to attract the conclusion that this is an offence of strict liability. Thus inflation (*R* v *St Margaret's Trust Ltd* [1958] 2 All ER 289), pollution (*Alphacell Ltd* v *Woodward* [1972] 2 All ER 475), and dangerous drugs (*Pharmaceutical Society of Great Britain* v *Storkwain*, above) are traditional areas where strict liability has been imposed. However, it does seem in recent years that the category of grave social concern is expanding to encompass new social activity to include acting as a director whilst disqualified (*R* v *Brockley* [1994] Crim LR 671) and unauthorised possession of a dangerous dog (*R* v *Bezzina* [1994] 1 WLR 1057).

However, the House of Lords have again emphasised the need for the prosecution to prove *mens rea* in *B* (*A minor*) v *DPP* [2000] 1 All ER 833, where Lord Hutton stated (at p. 855), 'the test is not whether it is a reasonable implication that the statute rules out mens rea as a constituent part of the crime — the test is whether it is a necessary implication'. Further in *R* v *Lambert* [2001] 3 All ER 577, the House held that although s. 28 of the Misuse of Drugs Act 1971 required the defence to prove a defence, this only meant introduce evidence of, rather than establish a defence on the balance of probabilities.

In view of these developments, it is submitted that it would be most unlikely for s. 1 of the Ancient Book Act 1997 to be an offence of strict liability, and therefore Arthur will only be guilty if the prosecution can establish that he had the necessary *mens rea*.

If the court decides that the prosecution must prove intention, it is submitted that Arthur cannot be guilty. As he has obtained the opinion of Ben, an expert, he clearly did not desire or even foresee the consequence. Arthur has made a mistake, and even if an accused makes an unreasonable mistake, in accordance with the House of Lords' decision in *DPP* v *Morgan* [1975] 1 All ER 8, he is entitled to be judged on the facts as he believed them to be.

If the court decides that the offence could be committed recklessly, it would still be very difficult for the prosecution to establish the appropriate *mens rea*. It is almost certainly the case that subjective recklessness would have to be proved — i.e., the prosecution must show that the accused foresaw the consequence and took an unjustified risk (*R* v *Cunningham* [1957] 2 All ER 412). Following the decision of the House of Lords in *R* v *G* [2003] 4 All ER 765, there would appear to be no scope for the application of the objective recklessness test, as expounded in *Metropolitan Police Commissioner* v *Caldwell* [1981] 1 All ER 961.

As Arthur sought the opinion of an expert it is difficult to see how it could be argued that he was consciously taking an unjustified risk.

It is therefore submitted that Arthur could be guilty of the offence only if the court decides that s. 1 of the Ancient Book Act 1997 creates an offence of strict liability. This would be a very harsh outcome bearing in mind that the real culprit in the circumstances is Ben, the expert. It is also ironic that Ben could not be guilty of aiding and abetting a strict liability offence as a result of the decision in *Callow* v *Tillstone* (1900) 19 Cox CC 576. In this case the defendant, a vet, was convicted of abetting the exposure for sale of unsound meat, an offence of strict liability. At the request of a butcher he examined the carcass of a heifer and negligently gave the butcher a certificate confirming that the meat was sound. Despite the fact that the butcher was convicted of the offence, the defendant's conviction for abetting was quashed, the court holding that *mens rea* was required for an accessory and that negligence was not sufficient; see also *Johnson* v *Youden* [1950] 1 KB 544. It is submitted that this is a further argument for holding that the Ancient Book Act 1997 does not create a crime of strict liability.

Q Question 4

Gloria, Wood's eccentric aunt, aged 57, was invited to stay with Wood and his girlfriend Mary at their property on the coast. It was agreed that Gloria would stay for three weeks and would occupy 'the lodge' in the garden of the Wood's house some 30 yards away. Gloria also agreed to pay £40 to cover the electricity she would use in the lodge.

Everything went well for two weeks with all three sharing meals at the house. However, a change of mood then came over Gloria who decided that she no longer wanted to have meals with Wood and Mary, and who spent more and more time by herself at the lodge.

After 20 days of the holiday Gloria, whose physical condition had visibly deteriorated, announced that she refused to leave the lodge and was going to stay there the rest of the winter. This so enraged Wood and Mary that the next day they told her to leave immediately, which she did.

Six hours later, at 11 pm, Gloria rang their bell pleading to be let in as she was cold and hungry and had nowhere else to go. Wood and Mary refused, and during that night Gloria was taken to hospital suffering from hypothermia.

While in hospital, Gloria fell unconscious and was placed on a life support machine. After five days she was correctly diagnosed by Dr Spock as being in a persistent vegetative state with no hope of recovery. He accordingly disconnected the machine.

Discuss the criminal responsibility (if any) of Wood and Mary.

Commentary

This problem concerns one of the more difficult areas of criminal law, criminal responsibility for omission to act. The Law Commission No. 143 proposed very detailed conditions concerning this topic, but these provisions were jettisoned in the revised Code (Law Com. No. 177) on the basis that the courts would be able to develop the correct principles. As Professor Glanville Williams pointed out, 'the law is in a state, if not of disarray, then of mystery'.

The question is based on the major case of *R v Stone and Dobinson* [1977] 2 All ER 341. A detailed knowledge of, and an ability to analyse this case is therefore essential in order to tackle the problem successfully.

As often is the case, a problem covering omission will also involve a consideration of causation.

Note: You are not required to consider the responsibility of Dr Spock.

- Involuntary manslaughter
  - Constructive
  - Gross negligence: *Adomako* [1994]

- Omission — general rule

- Duty of care

- Causation

✷ Suggested answer

The first issue to be resolved is causation. The question as to whether an omission, as opposed to an act, can actually cause a consequence is a moot point. There can be no criminal liability imposed on Wood and Mary in respect of their failing to care for Gloria unless the prosecution can establish that they were under a positive legal duty to care for her. The facts suggest two bases for this. First, that there was a contractual duty arising from the agreement between the parties regarding payment. The problem with this is that, as a domestic agreement, it may not be supported by any intention to create legal relations — therefore it does not give rise to any legally enforceable duty. The much more promising argument for the prosecution is that based on reliance and duty of care; see *R v Stone and Dobinson* [1977] QB 354. It could be argued that in allowing Gloria to stay, the defendants allowed a relationship of reliance to develop — but the present case can be distinguished from *Stone and Dobinson* on the grounds that Wood and Mary place a time-limit on Gloria's stay, and Gloria leaves of her own volition. Thus the argument as to whether or not there is any liability for failing to act is finely balanced.

Assuming that the failure to care for Gloria, or the refusal to readmit her to the house, can form the basis of liability, the prosecution will have to show that this omission caused Gloria's death. It is not necessary for the prosecution to prove that the omission was the sole or main cause, merely that it contributed significantly to the victim's death (*R v Cheshire* [1991] 3 All ER 670). The accused could argue that the doctor's turning off the life support system constituted a *novus actus interveniens*, breaking the chain of causation; but this argument was rejected by the House of Lords in *R v Malcherek; R v Steel* [1981] 2 All ER 422, where Lord Lane CJ stated that 'the fact that the victim has died, despite or because of medical treatment for the initial injury given by careful and skilled medical practitioners, will not exonerate the original assailant from responsibility for the death'.

It is therefore clear that the medical treatment, of itself, will not be held to have broken the chain of causation in law.

Wood and Mary could be charged with involuntary manslaughter. It is submitted that they could not be convicted of murder as from the facts there is no evidence that they intended either to kill or to cause grievous bodily harm, and they therefore lack the *mens rea* of murder (*R v Moloney* [1985] 1 All ER 1025).

They could not be charged with constructive manslaughter as the prosecution must establish an intention to do an act that is unlawful and dangerous (*R v Church* [1965] 2 All ER 72). In this problem, the accused have omitted to act, and in *R v Lowe*

[1973] 1 All ER 805 the Court of Appeal indicated that an omission could not constitute the unlawful act for constructive manslaughter.

The basis of manslaughter that would be argued is gross negligence, which was analysed by the House of Lords in *R v Adomako* [1994] 4 All ER 935, where their Lordships held that an accused would be guilty of manslaughter if the following four conditions were satisfied:

(1) the accused owed a duty of care to the victim;

(2) that duty was broken;

(3) the conduct of the accused was grossly negligent;

(4) that conduct caused the victim's death.

An issue that will have to be revisited, for these purposes, is the difficult one of whether Wood and Mary owed Gloria a duty of care.

Traditionally, the criminal law has always drawn a clear distinction between acts and omissions, being loath to punish the latter. Other European countries — e.g., Greece, France and Germany — do not exhibit the same reluctance, and there is dispute as to whether the English approach is correct. See in particular the different views of Professors A. Ashworth (1989) 105 LQR 424 and G. Williams (1991) 107 LQR 109. However, apart from the numerous statutes that impose a duty to act, e.g., s. 170 of the Road Traffic Act 1988, it appears that the common law will impose a duty to act only in very limited circumstances. Clearly a duty to act for the purposes of criminal responsibility can arise under a contract of employment, e.g., *R v Pittwood* (1902) 19 TLR 37, where a railway gate operator was found guilty of manslaughter when a person was killed crossing a railway line as a result of the accused leaving the gate open when a train was coming. Similarly, if the accused creates a dangerous situation he will owe a duty to try to minimise the danger. So, in *R v Miller* [1983] 1 All ER 978, the House of Lords upheld the accused's conviction for criminal damage where he had inadvertently started a fire and then, when he realised what he had done, simply left the building without making any attempt to prevent the fire spreading or to call the fire brigade.

In *R v Gibbins and Proctor* (1918) 13 Cr App R 134, the Court of Appeal held that parents owed a duty of care to their infant children living in the same household. As indicated above, the most relevant authority to this problem is the controversial case of *R v Stone and Dobinson* [1977] 2 All ER 341. Stone, a 67-year-old man of low intelligence, partially deaf and almost blind, lived in a house with his mistress Dobinson, who was 'ineffectual and inadequate', and Stone's subnormal son. Stone's sister Fanny came to live with them and contributed to the rent. Fanny suffered from anorexia nervosa, and was in other ways regarded as eccentric. In due course she refused to leave her room and her condition deteriorated. Stone and Dobinson made minimal efforts to check on her condition, and she was eventually found dead in bed by Dobinson in a scene of appalling filth.

The accused were found guilty of manslaughter and appealed on two grounds to the Court of Appeal, the first being that they had simply omitted to act and, as they did not owe Fanny a duty of care, there was no *actus reus*. This argument was rejected by the Court of Appeal, Lord Lane CJ stating: 'Whether Fanny was a lodger or not she was a blood relative of Stone; she was occupying a room in his house, and Dobinson had undertaken the duty of looking after her'.

Thus the court must decide if a duty of care was owed. In *R v Khan* [1998] Crim LR 830, the Court of Appeal stated that it was for the judge to rule whether, on the facts, a duty was capable of arising and for the jury to decide whether it did arise. However, in *R v Gurphal Singh* [1999] Crim LR 582, the Court of Appeal approved the practice of the trial judge deciding, as a matter of law, that a duty was owed.

The second contention of the accused's counsel was that they lacked the necessary *mens rea* required for manslaughter, as they did not foresee the risk of death or grievous bodily harm. Again the Court of Appeal rejected this argument, holding that the accused had acted in reckless disregard of danger to the health and welfare of an infirm person. Lord Lane CJ said: 'Mere inadvertence is not enough. The defendant must be proved to have been indifferent to an obvious risk of injury to health or actually have foreseen the risk but to have determined nevertheless to run it'.

As indicated above, however, Wood and Mary could point out that their situation is not identical to that of Stone and Dobinson. Gloria is not Wood's sister but only his aunt, and Mary does not appear to have undertaken to look after Gloria in the same way as Dobinson did Fanny. Further, they can argue that Gloria was not actually living in the same house, as she was staying in the lodge at the end of the garden. To impose the same duty on them as was imposed on Stone and Dobinson, where a different type of arrangement existed, would be very harsh, especially when it is generally agreed that *Stone and Dobinson* is a very difficult decision without a clear *ratio decidendi*.

Further, the House of Lords' decision in *R v Adomako* has altered the test in cases where a duty situation exists. Gross negligence and not recklessness is used, and the jury will have to consider whether the extent to which the accused's conduct departed from the proper standard of care incumbent upon them, involving as it must have done a risk of death to the victim, was such that it should be judged criminal. It is therefore much more difficult for the prosecution to prove that there was a risk of death as opposed to a risk of injury to health and welfare.

Q Question 5

Critically analyse with reference to decided cases, the reasons why the development and application of the criminal law is often unpredictable and inconsistent.

Commentary

Warning: do not attempt this type of question in an exam unless you are very competent and confident.

Occasionally an exam will contain a question which requires you to take a wider view of the criminal law. This is such a question. You cannot simply home in on a specific area and cover it in detail. You must try to think of instances throughout the syllabus that can be used in your arguments to answer the question. Avoid the common mistake of interpreting the question to read 'Choose one area of the criminal law where there are difficulties and write all about them'!

This question has been included as it enables you to think more widely about the role of the criminal law within the legal system and society as a whole. Not an easy task, but this author feels that the struggle is worth the effort. It is to be hoped that you agree.

- Constant change — *R* v *R* [1991]

- Lack of code — *Caldwell* [1981], *Morgan* [1975]

- Logic v Policy

- Role of House of Lords — *Clegg* [1995]

⚗️ Suggested answer

The development of many areas of law follows a consistent and logical course. The basic foundations, their concepts and application are accepted by the vast majority, and only fine tuning or adjustments of these principles are required to meet new situations. Unfortunately this cannot be said about criminal law, where the debate about fundamental concepts — such as whether recklessness should be interpreted subjectively or objectively and whether a mistake should have to be on reasonable grounds — and controversial issues — such as whether duress should be a defence to a charge of murder and whether a battered woman should have the defence of provocation — is still ongoing.

One of the problems is that the criminal law is subject to constant change. It has to adapt to cover new phenomena, such as stalking, and to reflect society's changing social and moral standards. As the House of Lords stated in *R* v *R* [1991] 2 All ER 257, abolishing the husband's marital rape exemption, the common law is capable of evolving in the light of social, economic and cultural developments, and the status of women has changed out of all recognition from the time (*Hale's Pleas of the Crown 1736*) when the husband's marital rape exemption was initially recognised. Similarly, society once believed that it was a crime to take your own life, and if you failed you were guilty of attempted suicide and should be punished. However, attitudes softened and it was recognised that such a person needed help, not a criminal trial; the law was consequently amended by the Suicide Act 1961. It is always likely that a newly elected government will introduce changes in certain aspects of the criminal law, e.g., public order offences.

There is no doubt that the development and application of the criminal law would be more consistent and predictable if we had an overall uniform approach. The problem is illustrated by two House of Lords' decisions: *Metropolitan Police Commissioner* v *Caldwell* [1981] 1 All ER 961, where an objective approach to recklessness was used, and *DPP* v *Morgan* [1975] 2 All ER 347, where a subjective approach to mistake was applied. Commentators may argue that two different areas of the criminal law were being considered (criminal damage and rape), but as the Law Commission has recognised (Law Com. No. 143) in suggesting codification: 'the criminal law could then exhibit a uniform approach to all crimes and defences'. At least in so far as recklessness is concerned, the House of Lords has now embraced the notion of subjectivity again in *R* v *G* [2003] 4 All ER 765, but the very fact that the legal definition of such a basic concept can change so much in the space of 20 years is itself startling.

Thus, perhaps above all other factors, the lack of a code is the source of the problem. All other major European countries (France, Germany, Spain) have a detailed criminal code, with a uniform approach providing a starting point for interpreting the law. Our criminal law has developed in a piecemeal fashion, with one offence's development showing little consistency with another's. So often it is difficult to say what our law actually is, even before we start to debate how it should be applied, e.g., *R* v *Savage and Parmenter* [1991] 4 All ER 698, interpreting (after over 130 years of use) the provisions of the Offences Against the Person Act 1861. A code could be expressed in clear language with definitions of fundamental concepts such as intention and recklessness, as suggested by the Law Commission's Draft Criminal Code; although, as the former chairman of the Law Commission Justice Henry Brooke stated ([1995] Crim LR 911): 'Nobody in their right mind would want to put the existing criminal law into a codified form'.

Often our criminal law follows a logical approach in its application; but as it does not exist in a vacuum and is not simply the application of academic principles, policy considerations sometimes prevail. As Lord Salmon stated in *DPP* v *Majewski* [1976] 2 All ER 142, regarding the defence of intoxication, 'the answer is that in strict logic the view [intoxication is no defence to crimes of basic intent] cannot be justified. But this is the view that has been adopted by the common law which is founded on common sense and experience rather than strict logic'. Policy considerations are also behind s. 1(3) of the Criminal Attempts Act 1981, whereby in the offence of attempt, the facts are to be as the accused believes them to be. Thus an accused objectively viewed may not be doing a criminal act but he or she can still be guilty of attempt, as in *R* v *Shivpuri* [1986] 2 All ER 334.

There is often no means of predicting which approach will prevail. In *Jaggard* v

Dickinson [1980] 3 All ER 716, the accused, who had been informed by her friend X that she could break into X's house to shelter, while drunk mistakenly broke into V's house. She was charged with criminal damage under s. 1(1) of the Criminal Damage Act 1971, but argued that she had a lawful excuse under s. 5(2) of the Act as she honestly believed that she had the owner's consent. Although the prosecution contended that this was a crime of basic intent and therefore drunkenness was no defence (citing the House of Lords' decisions of *Metropolitan Police Commissioner* v *Caldwell* and *DPP* v *Majewski* in support), the Court of Appeal quashed her conviction, giving priority to the statutory provision of s. 5(2) of the 1971 Act.

One important aspect of the criminal law process in recent years which has caused uncertainty is the role of the House of Lords in changing the criminal law. Clearly judges are there to say what the law is, not what it should be; but Lord Simon in *DPP for Northern Ireland* v *Lynch* [1975] 1 All ER 913 said: 'I am all for recognising that judges do make law. And I am all for judges exercising their responsibilities boldly at the proper time and place . . . where matters of social policy are not involved which the collective wisdom of Parliament is better suited to resolve'. Thus in *R* v *R*, the House of Lords changed the law of rape, by abolishing the husband's defence of marital rape immunity without waiting for Parliament to implement the Law Commission's recommendations. However, their Lordships took the opposite view in *R* v *Clegg* [1995] 1 All ER 334, where they refused to follow the Law Commission's suggestion that a person who was entitled to use force in self-defence but who used unreasonable force, thereby killing the victim, would be guilty of manslaughter, not murder. Lord Lloyd stated:

> I am not adverse to judges developing law, or indeed making new law, when they can see their way clearly, even where questions of social policy are involved. [A good recent example is *R* v *R*.] But in the present case I am in no doubt that your Lordships should abstain from law making. The reduction of what would otherwise be murder to manslaughter in a particular class of case seems to me essentially a matter for decision by the legislature.

It is difficult to appreciate the essential difference in issues in these two cases, despite Lord Lowery's justifications in *R* v *Clegg* that '*R* v *R* dealt with a specific act and not with a general principle governing criminal liability'. Clearly there is a difference in opinion amongst the Law Lords as to the correct application of these principles. This is well illustrated by the House of Lords' decision in *R* v *Gotts* [1992] 1 All ER 832. The majority decision not to allow duress as a defence to attempted murder was on the basis that duress was no defence to murder. The minority view to the contrary revealed a different analysis. They argued that duress is a general defence throughout the criminal law with the exceptions of the offences of murder and treason. It is for Parliament, and not the courts, to limit the ambit of a defence; and as attempted murder is a different offence to murder, duress must therefore be available.

It is submitted that these are the main reasons why the development and application of the criminal law is often uncertain and unpredictable. There are other factors, such as whether an issue is a question of law for the judge or fact for the jury, e.g., the meaning of 'administer' (*R* v *Gillard* (1988) 87 Cr App R 189); the difficulty in ascertaining the *ratio decidendi* of many cases, e.g., *R* v *Brown* [1993] 2 All ER 75 (consent); and the possible effect of the decisions of the European Court of Human Rights. But it is the lack of a code and uniform principles which are the main factors causing the inherent uncertainty.

Q Question 6

Arthur and Bert are the directors of Malo Ltd, a British ferry company. The directors know that their workforce is under enormous pressure during the tourist season, and that safety requirements are not always closely followed. They know that on several occasions their ferries have sometimes started their journeys with the bow doors slightly open, in breach of recognised procedure. However, as there have been no disasters or loss of life on its ferries, the company has not employed additional workers or improved its safety precautions.

Sid is the assistant bosun who is responsible for ensuring that all bow doors are properly shut, and Dave is the captain, responsible for all aspects of passenger safety. On one journey, Sid opened the bow doors, went to his cabin and fell asleep. As a result the bow doors remained open at the start of the voyage, in breach of safety requirements, and 10 passengers were killed when the sea flooded the lower deck. It later transpired that Dave had not bothered to make his customary check of the bow doors, as he had been too busy dealing with his other duties.

Discuss the criminal liability of Malo Ltd, Arthur and Bert for manslaughter.

Commentary

The outcomes of many recent disasters — such as Hillsborough, the *Marchioness*, Clapham Railway junction, the Kings Cross fire and the Zeebrugge ferry disaster — have focused attention on the question of corporate criminal responsibility. The results of these cases were considered by the vast majority of the public and commentators to be very unsatisfactory. Manslaughter charges were brought only after intense public pressure in one case alone, the Zeebrugge disaster, and those charges were dismissed. In the vast majority of the disaster cases the corporate body escaped with a fine. It is therefore not surprising that the Law Commission has turned its attention to this area (Law Com. No. 237) and that it can form the basis of an examination question.

Apart from covering the basis of corporate responsibility and the important case of *R* v *P&O European Ferries (Dover) Ltd* (1991) 93 Cr App R 72 (the Zeebrugge disaster), it is also necessary to state the existing bases of involuntary manslaughter and briefly consider causation.

If you were instructed to cover the criminal responsibility of the employees, you would need to analyse the issues of omission and causation in full. Detailed coverage of omission can be found in other suggested answers in this and the following chapter.

- **Corporate liability** — *Tesco Supermarkets* v *Nattrass* [1972]

- **Involuntary manslaughter**

- *R* v *P&O European Ferries (Dover) Ltd* [1991]

- *R* v *OLL Ltd* [1994]

- **Causation**

⋅Ọ⋅ Suggested answer

A corporation can be liable to the same extent as an individual for criminal acts carried out by certain employees: first, by holding that a corporation is vicariously liable for the acts of its employees where a natural person would similarly be liable, for example when a statute imposes criminal liability; secondly, by way of the judicially developed principle of identification.

An initial issue for the prosecution would be establishing causation. Malo Ltd and the directors would argue that the deaths were caused by the negligence of Sid and Dave, and therefore that the defendants should be exonerated. However, the prosecution need only establish that the defendants' conduct significantly contributed to the deaths. It is not necessary to prove that it was the main cause or even a substantial cause (*R* v *Cheshire* [1991] 3 All ER 670). Further, the court will rarely accept in criminal cases the *novus actus interveniens* argument (see, e.g., *R* v *Pagett* (1983) 76 Cr App R 141), and it is therefore submitted that it is quite probable that Malo Ltd, Arthur and Bert will be found guilty of manslaughter.

The fact that a company could be guilty of an offence requiring *mens rea* was recognised in *R* v *ICR Haulage Ltd* [1944] 1 All ER 691, where a company was convicted of a common law conspiracy to defraud, the court holding that the intent of the managing director represented the intent of the company. Denning LJ stated:

> a company may in many ways be likened to a human body. It has a nerve centre which controls what it does. The directors and managers represent the directing mind and will of the company and control what it does. The state of mind of these managers is the state of mind of the company and is treated by the law as such.

This principle was applied by the House of Lords in *Tesco Supermarkets* v *Nattrass* [1972] AC 153, where their Lordships held that the company may be criminally liable for the acts of only 'the board of directors and perhaps other superior officers of a company who carry out the functions of management and speak and act as the company'.

In *R* v *P&O European Ferries (Dover) Ltd* (1991) 93 Cr App R 72, Turner J recognised the need to look at the company's articles of association to ascertain the company's controlling mind; and although the courts have held that the company may not be identified with a branch manager of a supermarket (*Tesco* v *Nattrass*) or a depot engineer (*Magna Plant Ltd* v *Mitchell* [1996] Crim LR 396), it is quite clear that it will be identified with the company's directors. Indeed, the decisions by the Privy Council in *Meridian Global Funds Management Asia Ltd* v *Securities Commission* [1995] 2 AC 500 and the House of Lords in *Re Supply of Ready Mix Concrete* [1995] 1 AC 456, indicate that the courts are now more prepared to widen the identification principle to other employees within the company such as the company's financial investment manager.

It is therefore submitted that Arthur and Bert as directors would be identified as the company, but not Sid as assistant bosun of a ship. The position of Dave as ship's captain is less clear-cut, but the prosecution would argue that he should be included as control of the ship has been delegated to him. Nevertheless, the defence would counter with the submission that his position can be equated to that of the supermarket manager in *Tesco* v *Nattrass*, where the House of Lords held he could not be so identified.

Thus in order for Malo Ltd to be found guilty of manslaughter, the prosecution must prove that the directors Arthur or Bert (or possibly the captain Dave) had committed involuntary manslaughter. This can be defined as unlawful homicide without intention to kill or do grievous bodily harm and has two bases: first, constructive manslaughter, where the accused intended to do an act which was unlawful and dangerous (*DPP* v *Newbury and Jones* [1976] 2 All ER 365); secondly, where the accused has been reckless or grossly negligent (*R* v *Adomako* [1994] 3 All ER 79).

Quite clearly, this is not an example of constructive manslaughter as it is perfectly lawful to operate a ferry service; and even if the company was acting negligently so as to be committing a minor offence, this would still not be sufficient for constructive manslaughter. As Lord Aitkin said in *Andrews* v *DPP* [1937] 2 All ER 552: 'There is an obvious difference in the law of manslaughter between doing an unlawful act and doing a lawful act with a degree of carelessness which the legislature makes criminal'. Although this *dictum* has been heavily criticised, this House of Lords' decision is still good law and would apply here.

However, the prosecution would be able to present a strong case on the gross negligence basis. Following *R* v *Adomako*, the prosecution must prove that: (i) a duty of care was owed; (ii) there was a breach of that duty; (iii) the breach was grossly negligent and caused the victim's death. It is submitted that the first two conditions could be easily satisfied, and it is then a question for the jury to decide if the breach was grossly negligent. As Lord Mackay stated in *R* v *Adomako*:

This will depend on the seriousness of the breach of duty committed by the defendant in all the circumstances in which the defendant was placed when it occurred. The jury will have to consider whether the extent to which the defendant's conduct departed from the proper standard of care incumbent upon him, involving as it must have done a risk of death to the [victim] was such that it should be judged criminal.

The company would of course be judged on the standard of the reasonable prudent ferry operator, not that of the reasonable man.

The leading case on this topic is *R* v *P&O European Ferries (Dover) Ltd* (1991) 93 Cr App R 72. The roll-on roll-off ferry, *The Herald of Free Enterprise*, capsized just outside Zeebrugge harbour in March 1987, after leaving the harbour with its bow doors open, resulting in the death of many passengers. The assistant bosun whose job it was to ensure that the doors were shut was asleep in his cabin. The captain had no means of confirming from the bridge whether or not the doors had been shut. They, together with the directors and the company, were tried for manslaughter. Evidence was given that the system had worked without mishap for seven years in which there were upward of over 60,000 sailings. Further, although it would have been easy to reduce or eliminate the risk of the ship ever sailing with its doors open — by a system of positive reporting or the installation of bridge indicator lights — neither the Department of Transport nor Lloyds insurers required these measures, and P&O's system was no different to that of the other ferry operators. The Court of Appeal's ruling in *Attorney-General's Reference (No. 2 of 1999)* [2000] 3 All ER 182, makes it clear that liability for killing by gross negligence can be established without proof of a positive state of mind on the part of the defendant — the issue of fault is looked at objectively. This makes it far easier to impose liability for this type of manslaughter on corporate bodies. *R (on the application of Rowley)* v *DPP* [2003] All ER (D) 72, also confirms that subjective recklessness (actual foresight of risk) is not a pre-requisite for a conviction for gross negligence manslaughter.

The jury might well, therefore, find against Malo Ltd. As a result of Zeebrugge and other disasters, public opinion has hardened, and the dangers of defective systems are well known; secondly, in *R* v *OLL Ltd, Kite and Stoddart* (the Lyme Bay canoeing disaster — (1994), unreported), a company and its managing director were convicted of manslaughter at Winchester Crown Court after the jury had found that they were grossly negligent in allowing schoolchildren to go canoeing on the sea without proper supervision thereby causing their death; and thirdly, in a duty situation, the applicable test is, after *Adomako*, gross negligence and not recklessness.

Q Question 7

Critically assess the grounds upon which liability for failing to act will be imposed in English criminal law.

Commentary

Liability for omissions is a popular topic with examiners, either as an element of a problem question — typically linked to killing by gross negligence to bring out the duty of care issues — or as an essay topic in its own right. To deal comfortably with essay style questions on omissions it is necessary to have a good knowledge of the basic cases. For degree level examinations, however, it is likely that some element of analysis will be necessary. The extent to which this is the case will vary according to the level at which the paper is set. Second and third year undergraduates and CPE students would be expected to display more developed skills of critical evaluation. Try to avoid simply describing the law — make sure that you provide some comment on the examples you have given. There is not a great deal of material on law reform in this area — the Law Commission has not explored it in great detail, but it should not be difficult to identify some of the anomalies that the case law throws up.

- **Basic rule on liability for omissions**

- **Legal duty based on statute**

- **Legal duty based on contract**

- **Legal duty based on office**

- **Common law duty to act**

- **Where a duty ceases to exist**

- **Possible reforms**

⌾ Suggested answer

Every offence in criminal law requires proof of an *actus reus* on the part of the accused. In the vast majority of cases statute or common law defines this *actus reus* in terms of a positive act. Indeed, the expression *actus reus* literally translates as 'guilty act'. A moment's thought reveals, however, that a defendant can commit an offence by failing to act, just as readily as he can by positive action. If the parents of a newly born baby administer a lethal dose of poison to the child no one would seriously suggest that there would be a problem in establishing *actus reus*. Why should it be any different where the defendants decide not to feed the child, with the result that the child dies of starvation? The answer is that there is no difference in criminal law, but the method by which liability is established may differ where it is based on an omission as opposed to a positive act.

The basic rule in English criminal law is that there is no general positive duty to act to prevent the commission of criminal offences or to limit the effect of harm caused by the actions of others. This position reflects what is sometimes referred to as the individualistic approach to liability. If D is at a swimming pool, and he sees P (a young child with whom he has no connection) drowning in the deep end, why should D be required to go to P's aid? P has no special responsibility for P, and did not cause the risk to arise. It is pure chance that D is in a position to help. Why should fate be the basis for imposing a liability for failing to prevent P's death? Critics of the current position at common law argue for a 'social responsibility' approach. This view proposes that liability should arise for failing to attend those in peril partly because of the moral obligation to do so, but also because it reflects a more complex social pact. A positive duty to aid others would impose a responsibility but would also confer a corresponding benefit. D might one day find himself compelled to help P, but the next day he might be the beneficiary of the duty on P to aid D where D is in peril. At a macro level society benefits because less harm is suffered by individuals.

In reality English criminal law does impose criminal liability for failing to act, but it does so on the basis of exceptions. Thus D will not incur liability for failing to act unless the prosecution can point to a positive legal duty to act.

The most obvious source of such legal duties will be statute. Parliament creates liability for failing to act in two ways. At a very simple level it creates offences of omission. It is an offence for the owner of a vehicle to fail to display a valid tax disc. It is an offence to fail to submit a tax return, or to provide company accounts, etc. In these cases the omission itself is the crime. In many cases they are offences of strict or absolute liability. Alternatively Parliament may enact legislation that places a category of person under a duty to act in a particular way. A failure to comply with this duty may result in liability where the failure causes the commission of some prohibited consequence. Perhaps the best known example of this is provided by the Children and Young Persons Act 1933, which places parents and guardians under a legal duty to care for children. Suppose that parents go out for the evening leaving a four-year-old child alone. Whilst they are out he falls onto a fire and is killed. It is likely that the court would find that there was a culpable omission based on the breach of statutory duty, and liability could be imposed if causation and fault are also established.

An alternative basis for establishing a legal duty to act is where D is subject to a contractual duty or holds an office that suggests the imposition of a duty. In the case of employees the court will look at the express or implied terms of the contract to determine the extent and nature of the duties imposed on D. In *R v Pittwood* (1902) 19 TLR 34, a railway crossing gatekeeper opened the gate to let a cart pass, but then went off to lunch, forgetting to close the gate. A hay cart crossed the line and was hit by a train. The defendant was convicted of manslaughter. He argued that the only duty he owed was to his employers, with whom he had a contract. It was held, however, that his contract imposed a wider duty upon him to users of the crossing. Thus the duty arising under a contract inures to the benefit of those who are not privy to the contract — i.e., the passengers on the train. In *R v Dytham* [1979] 3 All ER 641, D was a police constable on duty. He witnessed V being ejected from a nightclub and beaten up by a doorman. D did not intervene. V died from his injuries. D was convicted of the common law offence of misfeasance in public office and his appeal against conviction was dismissed. The case begs the question — why was D not charged with causing the death of V by his failure to intervene? The answer may be that in cases of failing to act, proof of causation may be problematic. D obviously failed in his duty as a police officer — but would his intervention have prevented V's death? The mere fact that there is an agreement between parties does not necessarily mean that there will be a contractual duty to act. In *R v Instan* [1893] 1 QB 450, D was given money by her aunt to buy groceries. D failed to care for her aunt who subsequently died. It is unlikely that any contractual duty existed in this case, as the agreement was a domestic one — hence there would have been no intention to create legal relations.

Inevitably there are situations where, despite the absence of any statutory or contractual duty to act, it is felt that liability ought to be imposed. In such cases it falls to the common law to perform its residual function of supplying the omission. Judges 'discover' new common law duties to act because it is felt they ought to exist. *R v Instan* [1893] 1 QB 450, is a case in point. For the last 12 days of her life the aunt was suffering from gangrene in her leg and was unable to look after herself. Only D knew this. D did not provide her aunt with food nor did she obtain medical attention. This omission accelerated the aunt's death. D's conviction for manslaughter was upheld, the court proceeding on the basis that a common law duty was simply a moral duty so fundamental the courts had to enforce it. As Lord Coleridge CJ observed, a legal common law duty is nothing else than the enforcing by law of that which is a moral obligation without legal enforcement.

The problem with the common law is that it is reactive — it only develops because cases come to the courts on appeal. A narrow reading of *R v Instan* suggests that a common law duty is owed to one's blood relatives, but clearly the scope should be wider than that. The court in *R v Gibbins and Proctor* (1918) 13 Cr App R 134, accepted that a duty could be imposed upon a common law wife to care for her partner's child because, although the child was not hers, she had assumed a duty towards the child by choosing to live with the child's father and accept housekeeping money to buy food for them all. The problem with such rulings is that the limits of liability are left vague — what if D had lived with the child's father only on weekends?

Imposing liability for omissions where D undertakes to care for P and P becomes reliant on D may even be counter-productive. In *R v Stone and Dobinson* [1977] QB 354, the defendants were convicted of the manslaughter of Stone's sister Fanny because they took her in but failed to care for her adequately. With hindsight they might have been advised not to help her in the first place. The law therefore sends mixed messages. One ought to care for others, but one should not start to do so unless one is able to discharge that duty properly.

The common law duty to act was developed further by the important House of Lords' decision in *R* v *Miller* [1983] 1 All ER 978. D, who was squatting in an empty house, fell asleep whilst smoking a cigarette. Whilst he was asleep the cigarette set fire to the mattress. D woke, realised the mattress was on fire, but took no steps to dose the fire. The house was damaged in the ensuing blaze. He was obviously not under a statutory duty to put the fire out, nor was he under a contractual duty to do so. At the time the common law duties to act were based on duties owed to blood relatives, or arising from reliance. The House of Lords had little choice but to 'discover' a new legal duty at common law. Such a duty arises where D accidentally causes harm, realises that he has done so, and it lies within his power to take steps, either himself or by calling for the assistance to prevent or minimise the harm. The omission itself is not, of course, the offence. For criminal damage it must be shown that the omission caused the harm, and that D had the requisite *mens rea* at the time of the *actus reus*. Whilst the ruling in *R* v *Miller* is socially desirable — there is great social utility in D being required to limit the effect of his careless actions — there are many uncertainties. What is it that D is required to do once he realises he has caused harm? Is the test objective or subjective? Must he act as the reasonable person would have done, or does he simply have to do his best? The latter would certainly accord with the general trend towards subjectivity in criminal law.

Even where a positive legal duty to act can be identified, uncertainties may arise as to whether D has been or can be absolved from that duty. In *R* v *Smith* [1979] Crim LR 251, D's wife was seriously ill. She asked D not to seek help. Her condition worsened and she eventually asked D to get help, which he did, but it was too late to save her. D was charged with manslaughter and the trial judge directed the jury that D was under a duty by virtue of being the victim's husband, but he could be released from that duty if she so indicated and she was of sound mind at the time. This places the husband in a difficult legal position. At what point must he ignore his wife's wishes and obtain medical help? Some clarification is provided by the House of Lords' decision in *Airedale NHS Trust* v *Bland* [1993] AC 89, where it was held that doctors were under a duty to treat a patient where it was in the patient's best interests to do so. Where, however, all hope of the patient recovering had disappeared, the duty to nourish and maintain the patient would also cease.

To date the Law Commission has done little more than suggest a codification of the common law position as outlined above. It is submitted that a more radical approach would be to adopt the French model of creating a general statutory duty of 'easy rescue'. Essentially there would be liability for failing to prevent harm where such prevention would not be too onerous or difficult for D to achieve. The accident that led to the death of Princess Diana in the Paris underpass illustrates the point. French photographers were charged with manslaughter based on their failure to help because they allegedly photographed the crash scene when they could have been offering aid to the injured. Such a prosecution would not have been possible under English law.

Further reading

Amirthalingam, K., 'Caldwell Recklessness is Dead, Long Live Mens Rea's Fecklessness' [2004] MLR 491.

Ashworth, A., 'Interpreting Criminal Statutes' [1991] LQR 419.

Ashworth, A. and Blake, M., 'The Presumption of Innocence in English Criminal Law' [1996] Crim LR 306.

Kaveny, C.M., 'Inferring Intention from Foresight' (2004) LQR 120.

Norrie, A., 'Oblique Intent and Legal Politics' [1989] Crim LR 793.

Pedain, A., 'Intention and the Terrorist Example' [2003] Crim LR 549.

Smith, J.C., 'R v Woollin' [1998] Crim LR 890.

Sullivan, B., 'Corporate Killing — Some Government Proposals' [2001] Crim LR 31.

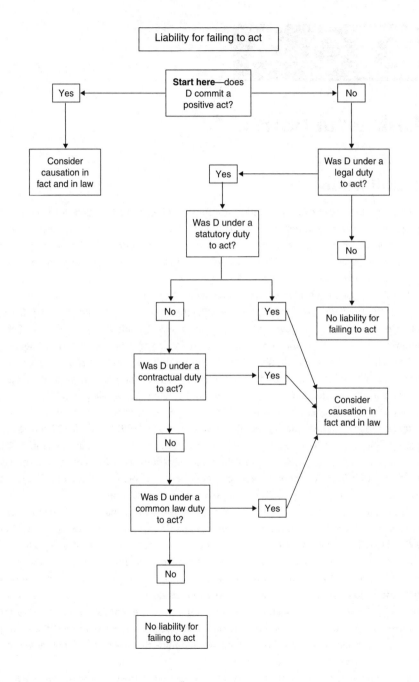

Unlawful homicide

Introduction

One of the themes of this book, and of the substantive criminal law itself, is the constant pressure for change and consequent uncertainty. This is aptly illustrated by the offences of murder and manslaughter, aspects of which have been considered by the House of Lords in recent years and have also been the subject of Law Commission reports (in particular involuntary manslaughter: No. 237 1996).

Despite the fact that Parliament has intervened in the past to amend aspects of homicide, e.g., in the Homicide Act 1957 and the Law Reform (Year and a Day Rule) Act 1996, the offence of murder is still governed by a common law definition. The *actus reus* of the offence is essentially causing the death of a human being. The *mens rea* is sometimes referred to as 'malice aforethought' — but it is suggested that this term should be avoided as it is likely to mislead. Murder does not require any proof of malice towards the victim on the part of the defendant, and there is no requirement that the killing should have been in any way premeditated. *R v Moloney* [1985] 1 All ER 1025, reaffirms that the *mens rea* is intention to kill or cause grievous bodily harm. *R v Woollin* [1998] 4 All ER 103 provides a gloss on this by providing that in cases where there may be some doubt as to intention the jury can have regard to the extent to which the defendant foresaw death or grievous bodily harm resulting from his actions. Intention should only be inferred where the defendant foresees a consequence as virtually certain to result from his actions.

The debate as to whether intention to kill or do grievous bodily harm should be the *mens rea* has been fuelled by Lord Mustill's *obiter dicta* in *Attorney-General's Reference (No. 3 of 1994)* [1997] 3 All ER 936. He was critical of the conspicuous anomaly that intention to cause grievous bodily harm is sufficient *mens rea* for murder. This anomaly has also been recognised by the Law Commission, whose Draft Code (cl. 54) provides that an intention to cause serious personal harm *being aware that death may occur* should be required. However, this suggestion, together with those abolishing the mandatory life sentence for murder, is likely to go unheeded on the basis that such changes would send the wrong message to society, in as much as the public would think that the crime of murder was no longer regarded as such a serious offence.

The need for legislation in this area was also recognised by the Law Lords in *Airedale NHS Trust v Bland* [1993] 1 All ER 821, concerning the criminal responsibility of doctors regarding euthanasia. This was another example of the problems caused by the absence of a criminal code, highlighting the fact that sometimes we do not actually know what the law is until it is formulated in a House of Lords' decision. It is certainly most unsatisfactory that their Lordships had to resort to the distinction between acts and omissions, in deciding that disconnecting the naso-gastric tube was an omission (to give further treatment), in order to hold that a doctor in these circumstances would not be committing murder or manslaughter.

The Law Commission has also recognised the urgent need to reform the law on involuntary manslaughter, to the extent that in their 1996 Report (Law Com. No. 237) they proposed the abolition of the common law offence and its replacement by two separate offences based on subjective recklessness and gross carelessness. It is an unusual step when the Law Commission decide to scrap all of the applicable principles, but in 1980 the Criminal Law Revision Committee stated that 'so serious an offence as manslaughter should not be a lottery'. Nevertheless, all the anomalies and inconsistencies must still be applied in trying to answer questions on this troublesome area. The author has accordingly included in this chapter typical problem questions concerning all the important aspects of these topics, as well as a full question on the partial defence of provocation, always an examination favourite.

Q Question 1

Mary, intending to give her neighbours Jill and Stan a fright, lit a fire in their letterbox not knowing whether anybody was in the house. In fact, Jill and Stan had gone out for the evening, but their aged parents, Meg and Hugh, who were staying at their home, were overcome by fumes. Owing to an administrative error, two ambulances arrived to take the victims to hospital; and the ambulance in which Hugh was transported was driven so negligently that it was involved in an accident and by the time it arrived at hospital Hugh had died.

Meg arrived at hospital and was informed that a blood transfusion would save her life. However, owing to religious beliefs, she refused and died two days later.

Discuss the criminal liability of Mary.

Commentary

Most criminal law exams will contain a question on murder, and this question is typical. Whenever you cover murder you should always consider the possibility of involuntary manslaughter as an alternative as examiners often leave the issue of *mens rea* for murder in doubt. In this answer the constructive basis of involuntary manslaughter is dealt with in detail.

The other major area that must be covered in detail is causation. Again this is a topic that you will often find included in questions based on unlawful homicide, and in this answer the cases concerning medical treatment as a *novus actus interveniens* must be analysed. In terms of construction of your answer, it generally aids clarity to deal with causation at the outset, as it is a common factor whatever form of homicide is involved.

Although there are difficulties surrounding these topics a well-prepared student would be confident of obtaining a high mark on a question of this nature.

- **Causation**

- **Murder — whether or not *mens rea* is made out**

- **Transferred malice**

- **Constructive manslaughter**

- **Causation**

- **Criminal Damage Act 1971**

:Q: **Suggested answer**

The most serious offences that Mary may be charged with are murder and manslaughter. Murder comprises causing the death of a human being within the Queen's peace with intention to kill or do grievous bodily harm. It has not been necessary since the coming into force of the Law Reform (Year and a Day Rule) Act 1996, that the death takes place within a year and a day of the unlawful act or omission.

The first issue to consider is that of causation. But for Mary starting the fire neither death would have occurred — hence causation in fact is established. As to causation in law, the prosecution does not have to prove that Mary's actions were the main cause or even a substantial cause of the victims' deaths, merely that they made a significant contribution to the consequence (*R* v *Cheshire* [1991] 3 All ER 670). Mary would argue in respect of Meg's death that her decision to refuse a blood transfusion was unreasonable and thus constituted a *novus actus interveniens* that broke the chain of causation. This point was resolved in *R* v *Blaue* [1975] 1 WLR 1411 where, on similar facts, the court applied the 'egg-shell skull' principle that you take your victim as you find him. Thus an accused will not be exonerated merely because the consequences of the accused's act are exacerbated by the susceptibilities of the victim. As Lawton LJ stated in *Blaue*: 'It has been the policy of the law that those who use violence on other people must take their victims as they find them. This in our judgement means the whole man, not just the physical man'. In *Blaue* the court refused to say that the victim's decision was unreasonable, but even if it were, on the authority of *R* v *Holland* (1841) 2 Mood and R 351, it would still not exonerate Mary. In this case the accused severely cut the victim's hand with an iron sword. The victim refused to have his fingers amputated although he was given medical advice that failure to do so would result in lockjaw and his death. Unfortunately, the diagnosis proved correct and the victim died. Nevertheless the accused was convicted of murder.

The position regarding Hugh's death is more complicated. Mary would argue the authority of *R v Jordan* (1956) 40 Cr App R 152, which decided that if the medical treatment received was the sole cause of death and was also grossly negligent, the chain of causation will be broken. However, later cases have isolated *Jordan*, demonstrating that it is very difficult to succeed with this argument. Thus in *R v Smith* [1959] 2 All ER 193, the accused stabbed the victim in a barrack room brawl. The victim was dropped twice while being taken to the medical orderly who failed to diagnose the full extent of his wounds. Not surprisingly the victim died, but the accused's conviction for murder was upheld as the court held that as the original wound was still an operating cause of death the chain of causation was not broken. Similarly in *R v Cheshire* (above), on facts similar to *R v Jordan*, the Court of Appeal upheld the accused's conviction for murder, Beldam LJ stating: 'it will only be in the most extraordinary and unusual case that such treatment can be said to be so independent of the acts of the accused that it could be regarded in law as the cause of the victim's death to the exclusion of the accused's act'.

So even if the evidence was capable of showing that the injuries sustained by Hugh in the ambulance accident were the sole cause of death, the court might still conclude that this was not 'so independent of the acts of the accused' and therefore not sufficient to break the chain of causation.

The *mens rea* for murder is satisfied by the prosecution establishing that the accused intended to kill or cause grievous bodily harm. This was stated in *R v Moloney* [1985] 1 All ER 1025 and confirmed by the House of Lords in *R v Hancock and Shankland* [1986] 1 All ER 641 and *R v Woollin* [1998] 4 All ER 103. This is a question of fact for the jury, and in *Moloney* the House of Lords stated that unless intention was a very complicated issue because of the facts of the case the trial judge should avoid any elaboration or paraphrasing of what is meant by intention, but simply leave it to the jury's good sense as intention is a word in common use and easily understood by the public.

If the issue is complex the trial judge might follow the guidelines laid down by the House of Lords in *Woollin*, where it was stated that if the simple direction was not enough, the jury should be further directed that they were not entitled to find the necessary intention unless they felt sure that death or serious bodily harm was a virtually certain result of D's actions (barring some unforeseen intervention) and that D had appreciated that fact.

However, Lord Scarman in *Hancock and Shankland* did emphasise that there is no magic formula that the trial judge must follow, although he should point out to the jury that the more probable the consequence the more likely the accused foresaw it and intended it. Nevertheless, foresight of consequence is not conclusive proof of intention, although it is evidence from which the jury may infer intention.

Mary may argue that she intended only to frighten the occupants of the house and not to cause death or grievous bodily harm. She may also argue that she did not intend to harm Hugh and Meg, but this argument will fail because of the doctrine of transferred malice, i.e., if Mary has the *mens rea* for a particular offence against a particular victim but she actually commits that crime against a different victim, the *mens rea* will be transferred to the actual victim and Mary will be guilty of that offence. Thus in *R* v *Mitchell* [1983] 2 All ER 427, the accused was found guilty of manslaughter when he deliberately hit a 72-year-old man who fell against an 89-year-old woman, knocking her over and causing her to break a femur. This required an operation and she died as a result of complications arising from it. The Court of Appeal rejected the accused's argument that the doctrine could only apply if the actual victim and the intended victim were identical; and more recently in *Attorney-General's Reference (No. 3 of 1994)* [1996] 1 Cr App R 351, the court held that the doctrine could apply to convict an accused of murder who stabbed a pregnant woman with the result that the baby was born alive but later died as a result of injuries inflicted by the accused (although this decision was reversed by the House of Lords: [1997] 3 All ER 936).

As intention is a question of fact for the jury, it is not possible to be certain that they would conclude that Mary had the necessary *mens rea*. A jury might accept that her action was directed at simply damaging the house or simply frightening the occupants. If this were the case, Mary could still be convicted of involuntary manslaughter, which is unlawful homicide without intention to kill or do grievous bodily harm. There are two broad categories of involuntary manslaughter. First, manslaughter by an unlawful and dangerous act, where the prosecution must prove that the accused intended to do an act that was unlawful and dangerous. Secondly, manslaughter by gross negligence or recklessness as to the risk of death (*R* v *Adomako* [1994] 3 All ER 79).

The constructive basis (as the first category is often known) is the one on which the prosecution would concentrate as it is easily established. It is not necessary for the prosecution to prove that Mary knew the act was unlawful or dangerous, simply that she intended to do that act — i.e., set fire to the house. Whether the act is unlawful is clearly a question for the judge and jury. It is clear that Mary has committed the *actus reus* of criminal damage, and although the jury must be satisfied that Mary had the necessary *mens rea* for this offence (*R* v *Jennings* [1990] Crim LR 588), she clearly intended to start the fire.

Mary may argue that she did not realise that this was dangerous, but this contention will not succeed as the House of Lords in *DPP* v *Newbury and Jones* [1976] 2 All ER 365 confirmed that this is a question of fact for the jury and the prosecution does not have to prove that the accused recognised the risk of danger. Further, the appropriate direction to the jury is that the accused's act is dangerous if, following *R* v *Dawson* (1985) 81 Cr App R 150, a sober and reasonable person, at the scene of the crime, watching the unlawful act being performed, knowing what the defendant knows of the circumstances, and seeing what the defendant sees, would have foreseen the risk of some physical harm resulting therefrom. It is quite clear that if one sets fire to a residential property not knowing whether the house is occupied there is a risk of physical harm, and therefore the prosecution would easily satisfy this condition.

In *R* v *Dalby* [1982] 1 All ER 916, the Court of Appeal appeared to introduce a third condition into constructive manslaughter — i.e., the act must be directed at the victim and likely to cause immediate injury. This was quickly amended by *R* v *Mitchell* to an act directed at another (not necessarily the victim). However, in *R* v *Goodfellow* (1986) 83 Cr App R 23, where the accused, intending to be re-housed by the council, set fire to his house, thereby causing the death of some of his family, the 'aimed-at doctrine' was rejected and the accused was convicted of constructive and reckless manslaughter. Thus it appears that as long as there is no intervening act, this condition is satisfied.

There has always been uncertainty as to what the appropriate *mens rea* for manslaughter should be, and indeed actually is. As Lord Aitkin stated in *Andrews* v *DPP* [1937] 2 All ER 552 at pp. 554–5, 'of all crimes manslaughter appears to afford most difficulties of definition, for it concerns homicide in so many and so varying conditions'. It is submitted that the *mens rea* for the unlawful act of criminal damage should suffice — thus following the decision of the House of Lords in *R* v *G* [2003] 4 All ER 765, Mary must be shown to have at least been aware of the risk of criminal damage.

In the unlikely event of Mary's arguments on causation succeeding, she would still be guilty of offences under the Criminal Damage Act 1971. In particular, arson under s. 1(3) and intentionally or recklessly endangering life under s. 1(2). On the other hand, it is unlikely that she would be convicted of attempted murder, as the prosecution must prove that Mary intended to kill — an intention to cause grievous bodily harm is not sufficient (*R* v *Jones* [1990] 1 WLR 1057).

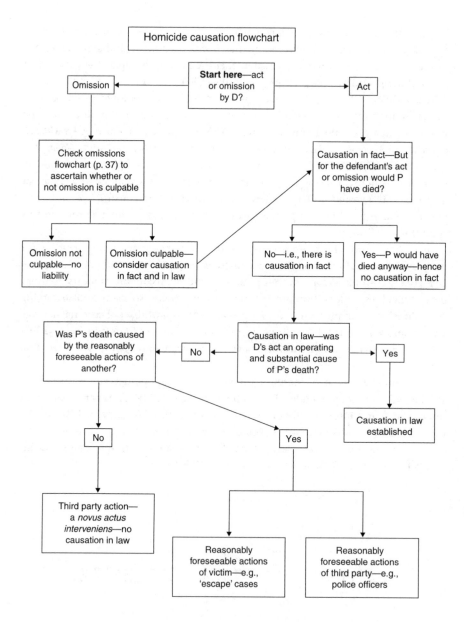

Q Question 2

Discuss Don's criminal liability for murder and manslaughter in the following circumstances.

On a very cold winter's night Don, accompanied by Mrs X, is driving along a lonely country road. Don's attention is distracted by his talking with Mrs X and he knocks down Tim, a pedestrian. Don is worried that Mrs X's husband may somehow learn of their relationship and therefore drives on although he can clearly see that Tim is injured and unconscious. Tim's body is not discovered until the following morning, by which time he has died from exposure to the exceptional cold. If he had received proper medical treatment the previous night, he would not have died.

Commentary

Even a cursory examination of this question should reveal that it raises issues of liability for failing to act, causation and manslaughter. The key to writing a good answer lies in getting the structure right and then calculating what emphasis to place on the various facets of the problem.

Note that the rubric requires candidates to address liability for homicide, hence avoiding getting side-tracked into a consideration of offences against the person. Candidates should recognise that there are two possible routes to liability based on the given facts. One relates to the positive act of colliding with Tim, the other relates to the consequences of Don's liability for failing to act.

In most answers you have to make decisions about how much material to include on specific elements. In this answer, as a conviction for murder is most unlikely, there is very little to suggest the necessary *mens rea*. (By contrast with the answer to the previous question, where this issue was in some doubt, and therefore required extensive coverage of the issue of intention.) Here, on the other hand, manslaughter is analysed in great detail, with an emphasis on applying the law to the facts of this problem.

Note that you are not required to consider the criminal responsibility of Mrs X, or offences other than murder or manslaughter, although clearly Don would be guilty of offences under the Road Traffic Act 1991.

- Act or omission

- Causation

- Murder

- Manslaughter

- Constructive manslaughter

- Manslaughter by gross negligence

- Duty of care

:Q: Suggested answer

Don's liability for the death of Tim could be based on his positive act of colliding with him. But for the collision Tim would not have died — hence Don in fact caused Tim's death. As to causation in law, the operating and substantial cause of death is hypothermia — in effect Tim being left out all night in the cold. He does not actually die from his injuries, although these obviously played a part. For this reason the prosecution would be advised to base Don's liability on his failure to care for Tim immediately following the collision.

There is no general liability for failing to act, but the law recognises exceptions where D is under a positive legal duty to act. Don would have been under a positive legal duty to report a road accident involving injury to another person, but this is an offence in its own right and is not the ideal basis for an allegation that he has committed homicide. More promising is the contention that Don accidentally caused harm to Tim, realised that he had done so, and thereby came under a common law duty to limit the extent of that harm so far as it was in his power to do so. The prosecution would argue that the facts satisfy the requirements for culpable omission laid down by the House of Lords in *R v Miller* [1983] 1 All ER 978. The House of Lords stated that a duty owed by someone who had created a danger was broken when that person deliberately failed to take steps to minimise that danger. Lord Diplock said:

> I see no rational ground for excluding from conduct capable of giving rise to criminal liability conduct which consists of failing to take measures that lie within one's power to counteract a danger that one has oneself created, if at the time of such conduct one's state of mind is such as constitutes a necessary ingredient of the offence.

This principle would apply to impose a duty on Don to summon medical assistance.

Although, Don might argue that the weather operated as a *novus actus interveniens*, the prosecution has to establish only that Don's conduct was a significantly contributing cause (*R v Cheshire* [1991] 3 All ER 670). The courts are also traditionally reluctant to accept the argument that a *novus actus interveniens* has broken the chain of causation and it cannot be envisaged that the extreme cold weather could be deemed the sole cause of death thereby exonerating Don.

Assuming causation can be established, attention turns to consideration of the type of homicide Don might be charged with. Murder seems most unlikely. In *R v Moloney* [1985] 1 All ER 1025, the House of Lords stated that only an intention to kill or cause grievous bodily harm would be sufficient to constitute the mens rea for murder. Their Lordships in *Moloney* also held that as intention is a word in common use, easily understood by the public, it should be left to the jury by the trial judge without any elaborate definition or direction. It is submitted that as Don was simply inadvertent when initially knocking Tim over, there is no question of the requisite intent being made out and accordingly this issue should not be left to the jury.

Manslaughter is divided into two categories: voluntary and involuntary. Voluntary manslaughter occurs when the accused causes the victim's death with intent to kill or do some grievous bodily harm, but successfully relies on one of the four partial defences arising under the Homicide Act 1957. These defences are: provocation; diminished responsibility; infanticide; or death arising as a result of a suicide pact. On the facts of this question there is no evidence of these elements and voluntary manslaughter would not be considered by the court.

Involuntary manslaughter is unlawful homicide without intent to kill or do some grievous bodily harm. The prosecution must prove that the accused caused the victim's death and, either that he intended to do an act that was unlawful and dangerous (constructive manslaughter), or that he was grossly negligent or reckless as to the risk of death (*R v Adomako* [1994] 3 All ER 79).

A manslaughter charge alleging constructive manslaughter could be problematic, as there is doubt as to whether an omission can constitute an unlawful and dangerous act for this purpose. The uncertainty stems from the Court of Appeal decision in *R v Lowe* [1973] 1 All ER 805; and in *R v Shepperd* [1980] 3 All ER 899, the House of Lords distinguished between omissions and commission stating:

> If I strike a child in a manner likely to cause harm it is right that if that child dies I may be charged with manslaughter. If, however, I omit to do something with the result that it suffers injury to its health which results in its death, we think that a charge of manslaughter should not be an inevitable consequence even if the omission is deliberate.

The prosecution would, therefore, be advised to concentrate on the allegation of killing by gross negligence, a form of manslaughter that can be based on a failure to act. The elements of the offence were established by the House of Lords in *R v Adomako*, where their Lordships decided that in cases of death resulting from a duty of care situation, the prosecution must prove the following conditions:

(a)   the accused owed a duty of care to the victim;

(b)   the accused acted in breach of that duty;

(c)   the accused's conduct was grossly negligent; and

(d)   that conduct caused the victim's death.

Whether or not conduct is grossly negligent is a question of fact for the jury and will depend on the seriousness of the breach in all the circumstances in which the accused was placed when it occurred. 'The jury will have to consider whether the extent to which the accused's conduct departed from the proper standard of care incumbent upon him involving as it must have done a risk of death to the victim was such that it should be judged criminal' (per Lord Mackay in R v Adomako).

As regards the collision, if Don had been only momentarily distracted while driving and the incident took place on a lonely country road where there was little possibility of other traffic or pedestrians, it is unlikely that the jury would find him grossly negligent as to the risk of death. However, Don's liability will be based on the fact that he realised that he had knocked Tim over and then deliberately left him. Was Don grossly negligent with regard to the risk of death? It is likely the jury will conclude that he was. The victim was unconscious; it was a lonely country road, and there was therefore little possibility of a passer-by coming to his assistance; and it was an extremely cold night, which meant that Tim's condition would rapidly deteriorate.

It is therefore submitted that the prosecution should now be able to establish all the ingredients of gross negligence and that Don would be found guilty of involuntary manslaughter.

Q Question 3

Prescilla is pregnant and Richard (as he well knows) is responsible for her condition. They become very depressed about the future and decide to commit suicide, by attaching themselves together by way of an electric cable which Richard connects to the mains. Richard then pulls the switch, but although a strong current passes through them and they are both badly burnt they are not killed. They are both taken to hospital and treated for first degree burns. Prescilla gives birth to a premature baby who, as a result of injuries caused by the electrocution, suffers severe respiratory problems. She is placed on a ventilator; but after five days, because she is now in a persistent vegetative state with no hope of recovery, Dr Spock decides to turn the machine off and the baby dies.

Discuss the criminal responsibility of Richard and Dr Spock.

Commentary

This question involves a number of interesting issues concerning unlawful homicide and the doctrine of transferred malice. It also requires detailed analysis of two controversial cases: Attorney-General's Reference (No. 3 of 1994) [1997] 3 All ER 936 and Airedale NHS Trust v Bland [1993] 1 All ER 821.

Candidates must also consider the question of suicide, and how the provisions of the Suicide Act 1961 and the Homicide Act 1957 affect the position. Consideration of the offence of abstracting electricity without the owner's consent under s. 13 of the Theft Act 1968 is not required!

- Causation

- Murder

- s. 2 Suicide Act 1961

- Transferred malice

- *Airedale NHS Trust* v *Bland* [1993]

⋮Q⋮ Suggested answer

Richard could be charged with a number of offences arising out of this incident. Regarding Prescilla, he could be charged with attempted murder, unlawful wounding under s. 18 of the Offences Against the Person Act 1861, and aiding and abetting suicide under s. 2 of the Suicide Act 1961. Regarding the baby who is born alive, he could (following *Attorney-General's Reference (No. 3 of 1994)* [1997] 3 All ER 936) be guilty of murder.

Turning first to causation, Richard may argue that he did not cause the baby's death, as the chain of causation was broken by Dr Spock turning off the life support machine. However, the prosecution only has to show that Richard's act significantly contributed to the baby's death (*R* v *Cheshire* [1991] 3 All ER 670). In *R* v *Steel and Malcherek* [1981] 2 All ER 422, Lord Lane CJ said (at pp. 696–7) that 'the fact that the victim has died despite or because of medical treatment for the initial injury given by careful and skilled medical practitioners will not exonerate the original assailant from the responsibility for the death'. It is therefore submitted that the prosecution would be able to establish causation by Richard.

Richard could be charged with murder of the baby. Murder is the unlawful killing of a human being within the Queen's peace, with intention to kill or do grievous bodily harm. If a foetus is injured in the womb and is not born alive, the appropriate charge is abortion or child destruction. However, in this problem, the baby had an existence independent of the mother, and Richard could be charged with murder. He will argue that he lacked *mens rea*, as he did not intend to kill or cause grievous bodily harm to the baby. Nevertheless, the prosecution can contend that the doctrine of transferred malice applies. Thus, where an accused has the *mens rea* for one particular crime but the actual victim is different from the intended victim, the accused will be guilty of the manslaughter of the actual victim. This long-established principle has been applied in many cases, e.g., in *R* v *Mitchell* [1983] QB 741, the accused was found guilty of the manslaughter of V when he deliberately hit X causing him to fall onto V thereby breaking her femur, an injury from which she eventually died.

Against this, however, the House of Lords held in *Attorney-General's Reference (No. 3 of 1994)* [1997] 3 All ER 936, that the doctrine of transferred malice could not be relied upon to secure a conviction for murder where an accused had stabbed a pregnant woman with the result that the baby was born alive but later died as a result of the injuries inflicted by his actions. The House reversed the decision of the Court of Appeal, reasoning that they could not extend the doctrine to what they regarded as a double transfer of intent — from the mother to the foetus, and from the foetus to the child. Lord Mustill stated that the doctrine 'is useful enough to yield rough justice in particular cases, and it can sensibly be retained notwithstanding its lack of any sound intellectual basis. But it is another matter to build a new rule upon it'.

Surprisingly, in view of their rejection of the Court of Appeal's reasoning, the House held that the accused could be guilty of the manslaughter of the baby. Thus Richard could be convicted of the manslaughter of the baby, on the basis that he intended to do an act that was unlawful and dangerous.

To be found guilty of attempted murder the accused must have done more than a merely preparatory act (Criminal Attempts Act 1981, s. 1) with an intention to kill (*R v Whybrow* (1951) 35 Cr App R 141); nor is an intention to cause grievous bodily harm sufficient (*R v Jones* [1990] 3 All ER 886). It is submitted that the jury would conclude that turning on the electricity after wiring up Prescilla is more than merely preparatory, and as Richard and Prescilla intended to die the prosecution could easily establish *mens rea*. However, in view of the alternative offences and the provisions of the Suicide Act 1961, the Crown Prosecution Service might decide that attempted murder is not the most appropriate charge. Incidentally, although the existence of a suicide pact (within the meaning of s. 4(3) of the Homicide Act 1957) is a defence, reducing murder to manslaughter, it is not available on a charge of attempted murder.

Instead Richard could be charged under s. 2 of the Suicide Act 1961, i.e., 'a person who aids, abets, counsels or procures the suicide of another shall be liable on conviction on indictment to imprisonment for a term not exceeding 14 years'. *R v McShane* [1977] Crim LR 737 demonstrates that Richard can be convicted of attempting to commit the offence, and it is submitted that as the facts clearly show that he has sufficient *mens rea* he will be found guilty of this offence.

Similarly there appears to be little doubt that a conviction under s. 18 of the Offences Against the Person Act 1861 would also follow. The severe burns would constitute either a wound or grievous bodily harm and Richard clearly has the intention to bring about this consequence (*R v Belfon* [1976] 3 All ER 46). It is most unlikely that Prescilla's consent would be a defence.

Dr Spock may also face charges of murder or manslaughter in respect of the baby's death, and his responsibility may depend on the application of the House of Lords' decision in *Airedale NHS Trust v Bland* [1993] 1 All ER 821. Although only a civil case, the House of Lords did consider at great length the criminal responsibility of a doctor who decided to disconnect the naso-gastric tube, which was feeding the victim who was in a persistent vegetative state. Their Lordships concluded that in the unlikely event of a prosecution for murder, there might be difficulties for the prosecution in establishing malice aforethought. However, the reason why they have believed there would be no conviction for murder or manslaughter was based on the traditional approach in dealing with omissions to act.

Their Lordships' reasoning was that disconnecting the naso-gastric tube would be viewed as discontinuing treatment and would therefore constitute an omission to act. Omissions are not punishable unless there is a duty to act, with breach of that duty causing the prohibited consequence. Clearly in a doctor/patient relationship the doctor owes a duty to act in the patient's best interests (R v *Adomako* [1993] 4 All ER 935), but it is not always in the patient's best interests to be kept alive in any circumstances. Thus if a doctor decides on bona fide grounds in accordance with accepted medical practice that it is in the patient's best interest to discontinue treatment and allow the patient to die with dignity, the doctor will not be acting in breach of his duty and cannot therefore be criminally responsible. Of course if he does a positive act which accelerates death this reasoning cannot apply and he could be found guilty of murder or manslaughter or attempted murder, as in the case of R v *Cox* [1992] *The Times*, 18 November (unreported), where a doctor, at the request of an incurably ill patient and with the consent of her relatives, gave her a drug with no analgesic (pain-relieving) qualities which in fact hastened the patient's death.

Q Question 4

Nick is married to Judith. Their marriage has been going through a difficult period because of Nick's prolonged impotence and violent mood swings. Nick has known for some time that Judith has been unfaithful to him but has said nothing to her. On a number of occasions he has lost his temper and assaulted Judith. A psychiatrist has examined Nick and advised that he suffers from a behavioural disorder that manifests itself in aggression towards women. Recently Nick has also become depressed because he has been made redundant and cannot find another job. One afternoon Nick returns home unexpectedly from work and finds Judith in bed having sex with David, his best friend. As he happens to be in an exceptionally phlegmatic mood, Nick calmly opens his wallet, takes out a £50 note and gives it to David, telling him to '. . . go and find a real whore . . .'. As Nick turns to leave the room Judith shouts 'At least he satisfies me, which is more than you can do!' Nick picks up a heavy hand-held mirror from Judith's dressing table and deals her a series of savage blows about the head, killing her. The glass from the mirror is dislodged by the impact with Judith's head and flies across the bed, hitting David in the neck. Nick sees what has happened but runs off in panic. David dies within minutes through loss of blood. Nick is apprehended by the police shortly afterwards.

Advise the Crown Prosecution Service as to the liability of Nick for the deaths of Judith and David.

Commentary

Provocation is a popular topic with criminal law examiners, whether as an essay question or as part of a homicide problem. Regarding essay questions, there is plenty of material for the candidate to comment upon. Decisions such as *R v Ahluwalia* [1992] 4 All ER 894 and *R v Thornton (No. 2)* [1996] 2 All ER 1023 (concerning battered women who kill their husbands) brought to public attention the deficiencies of the defence, leading many to call for reforms. These controversies have been reflected in the differences of opinion between the senior judges — particularly in respect of the extent to which provocation should be based on an objective standard as regards the degree of self-control to be expected from the accused. A good knowledge of decisions such as *DPP v Camplin* [1978] 2 All ER 168, *R v Morhall* [1995] 3 All ER 659, *R v Smith* [2000] 3 WLR 654 and *Luc Thiet Thuan v R* [1997] 2 All ER 1033, is therefore essential.

In terms of organising material to answer this question it is best to consider liability in relation to each victim separately, starting with causation and working through *mens rea* and defences. Note the way in which liability for omission arises in relation to the death of David. Note too the limitations of the rubric. There is no need to consider criminal damage as a free-standing offence, although it could play a part in the examination of unlawful act manslaughter.

- Causation

- *Mens rea*

- s. 3, Homicide Act 1957

- Subjective test for provocation

- Objective test for provocation *Smith* [2000]

- Issues related to transferred malice

:Q: Suggested answer

In relation to the death of Judith it would appear that Nick has caused the death in fact and in law. Nick commits a positive voluntary act that does cause her death. But for his actions she would not have died: *R v White* [1910] 2 KB 124. Nick's act is the cause in law of Judith's death. His act is the 'operating and substantial cause' of death: see *R v Smith* [1959] 2 QB 35. There is no evidence of any *novus actus interveniens*. In order for him to be found guilty of murder the prosecution must prove that Nick had either the intention to kill or to do grievous bodily harm; *R v Woollin* [1998] 4 All ER 103. Intent can be based on 'purpose/desire' or on evidence of foresight. It would appear to have been Nick's purpose to do some grievous bodily harm — this would suffice for the *mens rea* of murder. If necessary the trial judge could give a '*Woollin*' direction. Is there evidence that Nick foresaw death or grievous bodily harm as virtually certain? Foresight here is to be determined in accordance with s. 8 Criminal Justice Act 1967. Only if there were such evidence would a jury be entitled to infer that he intended death or grievous bodily harm. Assuming that Nick has the *mens rea* for murder attention will turn to possible defences.

The most obvious defence on the facts is provocation. This defence is only available to a defendant charged with murder, and if successfully pleaded will reduce his liability to manslaughter. The first stage in establishing the defence of provocation is the subjective test — was Nick provoked? It should be noted that anything, including words alone, can be provocation: see *R* v *Doughty* (1986) 83 Cr App R 319. There is no bar on provocation being induced by the actions of the defendant; see *R* v *Johnson* [1989] 2 All ER 859. The basic ingredients of this common law defence are to be found in the judgment of Devlin J in *R* v *Duffy* [1949] 1 All ER 932, coupled with s. 3 Homicide Act 1957. The first issue is whether or not there is evidence that Nick was provoked. If there is, as certainly seems to be the case here, the trial judge should leave the defence to the jury, with a suitable direction by way of guidance. There does not appear to be any problem with 'cooling time' — Nick's actions in respect of Judith seem to have been an immediate response to her comments. It is submitted that on the evidence presented in this question the subjective stage will be made out.

As to the objective stage the key decision is now that of the House of Lords in *R* v *Smith (Morgan)* [2000] 4 All ER 289. The issue for the House of Lords was whether characteristics other than age and sex were attributable to a reasonable man, for the purpose of s. 3 of the Homicide Act 1957, not only as regards the gravity of the provocation to the defendant but also as regards the standard of control to be expected of the defendant. By a majority it was held that the defendant's characteristics could be taken into account as regards both the gravity of the provocation and the degree of self-control to be expected. As regards Nick, therefore, characteristics such as his prolonged impotence, the marital problems, the fact that David is his best friend, and his lack of success in obtaining employment could all be taken into account as factors explaining why Judith's words were particularly provoking for him. As to the test for self-control, the effect of *R* v *Smith (Morgan)*, as explained in subsequent decisions such as *R* v *Weller* [2003] Crim LR 724, is that it would be wrong to tell the jury to ignore factors such as Nick's prolonged impotence, violent mood swings, his depression, and his behavioural disorder that manifests itself in aggression towards women. In effect the test becomes one of whether Nick exercised what was *for him*, reasonable self-control. How the jury will determine this is a matter of speculation, but two points should be made. The first is that, notwithstanding the liberal approach taken to the objective test in *R* v *Smith (Morgan)*, the courts should continue to exclude from the test of provocation mental illnesses that would of themselves constitute substantive defences — hence if a defendant were criminally insane it would seem odd to allow him to have this taken into account when assessing the defence of provocation. Secondly, Lord Hoffmann expressed the view that character traits such as an anti-social propensity to anger, male possessiveness and jealousy should not today be acceptable as reasons for loss of self-control leading to homicide. The trial judge will thus have a tortuous path to follow in determining whether any of the evidence relating to Nick points to a defect in character rather than a relevant characteristic.

Assuming that characteristics indicating mental illness should be excluded from the defence of provocation, Nick would be well advised to consider running diminished responsibility as an alternative defence. Under the Homicide Act 1957 s. 2(1) Nick would have to provide evidence that he was: '. . . suffering from such abnormality of mind (whether arising from a condition of arrested or retarded development of mind or any inherent causes or induced by disease or injury) as substantially impaired his mental responsibility for his acts and omissions in doing . . . the killing.' An abnormality of the mind would be a state of mind that the normal person would regard as abnormal — '. . . not only the perception of physical acts and matters and the ability to form rational judgement . . . but also the ability to exercise will-power to control physical acts in accordance with that rational judgement' — see *Byrne* [1960] 2 QB 396. Nick would appear to have the evidence to support this defence. His mental abnormality does not have to amount to borderline insanity: see *Seers* (1984) 79 Cr App R 261. Ultimately the jury will decide: see *Walton* v *R* [1978] 1 All ER 542. On the facts this would appear to be a far more appropriate defence than provocation.

In the unlikely event that the *mens rea* for murder cannot be established Nick could be charged with constructive manslaughter based on the unlawful act of maliciously inflicting grievous bodily harm contrary to s. 20 of the Offences Against the Person Act 1861. The act is clearly 'dangerous' (see below) and Nick would have had the *mens rea* for the unlawful act.

Turning to Nick's liability for the death of David, the first issue to consider is that of causation. There are two ways of approaching this. On the one hand Nick commits a positive act that causes David's death — i.e., smashing the mirror. Alternatively the prosecution could base liability on his failure to summon help — on the basis that he accidentally caused the shards of glass to pierce David's skin, realised what he had done, came under a responsibility to act and failed to discharge that responsibility: see *R* v *Miller* [1983] 1 All ER 978. His act, or failure to act, is the cause in fact of David's death: see *White* (above); and the cause in law, see *R* v *Smith* (above).

To be guilty of murder Nick must be shown to have had intention to kill or do grievous bodily harm: see *Vickers* (1957) and *Woollin* (1998) — both considered above. Nick does not appear to have had 'purpose' type intent, but there could be evidence of his having foreseen death or grievous bodily harm from which a jury could infer intent. One moot point is whether the prosecution could invoke the principle of transferred malice, whereby the *mens rea* directed at Judith can be used in relation to David: see *Latimer* (1886) 17 QBD 359. It may be easier for the prosecution to base liability for murder on Nick's failure to act — his knowledge of the injury to David, the loss of blood etc. and his failure to act is strongly suggestive of someone who foresees death as 'virtually certain'.

If Nick is charged with the murder of David he may seek to rely on the defences of provocation and diminished responsibility as outlined above.

Alternatively the prosecution could charge Nick with constructive manslaughter — this would have to be on the basis of the positive act of smashing the mirror, as opposed to an omission — see *Lowe* (1973). The positive act must be a crime — here this could be grievous bodily harm to Judith or criminal damage to her mirror. The criminal act must be dangerous as determined by the objective test laid down in *Church* [1965] 2 All ER 72, and *R v Dawson* (1985) 81 Cr App R 150. Would a sober and reasonable person at the scene of the crime, with the knowledge of the accused, have foreseen the risk of some physical harm? This is a question to be determined by the jury. Note that the unlawful act does not have to be directed at the actual victim: see *Mitchell* [1983] QB 741, and *R v Goodfellow* (1986) 83 Cr App R 23. Assuming the unlawful act is seen as dangerous, Nick must have the *mens rea* for the unlawful act — in the case of the grievous bodily harm. It would be enough that he was 'malicious' as in s. 20 of the Offences Against the Person Act 1861. Alternatively criminal damage could be used as the unlawful act. Following the decision of the House of Lords in *R v G* [2003] 4 All ER 765, the prosecution would have to show Nick was aware of the risk of criminal damage.

In theory Nick could be charged with killing David by gross negligence — see *R v Adomako* [1994] 3 WLR 288, especially if liability is to be based on his failure to summon help. This type of manslaughter tends to be charged in 'duty' situations, such as that arising between doctor and patient; householder and tradesman; landlord and tenant. The prosecution would presumably allege that having injured David, Nick came under a duty to care for him: see *R v Miller* (above). Assuming a duty of care did arise, the steps to liability, as set out in *R v Adomako*, would involve an examination of: (i) the extent to which Nick's conduct departed from the proper standard of care incumbent upon him; (ii) whether this involved a risk of death to David; and (iii) whether the breach of duty was so serious that it should be judged criminal.

Q Question 5

Kathleen, Fareed and Jimmy are all homeless, and at night they sleep rough near the railway station. Kathleen, a chronic alcoholic, has also been diagnosed as

suffering from paranoid schizophrenia. One night, after a heavy drinking session, Kathleen beds down in her usual spot. Once she is asleep Jimmy decides that it would be funny to urinate on Kathleen, something he has done several times before, to her great annoyance. Kathleen wakes to find Jimmy and Fareed laughing, and also notices Fareed drinking from a bottle of gin that she had hidden under her bedclothes. Kathleen flies into a rage, picks up a large piece of wood and chases after Fareed and Jimmy. Fareed, who is partially sighted, runs into the road and is hit by an oncoming bus. On admission to hospital the medical attendants fail to administer sufficient oxygen and he dies. In the course of running away Jimmy trips over a kerbstone and falls heavily. The bottle of cider in his coat pocket is smashed in the fall and he suffers severe cuts. Jimmy does not receive treatment for these cuts, which heal badly. Jimmy keeps picking at the wounds as they cause him discomfort and in due course he dies from blood poisoning caused by the resultant infection.

Advise the Crown Prosecution Service as to the criminal liability of Kathleen for both of these deaths.

Commentary

A fairly standard homicide question combining issues relating to causation, provocation and diminished responsibility, and constructive manslaughter. In terms of structure candidates would be advised to follow two simple rules. The first is to deal with each victim separately. It may be thought that this will involve a degree of duplication in that, for example, causation will have to be considered twice. In practice it is acceptable to go through an issue once in detail in relation to one incident, and then simply use the 'see above ' approach if the same issue arises later on, although care must be taken to ensure that any distinguishing factors are raised and dealt with. The second rule is to deal with causation first. As a matter of logic, if the defendant has not caused the death of the victim there is little point in considering other aspects of liability for homicide — different offences would need to be considered instead.

- Causation

- *mens rea* for murder

- Provocation and diminished responsibility

- Intoxication

- Constructive manslaughter

- Killing by gross negligence

:Ọ́: **Suggested answer**

Kathleen's liability for the death of Fareed

Did Kathleen cause the death of Fareed? On the facts one can assume that there was causation in fact. But for Kathleen chasing Fareed into the road would he have died? The obvious answer is no. Turning to causation in law, Kathleen will argue that Fareed is the author of his own misfortune. In legal terms this means her asserting that his actions in running into the road amounted to a *novus actus interveniens,* or a break in the chain of causation in law. The common law has been reluctant to recognise instances where the actions of the victim can be seen as amounting to a *novus actus,* but Kathleen might argue that this should be seen as an 'escape' case. Following *Roberts* (1971) 56 Cr App R 95, where the victim was injured after jumping from a moving car to escape from the defendant, the test for the jury will be to consider whether Fareed's escape was the natural result of what Kathleen said and did, in the sense that it was something that could reasonably have been foreseen as the con-sequence of what she was doing. In particular the jury would have to be directed that if Fareed had done something 'daft' or unexpected that no reasonable man could be expected to foresee, the harm he suffered could rightly be regarded as self-inflicted — i.e., the escape would be a *novus actus.* At this level running into the road into the path of an oncoming bus would be seen as 'daft', but the situation is complicated by other factors. The facts indicate that Fareed's judgement may have been impaired by alcohol consumption and that he was partially sighted. The Court of Appeal deci-sion in *Blaue* [1975] 1 WLR 1411 states that you must take your victim as you find him; *Williams* [1992] 2 All ER 183 provides that it should be borne in mind that a victim may in the agony of the moment do the wrong thing, and that the jury should bear in mind particular characteristics of the victim and the fact that in the agony of the moment he may act without thought or deliberation. *Corbett* [1996] Crim LR 594, suggests that this type of escape is within the range of foreseeable responses — even where the victim has been drinking. On balance, it is submitted that the chain of causation in law will not be broken by the escape attempt.

Medical treatment will not normally break the chain of causation. Although the medical treatment may be incompetent, the operating and substantial cause of death is still the injury inflicted by the defendant. In *R v Mellor* [1996] 2 Cr App R 245, the appellant contended that a substantial cause of the victim's death was the failure of the medical attendants at the hospital to administer sufficient oxygen to the victim. The appeal was dismissed, Schiemann LJ, observing that there was no onus on the Crown to prove that any supervening cause, such as medical treatment, was not a substantial cause of death. As he explained it is a question of fact and degree in each case for the jury to decide, having regard to the gravity of the supervening event, however caused, as to whether or not the injuries inflicted by the defendant were a significant cause of death.

Assuming causation in respect of the death of Fareed is made out, can Kathleen be guilty of murder? Given that she is chasing after Fareed with a weapon there is evidence that she intended some grievous bodily harm at least — consider the direction to the jury on intent in *R v Woollin* [1998] 4 All ER 103. The greater the probability of a consequence the more likely it is that the consequence was foreseen and that if that consequence was foreseen the greater the probability that that consequence was also intended. The jury will have to be reminded that the decision is theirs to be reached upon a consideration of all the evidence. In a case such as this the simple direction on intent may not suffice. The jury will need to be directed that they are not entitled to infer the necessary intention unless they feel sure that death or serious bodily harm was virtually certain (barring some unforeseen intervention) to result from Kathleen's actions and that she appreciated that such was the case.

Assuming she is charged with murder Kathleen could raise a number of defences. The most obvious of these is provocation. Following *R v Duffy* [1949] 1 All ER 932, and the provisions of s. 3 of the Homicide Act 1957, there is evidence that she lost her self-control. There is no obvious issue as to 'cooling time' and there is effectively no bar on what can amount to provocation: see *R v Doughty* (1986) 83 Cr App R 319. Section 3 of the 1957 Act sets out the role of the judge and jury. The question whether the provocation was enough to make a reasonable man do as he did will be left to be determined by the jury, and in determining that question the jury will take into account everything both done and said according to the effect which, in their opinion, it would have on a reasonable man. Note that the provocation can be cumulative. *R v Dryden* [1995] 4 All ER 987, endorses the 'the last straw' approach; as does *Humphreys* [1995] 4 All ER 889. On these facts it means that the jury should be directed to consider the history of events between the parties. This direction is important as the final act of provocation, if looked at in isolation, may not seem sufficiently grave to warrant the defence being allowed.

The correct approach to the objective stage of the test for provocation is now that endorsed by the majority of the House of Lords in *R v Smith (Morgan)* [2000] 4 All ER 289. The court should no longer distinguish between characteristics that relate to the gravity of the provocation and those that relate to the defendant's ability to exercise self-control. It is no longer appropriate to direct a jury to consider the objective stage by reference to how a reasonable person (with or without attributes of the defendant) would have reacted. The test for provocation should be described in terms that give the jury the discretion to act as justice requires. Hence it would be incorrect for a judge to direct a jury that certain characteristics of the accused are to be disregarded in assessing the degree of self-control to be expected. The emphasis is now on what degree of self-control it is fair and just to expect from the defendant, bearing in mind society's needs for consistent standards of behaviour. The House of Lords also noted that certain character traits, such as pugnacity and irritability were not to be seen as excuses for engaging in violent acts. Lord Hoffmann also argued that being 'thwarted or disappointed in the vicissitudes of life' or having anti-social propensities should not be taken into account. He also excluded 'male possessiveness and jealousy'. Lord Hoffmann and Lord Clyde accepted that certain character traits could not be taken into account by the jury, such as ' quarrelsome or choleric temperament'. There are difficulties with this 'cherry-picking' approach to the defendant's characteristics. As the more recent decision of the Court of Appeal in *R* v *Weller* [2003] Crim LR 724, indicates, it will not amount to a misdirection for the trial judge to decline to explicitly highlight such traits, but it might well be a misdirection for the trial judge to rule them out as matters that the jury was entitled to consider.

Intoxication, however, has never been a relevant characteristic for the purposes of assessing the objective stage of the test for provocation. Hence the court will take into account Kathleen's paranoid schizophrenia ('diagnosed' suggests expert medical evidence) and the fact that she may have been permanently damaged by her alcoholism. The court should ignore the fact that she was intoxicated for the purposes of applying the test for provocation.

Intoxication could be raised as a separate substantive defence to murder, reducing Kathleen's liability to manslaughter if successful. Murder is regarded at common law as a specific intent crime: see *DPP* v *Majewski* [1976] 2 All ER 142. There would have to be evidence that Kathleen did not form the specific intent because of the intoxication. It is submitted that it is far from clear on the given facts whether or not this was the case.

Arguably the more appropriate defence, given the medical evidence, would be diminished responsibility. Under s. 2 of the Homicide Act 1957 the burden would be on Kathleen to establish on the balance of probabilities, that she was suffering from such abnormality of mind (whether arising from a condition of arrested or retarded development of mind or any inherent causes or induced by disease or injury) as substantially impaired her mental responsibility for her acts. Note that her schizophrenia would probably satisfy this, but intoxication will not be taken into account, unless her alcoholism is a condition that has caused permanent harm to her mental health such that it affects her responsibility for her actions even when she is sober: see *Tandy* [1989] 1 All ER 267.

Tactically, given that it is easier to raise the defence of provocation as opposed to diminished responsibility, Kathleen is likely to opt for provocation — especially in the light of *R* v *Smith (Morgan)*.

A manslaughter charge against Kathleen in respect of the death of Fareed will be problematic. What is the unlawful act? If regard is had to *R* v *Arobieke* [1988] Crim LR 314, it will be seen that simply chasing someone is not enough. Even if the prosecution relies on assault (i.e., on the basis that the victim apprehended immediate physical harm), is the assault 'dangerous', viewed objectively? On the basis of *R* v *Watson* [1989] 1 WLR 684, it must be an act that the reasonable sober bystander, equipped with the knowledge of the defendant, would see as likely to cause some *physical* harm. In theory Kathleen could be charged with killing by gross negligence, but it is not the sort of duty of care situation envisaged in *R v Adomako* [1994] 3 WLR 288; see also *R v Khan (Rungzabe)* (1998) *The Times*, 7 April (unreported). Killing by gross negligence tends to be invoked in reliance situations or where the defendant is exercising a particular degree of skill and professionalism.

Kathleen's liability for the death of Jimmy

The prosecution would have little difficulty in establishing causation in fact — but for Kathleen's actions Jimmy would not have died. As to causation in law, the points raised above in respect of Fareed's escape would apply equally here. The argument would be as to whether or not the *R v Blaue* principle of 'take your victim as you find him' would cover the bottle in the pocket. It is submitted that there is no reason in principle why it should not. Hence the only remaining argument on *novus actus* and Jimmy's death relates to the consequent self-neglect. On the basis of *R v Dear* [1996] Crim LR 595, deliberately picking at wounds will not amount to a *novus actus interveniens*, provided they are the wounds inflicted by the defendant.

If causation is established the prosecution may charge Kathleen with murder, as outlined above, and she may raise the defences of provocation, diminished responsibility and even intoxication.

If the *mens rea* for murder is not made out, the prosecution could be in difficulties with unlawful act manslaughter. The unlawful act would presumably be the assault apprehended by Jimmy, but there may be doubts as to whether or not it satisfies the tests for dangerousness — see above. In particular, the reasonable sober person at the scene of the crime is imbued with the knowledge of the defendant. If Kathleen did not know Jimmy had a bottle in his pocket, the reasonable man does not have that knowledge. This makes establishing a dangerous unlawful act less likely. Killing by gross negligence remains a possibility, but it is not an obvious duty of care situation, and even if it were, could it be said that Kathleen's negligence in chasing Jimmy was so bad as to warrant being labelled criminal? This seems doubtful.

Q Question 6

Clive is a drug dealer. He gave a packet of prohibited drugs to Dennis, an experienced drug user. Dennis, aware of the contents of the packet, took the drugs to his house, injected himself and subsequently died of a drug overdose. Clive then injected Malcolm, at Malcolm's request, with a prohibited drug. Malcolm was aware of the nature of the drug being used by Clive. Later that same day Malcolm died from the effects of the drug as he had a weak heart. Finally Clive met Emma, aged 18, in the park. At her request, he gave her a syringe filled with prohibited drugs and encouraged her to inject herself. Emma, who had not taken drugs before, did this and then began to cough and shake uncontrollably. However, Clive simply left her and she died shortly after.

Advise Clive as to his criminal liability in respect of these deaths. Do not consider Clive's liability under the Misuse of Drugs Act 1971.

Commentary

This is an interesting homicide question centring on a number of recent Court of Appeal decisions, *R* v *Khan* [1998] Crim LR 830, *R* v *Kennedy* [1999] Crim LR 65, *R* v *Dias* [2002] Crim LR 490, *R* v *Rogers* [2003] 1 WLR 1374, and *R* v *Finlay* [2003] All ER (D) 142. Each of these cases highlights one of the recurring problems that periodically confronts the criminal law, i.e., the public's perception of the appropriate response of the law. All cases, in differing ways, involve the supply of drugs causing the death of a young victim who may have been experimenting with the drug for the first time. Obviously there are offences under the Misuse of Drugs Act 1971 which are designed to cover the illegal supply of drugs, but when a victim dies this leads the public to demand a more serious offence such as murder or manslaughter.

The many miscarriage of justice cases, especially those involving terrorism, which are surrounded by much public hysteria, demonstrate the criminal justice system in its most vulnerable state — with established procedures and safeguards often being disregarded. A similar situation applies to the substantive criminal law, and although in each case (other than *R* v *Dias*) the appellants were unsuccessful in their appeals, the courts had to resort to stretching the boundaries of some of the established principles concerning omissions and causation.

Apart from the decisions mentioned above, there are also two other important manslaughter cases involving the supply of drugs: *R* v *Cato* [1976] 1 All ER 260, and *R* v *Dalby* [1982] 1 All ER 916. A good answer to this question will therefore incorporate references to each of those cases, as appropriate, within the context of involuntary manslaughter. In addition, the concepts of omission and causation must be applied in order to arrive at conclusions for the three incidents.

Note that there is no need to consider Clive's substantive liability under the Misuse of Drugs Act 1971.

- Causation in each case

- Whether voluntary consumption breaks the chain of causation

- 'Thin Skull' rule

- *mens rea* for murder unlikely

- Involuntary manslaughter

- Whether any unlawful act

- Dangerousness

- *mens rea* for the unlawful act

- Killing by gross negligence

- Omission in respect of Emma

:Q̈: Suggested answer

Clive's liability in respect of Dennis

But for Clive supplying Dennis with the drugs Dennis would not have died—hence causation in fact is made out. The first real problem for the prosecution relates to causation in law. Dennis is an experienced drug user, and is aware of the contents of the packet. Hence Clive will contend that Dennis' voluntary and informed consumption of the drugs amounted to a *novus actus interveniens*. It is submitted that this argument is correct, and is reflected in the Court of Appeal's decision in *R* v *Dalby* [1982] 1 All ER 916. On similar facts it was held that the unlawful act of the supply of the dangerous drug by the defendant to the deceased did not constitute the *actus reus* of manslaughter. This was on the basis that the unlawful act of supplying drugs was not an act directed against the person of V, and did not cause any direct injury to him. This controversial decision appeared to add a new ingredient to constructive manslaughter in that the act had to be directed at the victim. However, in *R* v *Goodfellow* [1986] 83 Cr App R 23, the Court of Appeal rejected this submission and explained the decision in *R* v *Dalby* on the basis that the victim's actions had broken the chain of causation.

Although the prosecution has only to prove, in order to satisfy the causation in law element, that Clive's acts were a significant contribution to V's death (*R* v *Cheshire* [1991] 3 All ER 670), there is a powerful argument that a voluntary act by the victim operates as an intervening act. This view is stated by Professor Glanville Williams, *Textbook on Criminal Law* (2nd edition), at p. 39: 'what a person does (if he had reached adult years, is of sound mind and is not acting under mistake, intimidation or similar pressure) is his own responsibility and is not regarded as having been caused by other people. An intervening act of this kind, therefore, breaks the causal connection that would otherwise have been perceived between previous acts and the forbidden consequence'.

Against this the prosecution will rely on *R* v *Blaue* [1975] 1 WLR 1411, which demonstrates the principle that you take your victim as you find him (the 'egg-shell skull' or 'Thin Skull' principle). In effect the argument will be that if Dennis chose to be foolhardy and consume an excessive amount of the drug, so much the worse for Clive. It is submitted that the courts ought not to accept this argument no matter how reprehensible the supply of drugs might be. Dennis is responsible for his own welfare.

If Clive had unlawfully supplied Dennis with a knife that Dennis had in turn stabbed himself to death with, there is no serious argument that Clive would be regarded as having been the legal cause of Dennis' death. The reality is that a clear direction is needed on this issue from the House of Lords. On the one hand the rather dubious decision in *R* v *Kennedy* [1999] Crim LR 65 can be distinguished from the current facts on the ground that in that case D had made up the syringe containing the mixture of drugs that P chose to inject. On the other hand *R* v *Finlay* [2003] All ER (D) 142 presents Clive with a difficulty. Finlay prepared a syringe containing a heroin mixture that the deceased used to inject herself — a fatal overdose being the result. It was held that the self-injection did not break the chain of causation because it was reasonably foreseeable that the victim (an habitual drug user) would take advantage of the opportunity to consume the heroin provided.

If the argument as to the *novus actus interveniens* fails, Clive might be charged with unlawful act manslaughter (constructive manslaughter) in respect of Dennis' death, but there could be serious problems in identifying any criminal act by Clive that causes death. Supply is obviously an unlawful act under the Misuse of Drugs Act 1971, but it is not the supply that causes Dennis' death. It is the self-administration. Self-administration of drugs is not a crime.

Clive's liability in respect of Malcolm

Clive causes Malcolm's death in fact — but for his actions Malcolm would not have died. Clive's argument that it was Malcolm's weak heart that was the main cause of death would fail. *R* v *Cheshire* [1991] 3 All ER 670, states that the prosecution, to satisfy the causation test, only needs to prove that A's act was a significant contribution to V's death, and *R* v *Blaue* [1975] 1 WLR 1411 demonstrates the principle that you take your victim as you find him (the 'egg-shell skull' or 'Thin Skull' principle). Thus, the fact that Malcolm is exceptionally vulnerable because he has a weak heart does not mean that Clive did not cause his death.

It is unlikely that Clive would be charged with murder in respect of Malcolm's death. In *R* v *Moloney* [1985] 1 All ER 1025, the House of Lords confirmed the *mens rea* as intention to kill or cause grievous bodily harm. It is submitted that the prosecution would find it very difficult to establish beyond reasonable doubt that Clive had the necessary intention. It is therefore much more likely that Clive will be charged with constructive manslaughter. The prosecution must prove that Clive committed a dangerous criminal act that caused the death of Malcolm, and that Clive has the *mens rea* for that criminal act.

The circumstances in this question are very similar to those considered by the Court of Appeal in *R* v *Cato* [1976] 1 All ER 260. As in that case, there may be some dispute as to what constitutes the unlawful act. Even though Malcolm consented to Clive injecting him, this could still constitute aggravated assault under s. 47 of the Offences Against the Person Act 1861. This is because consent is not a defence to the deliberate infliction of actual bodily harm or more serious harm, unless it is in the course of a lawful activity (*R* v *Brown* [1993] 2 WLR 556). Clearly the injecting of drugs in these circumstances would not amount to a lawful activity and therefore is an unlawful act.

Clive, however, may argue that as he did not know that Malcolm had a weak heart, his act was not dangerous. This point arose in *R* v *Watson* [1989] 2 All ER 865, where the Court of Appeal decided that for the purpose of ascertaining whether there was an obvious risk of some physical harm, the reasonable man had to be put in the same circumstances as the accused. The reasonable person does not have the benefit of hindsight. So Watson's conviction was quashed, as he did not realise that the occupier of the house in which he was committing a burglary had a weak heart. It remains a question for the jury to determine whether there was a reasonably foreseeable risk that Malcolm might have a weak heart and thereby might suffer some physical harm by being injected with prohibited drugs.

Clive's action in injecting Malcolm with the drugs is clearly intentional, hence Clive would have the *mens rea* for the unlawful act causing death. It is likely, therefore, that Clive will incur liability for the manslaughter of Malcolm.

Clive's liability in respect of Emma

Clive's liability in respect of the death of Emma could be based on his supply of the prepared syringe, or on his failure to help her once she became distressed. Regarding his supply of the syringe, Clive clearly causes Emma's death in fact — but for supplying the syringe she would not have died. As with Dennis, however, Clive will argue that Emma broke the chain of causation by injecting herself. Both *R* v *Dalby* [1982] 1 All ER 916, and *R* v *Dias* [2002] Crim LR 490, support the argument that where drugs are supplied to P by D, death results from the voluntary consumption of the drugs by P (i.e., P's self-administration of the drugs is a *novus actus interveniens*).

The problem for Clive, however, is that subsequent cases have sought to extend the liability of drugs suppliers. In the Court of Appeal decision in *R* v *Kennedy* [1999] Crim LR 65, *Dalby* was distinguished to uphold the appellant's conviction for manslaughter. His act in supplying the drug and encouraging P to inject himself was deemed an unlawful act (under s. 23, Offences Against the Person Act 1861) and preparing the mixture and handing it to P for immediate injection was held to be capable of amounting to a significant cause of death. Further, as noted above, in *R* v *Finlay* it was held that the reasonably foreseeable actions of the victim would not break the chain of causation in law. In Clive's case the prosecution will argue, probably with success, that it was reasonably foreseeable that an inexperienced drug user would rely on Clive for guidance and consume what he supplied.

Assuming causation is established, liability for murder is most unlikely, given the facts — see above. The prosecution might be in some difficulty establishing an unlawful act. The supply of drugs is an offence, but it is the self-administration of the drugs that causes the death. Self-administration of drugs is not criminal, beyond the technical offence of possession at the moment of administration.

The prosecution can circumvent these difficulties by basing Clive's liability on his failure to care for Emma. His liability for failing to act could be based on a common law duty arising from her reliance on him: see *R* v *Stone and Dobinson* [1977] QB 354. Alternatively, and more promisingly, the prosecution could rely on *R* v *Miller* [1983] 1 All ER 978, where the House of Lords decided that if A created a dangerous situation and realised this, he was under a legal duty to take steps to minimise the danger. So, Miller, who inadvertently set fire to property, was guilty of criminal damage when, realising what he had done, failed to call the fire brigade. The same principle should be applied to Clive. He has created the dangerous situation, and it would be easy for him to summon medical attention to minimise the danger he has caused Emma. This would tie in with the prosecution charging him with killing by gross negligence, as constructive manslaughter requires proof of a positive criminal act.

Following the House of Lords' decision in *R* v *Adomako* [1995] 1 AC 171, in order to prove gross negligence manslaughter the prosecution would have to establish the following four conditions:

(a)   Clive owed Emma a duty of care;

(b)   Clive was in breach of that duty;

(c)   Clive's conduct was grossly negligent, i.e., having regard to the risk of death, Clive's conduct fell so far beneath the required standard, and was so bad as to amount to criminal negligence;

(d)   Clive's conduct caused Emma's death.

It is submitted that the prosecution would easily establish conditions (b), (c) and (d) but there are difficulties in deciding whether a duty of care was owed. This is because the general rule in criminal law is that a duty to help others is not owed by members of the public. Thus in *R* v *Khan* [1998] Crim LR 830, the Court of Appeal quashed A's conviction because of a misdirection by the trial judge who failed to give a direction on the duty of care point, and the Appeal Court was reluctant to assume that such a duty existed. The Court stated that to extend a duty to summon medical assistance to a drug dealer who supplies heroin to a person who subsequently dies, would enlarge the class of persons to whom on previous authorities, such a duty does arise.

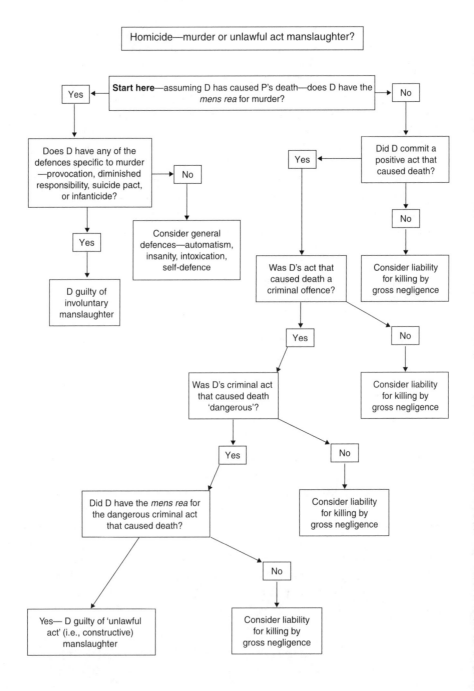

Further reading

Chalmers, J., 'Merging Provocation and Diminished Responsibility: Some Reasons for Scepticism' [2004] Crim LR 198.

Doran, S., 'Alternative Defences — the Invisible Burden on the Trial Judge' [1991] Crim LR 878.

Edwards, Susan, M., 'Abolishing Provocation and Reframing Self-Defence — the Law Commission's Options for Reform' [2004] Crim LR 181.

Gardner, T. and Macklem, T., 'Compassion Without Respect? Nine Fallacies in R v Smith' [2001] Crim LR 623.

Gardner, J. and Macklem, T., 'No Provocation Without Responsibility: A Reply to *Mackay* and *Mitchell*' [2004] Crim LR 213.

Heaton, R., 'Dealing in Death' [2003] Crim LR 497.

'Legislating the Criminal Code: Involuntary Manslaughter', Law Com. No. 237 (1996).

Mackay, R.D., and Mitchell, B.J., 'Replacing Provocation: More on a Combined Plea' [2004] Crim LR 219.

Norrie, A., 'After Woollin' [1999] Crim LR 532.

O'Doherty, J.P. Stephen, 'Involuntary Manslaughter: Where to Now?' [2004] JP 168.

Non-fatal offences against the person

Introduction

Apart from motoring and theft-related offences, criminal assaults, batteries and woundings are the staple diet of the criminal courts, with more than 100,000 prosecutions a year. Because of the historical increase in crime there has been an increase in the number of Crown Court judges, recorders and assistant recorders, many of whom have been recruited from outside the ranks of specialist criminal practitioners. It is therefore imperative that the offences are clear, fair and easily applied. However, as the Law Commission has pointed out (Law Com. No. 177):

> the existing interface between common law and statutory provisions undoubtedly contributes to make the law obscure and difficult to understand for everyone concerned. This may lead to inefficiency, the cost and length of trials may be increased, because the law has to be extracted and clarified and there is greater scope for appeals on misdirections on points of law.

Sir Henry Brooke, the former head of the Law Commission, in announcing the Law Commission's proposals for reform of offences against the person (Law Com. No. 122) stated that it was intolerable that the courts were still wrestling with the intricacies and inconsistencies of the Offences Against the Person Act 1861, which is full of antique and obscure language and which has been the subject of many recent appeals that displayed serious disagreement as to the basic content of the law. Even after the House of Lords' decisions in *R v Savage and Parmenter* [1991] 4 All ER 698, *R v Brown* [1993] 2 All ER 75 and *R v Burstow* and *R v Ireland* [1997] 4 All ER 225, many aspects of the law are unsatisfactory and its application erratic (for example, see *R v Wilson* [1996] 3 WLR 125 where the Court of Appeal in quashing a conviction decided that the trial judge was wrong to apply *Brown* on the facts of the case).

The Law Commission's work on this topic has taken over 20 years and has massive support amongst judges, magistrates, the police and solicitors and barristers. If implemented the recommendations would save the waste of enormous amounts of valuable court, lawyers', and citizens' time and money simply on attempts to find out what the law is, and in correcting errors where the administration of justice has gone wrong when obscure law has been wrongly applied. The report was published in 1994, but as yet no Draft Bill has been placed before Parliament, so it appears that the problems will remain.

The questions included in this chapter cover all the typical offences against the person you would expect to find on a standard criminal law syllabus. There is no specific coverage of the Public Order Act 1986, as this will normally be covered in a Constitutional Law, or Civil Liberties syllabus. The emphasis is, therefore, on the Offences Against the Person Act 1861, in particular ss. 18, 20 and 47. Candidates will normally be expected to show an awareness of the Protection from Harassment Act 1997, although it is likely that the more serious incidents will be prosecuted under the 1861 Act. This again demonstrates the need for a code as the present development of principles depends on the accidents of litigation and piecemeal legislation. The common law method of resolving uncertainty by retrospective declaration of the law is objectionable in principle as it may lead to the conviction of a defendant on the basis of criminal liability not known to exist in that form before he acted.

The one area of non-fatal offences against the person that has been thoroughly over-hauled by Parliament is sexual offences. The Sexual Offences Act 2003 came into effect in May 2004, hence candidates can expect its provisions to be applied in examination papers from the start of the 2004/5 academic year. The significance of the legislation is hard to overstate. Broadly it sweeps away the Sexual Offences Act 1956 to create, *inter alia*, new offences of rape and serious sexual assault. A completely new approach to consent in relation to sexual offences is introduced, one that puts the onus firmly on the defendant to ascertain free and informed consent prior to engaging in sexual activity.

Q Question 1

Femi is driving his car through central London. At a point where the road narrows from two lanes down to one, a car driven by Roy cuts in front of Femi's car. Femi is infuriated. As the traffic is at a standstill Femi gets out of his car, pulls open Roy's car door and shouts abuse at him. Roy is very frightened by this. Louise, a passenger in Roy's car, gets out to remonstrate with Femi, whereupon Femi head-butts her. Louise is wearing steel rimmed glasses and, as a result of this attack, both she and Femi suffer deep cuts to their foreheads, the frame of the glasses having caused the lacerations. Chiquitta, an elderly woman, sees this disturbance and tries to intervene. Femi pushes her away, causing Chiquitta to lose her balance and fall heavily. Chiquitta suffers a fractured hip and receives hospital treatment. Complications set in and Chiquitta dies a few weeks later from a blood clot on the brain. Louise becomes increasingly ill in the weeks following the attack, and tests reveal that she has become HIV+. Subsequent tests prove that she contracted the condition from Femi who, it transpires, is a drug addict. As a result of sharing needles, he became HIV+ some months prior to his attack on Louise.

Advise the Crown Prosecution Service as to the criminal liability of Femi.

Commentary

Most assaults problems are designed to take candidates through the range of mainstream offences under the Offences Against the Person Act 1861, namely s. 18, s. 20 and s. 47. As a matter of technique it is advisable to start by looking at the harm suffered by the victim. That will lead you into consideration of the most suitable offence. Hence if the harm suffered was a bruise, it would be foolish to start with s. 18 as this requires either grievous bodily harm or wounding. Once you have identified the harm done, it makes sense to start with the most serious offence that might have been committed in causing the harm, and then work down to the less serious offences. In short, 'start high and work down'. Be prepared to argue in the alternative — it may be one offence, but if a particular element cannot be proved it may be another. In this particular question it makes sense to take the incidents in the order in which they occur. The point about words alone constituting an assault is a very popular one with examiners so it pays to be prepared to deal with this. Avoid the common mistake of assuming that offensive or threatening words amount to an assault. Look at the effect on the victim — did he apprehend immediate physical violence? You should also avoid unwarranted assumptions. On the given facts it might be tempting to discuss Femi's liability for the inevitable death of Louise. As far as the question is concerned, however, she is still alive and you should limit your answer to Femi's liability for non-fatal offences. Although you are told that Femi is a drug addict there is no evidence that he acts under the influence of drugs at the time of the assaults outlined in the question. The defence of intoxication should not, therefore, be considered in any depth.

- Femi's attack on Roy — possible liability for assault

- Whether Roy suffers psychological harm

- Injuries to Louise — s. 18 and s. 20

- Death of Chiquitta — causation and constructive manslaughter

- Louise becoming HIV+ — liability for grievous bodily harm

:Q: Suggested answer

The facts state that Femi shouted abuse at Roy, frightening him. Femi may have incurred liability for common assault. The *actus reus* requires proof that Roy apprehended immediate physical violence. The events will be viewed from the perspective of the victim, not the reasonable person: see *Smith* v *Chief Supt Woking Police Station* (1983) 76 Cr App R 234. It is possible to commit a 'narrow' assault by words alone. The authority for this is the House of Lords' decision in *R* v *Burstow*; *R* v *Ireland* [1998] AC 147. Overturning earlier decisions such as *R* v *Meade & Belt* (1823) 1 Lew CC 184, Lord Steyn described the proposition that a gesture may amount to an assault but that words can never suffice as unrealistic and indefensible. The *mens rea* for assault is intention to cause the victim to apprehend immediate physical harm, or recklessness as to whether the victim apprehends such harm: see *R* v *Savage*; *R* v *Parmenter* [1991] 3 WLR 914. The recklessness is subjective — Femi must at least be aware of the risk that Roy will fear immediate physical violence. It is submitted that Femi could be guilty of common assault on these facts and should be charged under s. 39 of the Criminal Justice Act 1988; see further *DPP* v *Little*; *DPP* v *Taylor* [1992] 1 QB 645.

Reference to Roy being very frightened raises the possibility that Roy may have suffered some psychological harm as a result of the abuse from Femi. Both *R* v *Chan-Fook* [1994] 2 All ER 760, and *R* v *Burstow*; *R* v *Ireland* (above), make it clear that psychological disturbance can amount to actual bodily harm, or even grievous bodily harm, provided there is medical evidence to substantiate this. Merely being upset will not suffice. As Lord Steyn explained, in *R* v *Burstow*; *R* v *Ireland*: '. . . neuroses must be distinguished from simple states of fear, or problems in coping with everyday life. Where the line is to be drawn must be a matter of psychiatric judgment.' If Roy's fright amounts to actual bodily harm Femi could be charged under s. 47 of the Offences Against the Person Act 1861 with assault occasioning actual bodily harm. The assault is apparent, as explained above. It would be for the prosecution to establish that this assault caused the actual bodily harm. The *mens rea* would be as for common assault — outlined above. It is not necessary to prove that Femi foresaw the risk of actual bodily harm: see further *R* v *Savage*; *R* v *Parmenter* (above).

Femi then headbutts Louise causing her to suffer deep cuts to her forehead because of the contact with the frame of her glasses. The harm done could amount to grievous bodily harm, if the lacerations are categorised as 'serious harm': see *R* v *Saunders* [1985] Crim LR 230. Femi could therefore be charged with an offence under s. 18 Offences Against the Person Act 1861. The difficulty with a s. 18 charge would be proof of the necessary intent. Did Femi intend grievous bodily harm? The prosecution would have to prove that it was either his purpose to do some grievous bodily harm, or that in attacking Louise he foresaw such harm as at least virtually certain — thus permitting a jury to infer intent, as per *R* v *Woollin* [1998] 4 All ER 103.

The more likely charge is under s. 20 of the Offences Against the Person Act 1861. The lacerations would clearly amount to 'wounding' — see *JCC* v *Eisenhower* [1983] 3 WLR 537. There has been a break in the surface of the skin. The *mens rea* requires proof that Femi acted maliciously. On the basis of *R* v *Mowatt* [1967] 3 All ER 47, the prosecution must prove that Femi foresaw that some physical harm to some person, albeit of a minor character, might result from his actions. This direction was subsequently endorsed by the House of Lords in *R* v *Savage*; *R* v *Parmenter* [1992] 1 AC 699. On the facts there appears to be little doubt that the *mens rea* for s. 20 will be established. There is overwhelming evidence that Femi foresaw at least some physical harm being caused to Louise. The fact that he may not have foreseen lacerations being caused by contact with the frame of her glasses is neither here nor there.

It should be noted that, if the lacerations are seen as amounting to grievous bodily harm, as discussed above, Femi might also be guilty of maliciously inflicting grievous bodily harm contrary to s. 20 of the 1861 Act. Femi could also be charged with criminal damage in relation to the spectacles worn by Louise, provided he was aware of the risk that property might be damaged: see the decision of the House of Lords in *R* v *G* [2003] 4 All ER 765, where the subjective approach to recklessness was approved in preference to the objective approach previously dictated by *Metropolitan Police Commissioner* v *Caldwell* [1981] 1 All ER 961.

Femi may incur liability in respect of the death of Chiquitta. But for his actions she would not have died — hence causation in fact is established. As to causation in law, Femi will argue that Chiquitta dies from a blood clot, not the injuries he caused. The question that arises, therefore, is whether or not the blood clot amounts to a *novus actus interveniens*. Medical evidence will be required as to the likelihood of Chiquitta having suffered the blood clot in any event. It is submitted that unless the blood clot can be identified as an independent and potent cause of death the chain of causation will be intact. The blood clot will be seen as 'part and parcel' of the injuries caused by Femi. He clearly commits a battery. *R* v *Blaue* (1975) 61 Cr App R 271, makes it clear that a defendant must take his victim as he finds him. The 'thin skull' rule would extend to cover the victim's propensity to complications following an attack by the defendant. Assuming Femi is found to have caused Chiquitta's death, it is unlikely he would be charged with murder. There is little evidence that it was his intention to kill or do grievous bodily harm: see *R* v *Woollin* (above).

Liability for constructive, or unlawful act, manslaughter could be based on his assault. This is obviously a criminal act, but there may be difficulties in establishing that it is objectively dangerous.

On the basis of *R* v *Church* [1965] 2 All ER 72, and *R* v *Dawson* (1985) 81 Cr App R 150, the jury would be directed to consider whether a sober and reasonable person, present at the scene of and watching the unlawful act being performed, knowing what the defendant knows, and seeing what the defendant sees, would have foreseen the risk of some physical harm. Given Chiquitta's age, the reasonable person might have foreseen physical harm as a result of her being pushed away by Femi — this would accord with the reasoning in *R* v *Watson* [1989] 2 All ER 865. The *mens rea* for constructive manslaughter would be the *mens rea* for the assault — as to which see above. There seems little doubt that the prosecution could establish this.

Can Femi incur further liability in respect of Louise becoming HIV+? The condition itself would undoubtedly amount to grievous bodily harm — see above. The most straightforward charge would be under s. 18 of the 1861 Act. The prosecution would have to prove that Femi caused grievous bodily harm (evident) and intended to do so. The complication would be the *mens rea*. There is no evidence that Femi knew he was HIV+, although it might be tempting to infer this from his having shared needles.

As an alternative the prosecution might consider liability under s. 23 of the

Offences Against the Person Act 1861. Section 23 requires proof that Femi unlawfully and maliciously administered to Louise any poison or other destructive or noxious thing, so as thereby to endanger her life, or inflict grievous bodily harm on her. It is submitted that the term 'administration' is liberally interpreted. The AIDS virus could be the 'noxious substance'. Causing Louise to become HIV+ would amount to endangering her life. Again the problem would be whether or not Femi was aware of his condition. If not there could be difficulties in establishing that he foresaw the risk of the harm specified in s. 23, assuming the courts apply *R* v *Mowatt* (above).

Q Question 2

Wayne, aged 15, calls at houses in his neighbourhood on Halloween night for 'trick or treat'. He knocks at the door of John, a visibly frail old-aged pensioner, who offers Wayne some bars of chocolate. Wayne indicates that he expects to be given money, but John tells him that he can have the bars of chocolate or nothing. Wayne spits in John's face, and leaves empty-handed. He later decides to punish John by telephoning him repeatedly in the middle of the night, ringing off when the receiver is lifted. John's wife Trudy becomes very distressed by these calls and has to receive treatment from her doctor for palpitations, sweating and breathlessness as a result.

The following week Wayne goes to a party where he consumes large quantities of alcohol. On the way home he takes a small bronze statue from John's front garden and throws it, causing the statue to hit the living room window at the front of John's house. The window shatters. John, who was watching television in the room at the time, is blinded in one eye when he is hit by flying glass.

Advise the Crown Prosecution Service as to the offences committed by Wayne.

Commentary

This is a mixed question in that candidates have to consider a number of Theft Act and assault offences, but it does raise some typical points relating to the latter. In terms of structure it is sensible to take the incidents in the order in which they come. As regards the blackmail issue, note the significance of the defendant's age in respect of the subjective test as to whether the demands were warranted. Words as an assault, and assaults by telephone are always popular issues with examiners, hence a good knowledge of *Burstow; Ireland* [1997] 4 All ER 225 is essential. Avoid the common error of assuming that the phone calls cause an assault. Remember that the victim must actually apprehend immediate physical violence for the *actus reus* to be made out. Simply being upset will not suffice. Note the change to criminal damage following the abandoning of '*Caldwell*' recklessness — *R* v *G* establishes that subjective fault now prevails, but the decisions in *R* v *Caldwell* regarding intoxication and criminal damage still hold good.

- Possible liability for blackmail

- Wayne assaulting John by spitting

- Trudy's neuroses as a result of the telephone calls

- Criminal damage to the window

- GBH suffered by John

- Intoxication as a defence to criminal damage and the assault offences

:Q: Suggested answer

Although 'trick or treat' is seen by some as a harmless prank, there is evidence to suggest that many older people find the behaviour of youths who indulge in the practice to be quite intimidating. There is obviously a fear that if something is not provided to those playing 'trick or treat' there may be unpleasant consequences. This raises the possibility that Wayne may have committed the offence of blackmail, especially where Wayne indicates that he was expecting money. Under s. 21 of the Theft Act 1968, blackmail requires proof that the defendant made a demand, although this can be implied — see *R* v *Collister and Warhurst* (1955) 39 Cr App R 100. The trick or treat game would be the demand in this case. The demand must be menacing. On the basis of *Thorne* v *MTA* [1937] AC 797, it would suffice that the demand was accompanied by a threat that would have unpleasant consequences (i.e., the 'trick' element of trick or treat).

The basic objective test for menaces is that laid down in *R* v *Clear* [1968] 1 QB 670; and *Garwood* [1987] 1 WLR 319. However, in the latter case Lord Lane CJ observed that: '. . . where the threats in fact affected the mind of the victim, although they would not have affected the mind of a person of normal stability . . . the existence of menaces is proved providing that the accused . . . was aware of the likely effect of his actions upon the victim.' The fact that Wayne knows the victim to be elderly and frail may assist the prosecution here. Hence the demand may be menacing even though a reasonable person would not have been concerned. Wayne may have deliberately picked on John believing an old-aged pensioner to be more likely to accede to his demands.

Although he clearly makes the demand with a view to gain, Wayne might be able to argue that the demand was warranted — see s. 21(1), Theft Act 1968. For these purposes a demand with 'menaces' is unwarranted unless the person making it does so in the belief: '(a) that he has reasonable grounds for making the demand; and (b) that the use of the menaces is a proper means of reinforcing the demand.' Wayne, being 15 years of age, may honestly believe that the custom of 'trick or treat' gives him reasonable grounds for making the demand, and he may also believe that relying on 'trick or treat' is a reasonable way of enforcing the demand. There is no intimation here that he is suggesting that he will commit a serious offence if not given the money.

In spitting at John it is likely that Wayne will have committed the offence of battery. The *actus reus* of common battery simply requires proof of unlawful physical contact; see *Cole* v *Turner* (1705) 6 Mod Rep 149, and *Coward* v *Baddeley* (1859) 28 LJ Ex 260. There is little doubt that spitting would constitute the *actus reus* for these purposes. The action appears to be entirely intentional, hence the *mens rea* would also appear to be evident (intention or subjective recklessness): see *R* v *Savage*; *R* v *Parmenter* [1991] 3 WLR 914. Common assault could be considered as an alternative charge if John apprehended immediate physical violence, but the facts do not suggest this. Neither is there evidence that the spitting caused what could be regarded as actual bodily harm — thus a charge under s. 47 of the Offences Against the Person Act 1861 of assault occasioning actual bodily harm would not be appropriate.

Wayne's subsequent nuisance telephone calls cause John's wife Trudy to become very distressed, culminating in her receiving medical treatment for palpitations, sweating and breathlessness. The issue for the prosecution will be whether or not these conditions can amount to actual bodily harm. On the basis of *R* v *Burstow*; *R* v *Ireland* [1997] 4 All ER 225, approving *R* v *Chan-Fook* (1994) 99 Cr App R 147, psychiatric harm can be grievous bodily harm or actual bodily harm, depending on its severity. In either case there must be expert medical evidence as to the extent of the harm. In *R* v *Burstow*; *R* v *Ireland* (above) Lord Steyn observed that neuroses should be '. . . distinguished from simple states of fear, or problems in coping with everyday life. Where the line is to be drawn must be a matter of psychiatric judgment.' It is a moot point, therefore, as to whether or not Trudy has suffered actual bodily harm. In any event, a charge under s. 47 would require proof that Wayne had committed an assault, at least in the narrow sense of causing his victim to apprehend immediate physical violence. That this can be caused by means of a telephone call, even a silent call, was clearly established in *R* v *Burstow*; *R* v *Ireland* (above). The difficulty lies in establishing the assault itself. Trudy is distressed by the calls, but that does not necessarily mean that the calls caused her to apprehend physical violence, let alone immediate physical violence. Causing her to feel generally uneasy will not suffice for these purposes. If the *actus reus* of assault is not made out, not only does the charge under s. 47 of the 1861 Act fail, but also the common assault charge.

Even if Trudy did apprehend immediate physical violence, Wayne must be shown to have intended this, or to have at least been aware of the risk that his victim might suffer such harm; see *R* v *Savage*; *R* v *Parmenter* (above). The fact that the intended victim of his calls might have been John, not Trudy, is immaterial. Under the principles of transferred malice the identity of the victim is irrelevant; see *R* v *Latimer* (1886) 17 QBD 359.

There is no likelihood of Wayne incurring liability for theft of the statue, under s. 1 of the Theft Act 1968. The statue is property belonging to another, and he does appropriate it. Assuming he was dishonest, the problem for the prosecution would be in establishing intention to permanently deprive John.

Wayne does commit criminal damage in smashing the window. Under s. 1 of the Criminal Damage Act 1971 he damages or destroys property belonging to another. There is evidence that his actions were intentional, but recklessness would suffice. Following the House of Lords' decision in *R* v *Caldwell* [1982] AC 341, it would have sufficed to show that Wayne gave no thought to an obvious risk of property being damaged. This formulation of recklessness has now been abandoned, however, and the decision of the House of Lords in *R* v *G* [2003] 4 All ER 765, makes clear that Wayne will have to be at least aware of the risk of criminal damage in order to have the necessary *mens rea*. On the facts it is submitted that this will be established. Wayne may seek to rely on his self-induced intoxication as a defence. The mere fact that he has been drinking does not necessarily mean that he will succeed with the defence. There must be evidence that, as a result of the alcohol consumption, he could not and did not form the necessary *mens rea*; *R* v *Cole and Ors* [1993] Crim LR 300. Further, 'simple' criminal damage contrary to s. 1(1) of the Criminal Damage Act 1971 is a basic intent crime — i.e., one where the *actus reus* does not go beyond the *mens rea*. Hence self-induced intoxication will not provide a defence unless Wayne was not reckless in consuming the alcohol (not likely on the facts), or if the risk of harm would not have occurred to him even if he had been sober (again, no evidence of this).

On the basis of the leading authority, *DPP* v *Majewski* [1976] 2 All ER 142, therefore, Wayne would not have a defence of self-induced intoxication as regards a s. 1(1) charge. A charge of aggravated criminal damage could be brought if Wayne was at least reckless as to whether the damaging of the property would endanger life: see *R* v *Steer* [1987] 3 WLR 205. This means that Wayne would have to be reckless as to whether the smashing of the window would endanger life. Recklessness here would be subjective: see *R* v *G* (above). Given that John is injured by the broken glass the prosecution has the evidential basis for charging the aggravated offence under s. 1(2). In *R* v *Caldwell* (above) the House of Lords held that aggravated criminal damage, where the defendant was reckless as to whether or not life would be endangered, was to be regarded as a basic intent crime. The recklessness in becoming intoxicated providing the necessary fault. Hence again, Wayne would not be able to plead intoxication as a defence.

John losing the sight in one eye would amount to grievous bodily harm. Wayne clearly causes this harm, hence the *actus reus* of the offence under s. 18 of the Offences Against the Person Act 1861 would be made out. *Mens rea* would be the problem — especially as Wayne had been drinking. The prosecution would have to prove an intent to do some grievous bodily harm. It is submitted that this is most unlikely on the facts. In any event, s. 18 is a specific intent crime. On the basis of *R* v *Majewski* (above) Wayne would be able to plead self-induced intoxication as a result and if successful this would reduce his liability to s. 20 of the Offences Against the Person

Act 1861. The blinding constitutes the required harm. Wayne will be malicious if he foresaw the risk of some physical harm, albeit slight; see *R* v *Mowatt* [1967] 3 All ER 47. One argument he might raise is that he foresaw someone being frightened by his actions, but it did not occur to him that anyone would be hurt. *R* v *Sullivan* [1981] Crim LR 46, confirms that an intention to frighten will not suffice under s. 20 unless it encompasses foresight of some physical harm. If this is the case the prosecution may have to pursue a s. 47 charge instead. Self-induced intoxication is normally no defence to a charge under s. 20 as the crime is one of basic intent: see *R* v *Majewski* (above). Regarding a s. 47 charge, the harm done to John clearly amounts to actual bodily harm. Assault for the purposes of s. 47 encompasses battery, hence the indirect physical contact with the glass will supply the 'assault' element. There are no causation issues. Wayne will therefore have committed the *actus reus* of the s. 47 offence. On the basis of *R* v *Savage*; *R* v *Parmenter* (above), Wayne can be shown to have had the *mens rea* for assault provided he was aware of the risk that he would commit a battery, or cause another to apprehend immediate physical violence. Only if this never crossed his mind would he be able to deny *mens rea*. There is no need to show he foresaw the harm done, or even actual bodily harm. Again, self-induced intoxication would not normally be a defence to a charge under s. 47 as it is a basic intent crime.

Q Question 3

Mike and Karen are both lecturers at Crammershire University. Karen is a member of the university's karate club and she persuades Mike to join. The day of the next karate club meeting is Karen's birthday. Before the club meeting she spends a few hours in the bar drinking with friends. By the time she leaves the bar to go to the training sessions Karen has drunk six pints of lager and several Vodka 'shots'. During the training session Karen hits Mike in the face with her forearm. Mike falls awkwardly hitting his head on a nearby bench. Mike's girlfriend Gaye, who had come along to watch the session, witnesses the attack on Mike and runs towards Karen screaming abuse. Karen, who is intensely jealous of Gaye's relationship with Mike, throws Gaye to the ground and kicks her in the head. Gaye suffers minor bruising and grazes. Karen, who is distressed, runs off to the changing rooms without bothering to attend to Mike. Other club members call for medical help. It later transpires that Mike has a broken leg and has lost the hearing in one ear.

The following week Mike sees Karen coming towards him in the corridor at the university. As she approaches Karen raises her arm intending to give Mike a hug and apologise for what she has done. Mike fears that she is about to hit him again. He pulls his mobile telephone out of his pocket and thrusts it towards Karen's face with the result that Karen suffers several broken teeth and her glasses are smashed.

In the weeks following these incidents Gaye becomes increasingly depressed and neurotic and has to seek professional psychological help to cope with the trauma caused by Karen's attack.

Advise the Crown Prosecution Service as to the respective criminal liabilities of Karen, Gaye and Mike.

Commentary

This question brings together issues one would normally expect to see in a problem question concerned with non-fatal assaults. The link between violence and intoxication is well known, hence candidates can expect examiners to use the framework of the 1861 Act to test their knowledge of the basic intent/specific intent dichotomy. Consent is also a regular theme, and here it has to be explored in the context of sporting activities. It is natural for victims who are attacked to seek to defend themselves in some way if they can. Hence candidates should also expect to see issues relating to self-defence arise in the context of assaults questions. The basic test for self-defence is very simple, hence examiners often add a 'twist' by including an issue of mistake relating to self-defence. Note also that the question contains a trap for the unwary in respect of omissions. It is not enough to identify a duty and a corresponding failure to act. Where the defendant is charged with a 'result' crime it has to be proved that the omission was one of the causes of that result if the omission is to be used as the basis for liability.

- Grievous bodily harm suffered by Mike — possibility of s. 18 or s. 20, 1861 Act

- Section 47 and common law offences as residual basis for liability

- Karen's defences — consent and intoxication

- Assaults on Gaye and possible self-defence raised by Karen — intoxication and self-defence

- Gaye's liability for verbal assault and possible self-defence arguments

- Mike's liability for actual bodily harm to Karen, and criminal damage to her glasses

- Mike's self-defence argument

⚙ Suggested answer

Turning first to incidents arising out of the karate session, Mike suffers a broken leg and loss of hearing as a result of the fall. The broken leg and loss of hearing could each be classified as 'grievous bodily harm' — i.e., serious harm: see *R v Saunders* [1985] Crim LR 230. This opens up the possibility of charges under s. 18 and s. 20 of the Offences Against the Person Act 1861. Section 18 requires proof that Karen caused grievous bodily harm — but for her actions Mike would not have suffered the harm.

Causation in law requires proof that the harm was a reasonably foreseeable consequence of her actions. The fact that Mike falls and hits his head etc. will not break the chain of causation. In any event *R v Blaue* [1975] 1 WLR 1411 makes it clear that Karen must take Mike as she finds him — including his propensity to fall over when hit! The *mens rea* for s. 18 is intent — although there is no clear authority at the moment as to what intent means in the context of s. 18 it would be intolerable if the courts adopted any approach other than that in *R v Woollin* [1998] 4 All ER 103. If intention to do grievous bodily harm is sufficient for murder, the intent must be the same under a s. 18 charge. On the facts it may be difficult to establish that Karen intended to do grievous bodily harm — in any event intoxication will be a complicating factor as explained below.

A charge under s. 20 Offences Against the Person Act could be brought as an alternative. The harm required is either grievous bodily harm (see above) or wounding. The injuries suggest that he has suffered a wound. On the basis of *JCC v Eisenhower* [1984] QB 331 this requires proof of a rupture of the dermis and the epidermis. Under s. 20 the grievous bodily harm must be inflicted — but for these purposes this would be satisfied by proof of causation: see *R v Burstow; R v Ireland* [1997] 4 All ER 225. The *mens rea* under s. 20 is satisfied by proof that Karen was malicious: see *R v Mowatt* [1968] 1 QB 421. Karen must at least have been aware of the possibility of causing some physical harm. She does not need to have foreseen the harm actually caused. It should be possible to establish this on the facts.

In the unlikely event that the *mens rea* for s. 20 cannot be established a charge under s. 47 Offences Against the Person Act 1861 could be sustained on the basis that Karen committed an assault (see below) and the assault caused actual bodily harm — see below. Note that under s. 47 Karen need not have any *mens rea* in respect of the actual bodily harm — she only needs the *mens rea* for the assault (either broad or narrow): see *R v Savage; R v Parmenter* [1991] 3 WLR 914.

As to lesser offences, hitting Mike in the face would constitute a battery. Any unlawful touching will suffice: see *Cole v Turner* (1705) 6 Mod Rep 149. The *mens rea* is intention or (subjective) recklessness: see *R v Savage; R v Parmenter* [1991] 3 WLR 914. There is *prima facie* evidence of *mens rea*, subject to what is said below regarding intoxication. If Mike sees the blow coming and apprehends immediate physical violence Karen may also have committed an assault in the 'narrow' sense — the *mens rea* is as for battery.

Karen's failure to help Mike once she has injured him may not be significant. In theory she has caused harm and comes under a responsibility to limit the effect of that harm: see *R v Miller* [1983] 2 AC 161. Note, however, that there is no liability for the omission *per se* — the omission must cause some harm. If the facts are that her failure to act has only a *de minimis* effect in terms of making the harm worse it should be ignored as a basis for liability.

Turning to consider the defences that Karen might raise in respect of the harm done to Mike, she may seek to rely on his consent to harm. On the basis of *R v Donavon* [1934] 2 KB 498, a victim cannot validly consent to physical harm if it amounts to actual bodily harm or worse unless the activity comes within a range of policy-based exceptions. The obvious one here is 'manly diversion' or sport. The issue would be whether or not karate classes come within this exception. Even if they do, a further issue would be the extent of the harm or risk of harm consented to by participants. In *R v Billinghurst* [1978] Crim LR 553 it was suggested that the question should be one of reasonable foreseeability — i.e., the nature of the sport and likelihood of injury. Injuries deliberately inflicted outside the normal course of the activity would definitely fall outside the scope of the defence of consent. At common law the defence of consent is also permitted where parties engage in mutual 'horse-play' and practical jokes: see *R v Aitken* [1992] 1 WLR 1066, and *R v Richardson and Irwin* [1999] Crim LR 494. If the defence succeeds on either basis Karen will have a complete defence to charges under s. 18, s. 20 and s. 47 of the Offences Against the Person Act 1861.

The alternative defence would be self-induced intoxication. If Karen was merely drunk she has no defence as such — intoxication requires evidence that she was incapable of forming, and did not form, the necessary intent. On the basis of *DPP v Majewski* [1977] AC 142, her voluntary intoxication could be a defence to crimes of specific intent but not crimes of basic intent. Section 18 of the Offences Against the Person Act 1861 is a specific intent crime because the *mens rea* goes beyond the *actus reus*. If Karen was charged under s. 18 and successfully pleads intoxication her liability will be reduced to the 'lesser included' offence of s. 20 Offences Against the Person Act 1861 — a basic intent crime. Hence if she is charged under s. 20 or s. 47 Offences Against the Person Act 1861 or charged with common assault or battery she will not escape liability on the grounds of self-induced intoxication, as these are all basic intent crimes. She cannot claim that her consumption of the alcohol was anything other than reckless: see *R v Hardie* [1984] 3 All ER 848. The only possible escape route would be an argument that she would not have been aware of the risk of harm even if she had been sober. There is no evidence to suggest this. Her liability will, therefore, be imposed on the basis that she was reckless in becoming intoxicated and recklessness is sufficient *mens rea* in respect of any one of the basic intent offences.

Karen may also have incurred liability in respect of the harm caused to Gaye. Psychological harm can amount to grievous bodily harm or actual bodily harm depending on its seriousness: see *R v Burstow; R v Ireland* [1997] 4 All ER 225. The prosecution will have to produce medical evidence to show that the harm is not transient and minor. On the facts, bearing in mind the *mens rea* requirements outlined above, a charge under s. 47 of the Offences Against the Person Act 1861 seems the most likely here.

Minor bruising and grazes would most likely constitute actual bodily harm contrary to s. 47 of the Offences Against the Person Act 1861: see *R v Miller* [1954] 2 QB 282. Grazing would not amount to a wound unless the definition in *JCC v Eisenhower* (above) was satisfied. As indicated above the *mens rea* for s. 47 would be intention or subjective recklessness. Provided Karen intended to assault Gaye it does not matter that she might not have foreseen the actual bodily harm that actually transpired; see *R v Savage; R v Parmenter* [1991] 3 WLR 914.

Karen may raise the defence of self-defence in respect of Gaye. Karen is entitled to use reasonable force to protect herself — see e.g., *R v Julien* [1969] 1 WLR 839. The question will be whether or not the force she used was reasonable in the circumstances. She cannot avail herself of the fact that she misjudged the amount of force required due to her being intoxicated: see *R v O'Grady* [1987] 3 WLR 321.

As to Gaye's possible liability, she makes no physical contact with Karen, hence the only possible charge could be in relation to 'narrow' assault based on her threats. The House of Lords has made it clear that words can constitute an assault — see *R v Burstow; R v Ireland* [1997] 4 All ER 225. The problem for the prosecution would be in establishing that Karen actually apprehended any immediate physical harm. She may not have been perturbed by Gaye's threats. Gaye would need to have the *mens rea* for assault — see above. Gaye could rely on self-defence (i.e., reasonable force used in defence of another), on the basis that she was acting to protect Mike. Alternatively she could invoke the statutory defence under s. 3 of the Criminal Law Act 1967 — using reasonable force to prevent the commission of a criminal offence.

In breaking Karen's teeth Mike may have caused actual bodily harm contrary to s. 47 of the Offences Against the Person Act 1861. He appears to have caused the harm with the necessary *mens rea* — i.e., he was at least aware of the risk of harm: see *R v Savage; R v Parmenter* (above). The obvious defence would be self-defence at common law — considered above. The issue to note here is that Mike is mistaken — there is in fact no need for him to defend himself. Following *Beckford v R* [1987] 3 WLR 611, Mike would be judged on the facts as he honestly believed them to be — hence if he honestly believed he was about to be attacked again by Karen he could use force that would have been reasonable to defend himself in such circumstances.

In damaging Karen's glasses Mike may have committed the offence of criminal damage contrary to s. 1(1) Criminal Damage Act 1971. Mike has committed the *actus reus* by damaging property belonging to another — the main issue for argument would be *mens rea*. He does not appear to have intended the harm, hence the prosecution will have to establish that he was at least reckless. *MPC v Caldwell* [1982] AC 341 no longer applies here, following the decision of the House of Lords in *R v G* [2003] 4 All ER 765. Hence the prosecution will have to show that Mike was at least aware of the risk that property might be damaged by his actions. If he gave no thought to the risk he might escape liability. Again Mike could argue that he was using reasonable force to prevent harm to himself (e.g., where D destroys a gun that X is about to use to shoot D).

Q Question 4

The majority decision of the House of Lords in *R v Brown* [1993] 2 All ER 75 concerning consent as a defence to the deliberate infliction of physical harm, does not follow the legitimate aims and functions of the criminal law.

   Discuss.

Commentary

This is a challenging question on a difficult issue. Consent as a defence in criminal law has always caused problems, and since *Brown* there have been two very detailed Law Commission reports on the subject. It is always likely, therefore, to be the subject of an exam question.

   There is also the added complication of reference to the legitimate aims and functions of the criminal law. As English criminal law is not codified, there is no statute that sets out the law's aims and functions, so it is necessary to consider case law, Law Commission reports, and the views of commentators to ascertain these. In this answer, candidates must attempt to cover all aspects of this issue, as the question is not simply an invitation to write all you know about *Brown*.

   There are various versions of aims and functions for criminal law (as well as criminal justice and sentencing), but the author has chosen those set out in the American Law Institute Penal Code, which are as good as any. Obviously you cannot relate all of them to the decision in *Brown*, but it provides a basis and point of reference.

   You must then deal fully with the *ratio decidendi* of the case, with a detailed analysis of Lord Templeman's judgment on behalf of the majority. A discussion as to whether this does represent the legitimate aims and functions of the criminal law must then follow.

   Obviously opinions on this issue will greatly differ, as of course they did in the House of Lords with Lords Mustill and Slynn dissenting. Your conclusion could therefore be totally different from this author's; but provided it is logically developed from your earlier analysis, it would not mean that your answer would necessarily obtain a lower mark. Indeed, it might result in a higher one!

- Aims of the criminal law

- House of Lords' decision in *Brown* [1993]

- Lord Templeman's rationale

- Law and morals

- Role of the House of Lords

- Public interest

:Q: **Suggested answer**

There will never be complete agreement as to the correct aims and functions of the criminal law and, in the absence of a criminal code setting out a rationale containing fundamental principles, this issue will remain a topic of debate. However, the aims and functions of English criminal law, it is submitted, are similar to those stated in the American Law Institute Model Penal Code, i.e.:

(a) To forbid and prevent conduct that unjustifiably and inexcusably inflicts or threatens substantial harm to individual or public interests.

(b) To subject to public control persons whose conduct indicates that they are disposed to commit crime.

(c) To safeguard conduct that is without fault from condemnation as criminal.

(d) To give fair warning of the nature of the conduct declared to be an offence.

(e) To differentiate on reasonable grounds between serious and minor offences.

In addition to protecting the public from harmful activity, we also expect the criminal law to respect certain individual liberties such as freedom from coercion, deception or fear; the right to protest, demonstrate etc. Individual freedom of choice is also a liberty that we place high on our list of priorities, and it is this conflict between individual freedoms and collective interests which was one of the major issues in *R* v *Brown* [1993] 2 All ER 75.

In *Brown*, a group of middle-aged men willingly participated in sado-masochistic activities that involved the deliberate infliction of wounds. Videos were made of their activities and circulated to members of the group, but not to outsiders. The men were charged with various offences including assault occasioning actual bodily harm (Offences Against the Person Act 1861, s. 47) and malicious wounding (Offences Against the Person Act 1861, s. 20) and pleaded guilty when the trial judge ruled against their defence of consent. The Court of Appeal upheld their conviction but certified the following point of law of general public importance: 'Where A wounds or assaults B occasioning him actual bodily harm in the course of a sado-masochistic encounter, does the prosecution have to prove lack of consent on the part of B before they can establish A's guilt under section 20 or section 47 Offences Against the Person Act 1861?'. The House of Lords answered this question in the negative and dismissed the appeal. Lord Templeman, who gave the majority judgment, decided the issue using a mixture of precedent and public policy. He stated that consent is not a general defence where actual bodily harm or wounding has been caused. There are exceptions to this rule, and violence intentionally inflicted will not be a criminal offence if it occurs in the course of a lawful activity, such as contact sports, surgical operations, rough horseplay or tattooing. The question for the House therefore was, can such sado-masochistic behaviour as occurred in *Brown* be a lawful activity?

Lord Templeman concluded that this could be answered only by considerations of policy and public interest. The criminal law must provide sufficient safeguards against exploitation and corruption of others, particularly those who are young, weak in body or mind, inexperienced or in a state of special physical, official or economic dependence. He referred to three reasons leading to the conclusion that such conduct was not in the public interest:

(a) It glorified the cult of violence ('pleasure derived from the infliction of pain is an evil thing').

(b) It increased the risk of AIDS and the spread of other sexually-transmitted diseases.

(c) It could lead to the corruption of youth.

Lord Templeman concluded: 'I am not prepared to invent a defence of consent for sado-masochistic encounters which breed and glorify cruelty and result in offences under section 47 and section 20 of the Act of 1861'.

The minority (Lords Mustill and Slynn) interpreted the relevant cases (*R* v *Coney* (1882) 8 QBD 534; *R* v *Donovan* [1934] 2 KB 498; and *Attorney-General's Reference (No. 6 of 1980)* [1981] QB 715) and the public interest requirements differently. Lord Mustill decided that the decks were clear for the House to tackle completely anew the question of whether the public interest required s. 47 to be interpreted as penalising the conduct in question. He concluded that:

> the state should interfere with the rights of the individual to live his or her life as he or she may choose no more than is necessary to ensure a proper balance between the special interests of the individual and the general interests of the individuals who together comprise the populace at large.

In relating the majority decision to aims and functions, many questions arise. First, in ascertaining public interest, how far should the Law Lords take into account society's morals? This involves reference to the Hart–Devlin debate (see Lord Devlin, *The Enforcement of Morals*) as to whether conduct should be criminalised simply because it is a moral wrong, and whether the criminal law should simply reflect society's moral standards or try to improve them. This is virtually impossible to answer briefly, but it is submitted that as it cannot be deemed morally right to encourage deliberate injury through sado-masochistic activity, the majority decision does not conflict with this objective. If the majority had not declared it unlawful, their decision could have been interpreted as condoning or even encouraging such activities.

Secondly, was the House of Lords' decision in *Brown* creating new law, or was it giving effect to the will of Parliament expressed in the 1861 Act? Again, this is difficult to answer, but the application of the defence of consent is probably correct as there has been traditionally a reluctance to extend its boundaries, partially because of the difficulties in deciding whether consent was freely given by a victim capable of understanding the nature of the act (see *Burrell* v *Harmer* [1967] Crim LR 169 — consent to tattooing given by boys aged 12 and 13 held invalid). It is submitted that their Lordships were not abolishing an existing defence (as they did when they removed the husband's marital rape immunity in *R* v *R* [1991] 4 All ER 481) but were simply declaring the boundaries of an existing offence.

Thirdly, was this a situation where respect for individual freedom should have been outweighed by the need to protect society from such conduct? The participants were middle-aged men who were in control of the activities, but the Law Lords considered that because of the risk of future, younger, inexperienced participants, the accused's individual liberty had to be sacrificed. This aspect of the decision was heavily criticised (e.g., N. Bamforth, 'Sado Masochism and Consent' [1994] Crim LR 661) and was considered by the Court of Appeal in *R* v *Wilson* [1996] 3 WLR 125. In that case, a husband, who at his wife's request had branded his initials on her buttocks with a hot knife, had his conviction under s. 47 of the 1861 Act quashed. The court took the view that *Brown* was not to be taken as authority for the proposition that consent is no defence to a charge under s. 47 in all circumstances where actual bodily harm is inflicted. Russell LJ stated:

> we are firmly of the opinion that it is not in the public interest that activities such as the appellant's in this appeal should amount to criminal behaviour. Consensual activity between husband and wife, in the privacy of the matrimonial home, is not, in our judgement, normally a proper matter for criminal investigation, let alone criminal prosecution.

In *Wilson*, therefore, individual liberty was the deciding factor; whereas in *Brown*, the deciding factor was protection of the public. Both decisions were based to some extent on the concept of public policy, which has been described as an 'unruly horse'. Both cases demonstrate the difficulties of applying the criminal law and in deciding whether a judgment is right or wrong.

Q Question 5

Jack and Brian argue fiercely. Brian deliberately throws a pint of beer over Jack and then forcibly pushes Jack, causing him to gash his head and fall to the floor. Jack, feeling a little dazed, picks up a bottle and throws it at Brian. The bottle hits Brian causing him minor bruising, but then ricochets into PC 49, a police officer who is on duty, causing him to fall and suffer concussion.

Discuss the criminal responsibility of Jack and Brian.

Commentary

This is a typical question on assault and aggravated assault, an area of law that would be very straightforward had the Law Commission's recommendations (No. 122) been implemented. As they have not, we still have to grapple with the notorious Offences Against the Person Act 1861, a statute riddled with inconsistencies and anomalies.

A good answer must reveal an understanding of the elements of, and differences between, s. 18, s. 20 and s. 47 of the 1861 Act, and an ability to apply them to the facts of the problem. This will be the heart of the answer, although you must also cover common assault under s. 39 of the Criminal Justice Act 1988 and assault on a police officer in the execution of his duty (Police Act 1996, s. 89). The defences of automatism and self-defence should also be considered briefly before being rejected (for obvious reasons).

No doubt the Crown Prosecution Service would consider charges under the Public Order Act 1986 in an incident of this nature, but as this topic is more likely to be found on a Public Law (or Constitutional Law) syllabus, it has been excluded from this answer.

- **Common assault — Criminal Justice Act 1988, s. 39**

- **Offences Against the Person Act 1861, s. 18**

- **Offences Against the Person Act 1861, s. 20**

- **Offences Against the Person Act 1861, s. 47**

- *Savage* v *Parmenter* [1991]

- **Police Act 1996, s. 89**

- **Defences**

:Ọ: Suggested answer

When Brian throws a pint of beer over Jack he will have committed a common assault under s. 39 of the Criminal Justice Act 1988. This summary offence comprises both technical assault and battery. Quite clearly Brian's act would constitute a battery, i.e., 'an act by which the defendant intentionally or recklessly inflicts unlawful personal violence upon the victim' (*Fagan* v *Metropolitan Police Commissioner* [1968] 3 All ER 442). A battery can be the direct application or (as in this case) indirect application of personal violence. Thus in *R* v *Martin* (1881) 8 QBD 54, where the accused placed an iron bar across the exit of a theatre and then turned out the lights, he was guilty of inflicting grievous bodily harm (under s. 20 of the Offences Against the Person Act 1861) as the escaping audience were injured when they ran into the bar.

It is possible that Brian also committed a technical assault on Jack, i.e., 'any act by which the defendant intentionally or recklessly causes the victim to apprehend immediate and unlawful personal violence' (*Fagan*). This would of course depend upon whether Jack apprehended the impending force of the beer!

However, the more serious consequence which Brian has caused by pushing Jack is the gash to Jack's head, and as a result he will face charges under the Offences Against the Person Act 1861. It is unlikely that this injury would constitute grievous bodily harm (words which should be given their ordinary and natural meaning, according to the House of Lords' decision in *R* v *Smith* [1960] 3 All ER 161) but it could amount to a 'wound', which requires only that the continuity of the whole skin be broken (not simply an internal rupturing of blood vessels: *C (A Minor)* v *Eisenhower* [1984] QB 331). If this is the case, Brian could be charged under s. 18 of the 1861 Act: 'Whosoever shall unlawfully and maliciously by any means whatsoever wound or cause any grievous bodily harm to any person with intent to do some grievous bodily harm . . . shall be guilty of [an offence]'. Nevertheless, the prosecution must prove an intention to cause grievous bodily harm, and it is submitted that, on the facts, this would be very difficult to establish (even though it is a question of fact for the jury in accordance with *R* v *Moloney* [1985] 1 All ER 1025).

It is more likely that Brian would be charged under s. 20 of the 1861 Act: 'Whosoever shall unlawfully and maliciously wound or inflict any grievous bodily harm upon any other person . . . shall be guilty of [an offence]'. Whereas in *R* v *Mowatt* [1967] 3 All ER 47, the House of Lords stated that the word 'maliciously' adds nothing to the *mens rea* requirement of s. 18, it is the only word used to define the *mens rea* of s. 20, and its meaning has been the subject of intense debate. The key decision on this point is the House of Lords' decision in *R* v *Savage and Parmenter* [1991] 4 All ER 698, where the facts were similar to this problem. Their Lordships decided that in order to establish the *mens rea* for s. 20, all the prosecution had to prove was that the accused actually foresaw that some harm might result. This is an easy test to satisfy, as it is not necessary for the prosecution to prove that the accused foresaw the risk of grievous bodily harm or a wound (the prohibited consequences under s. 20), simply that some harm might result. However, this test is subjective, the House of Lords having rejected the argument that *Caldwell* recklessness was applicable.

It is therefore submitted that as a forcible push involves the risk of some physical harm, the prosecution (if the gash was held by the judge to constitute a wound) would be able to establish the ingredients of s. 20 of the 1861 Act.

On the other hand, if the court concluded that the gash was not a wound, Brian could be found guilty under s. 47 of the Act (assault occasioning actual bodily harm). The consequence, actual bodily harm, can include psychiatric harm (*R* v *Mike Chan-Fook* [1994] 2 All ER 552) and minor, but not merely superficial, cuts of a sort probably requiring medical treatment. As the maximum period of imprisonment (five years) is the same for a conviction under either s. 20 or s. 47, the prosecution would probably be satisfied with a conviction under s. 47. *R* v *Savage and Parmenter* [1991] 4 All ER 698 confirms that a s. 47 conviction is a permissible alternative verdict on a count alleging unlawful wounding contrary to s. 20, and also clarified the *mens rea* requirement for s. 47 — which is satisfied by the prosecution proving that the accused had the *mens rea* for common assault. It is not necessary for the accused to have intended or foreseen the risk of actual bodily harm. Thus, as long as Brian caused the consequence with the *mens rea* of common assault, Brian will be guilty under s. 47.

Jack will also face charges under the 1861 Act. Brian's injuries would seem to constitute actual bodily harm, but the concussion suffered by PC 49 could amount to grievous bodily harm. This is a question of fact for the jury and would obviously depend on the medical evidence. If it was deemed grievous bodily harm it is likely that Jack could be found guilty under s. 18 of the Offences Against the Person Act 1861, as throwing a beer bottle at someone is evidence of intention to cause grievous bodily harm. The fact that Jack did not intend to harm PC 49 will not assist him, as the doctrine of transferred malice will apply. This doctrine can also be used if Jack was charged under s. 89 of the Police Act 1996 (replacing s. 51 of the Police Act 1964) with assaulting a police officer in the execution of his duty. Thus in *McBride* v *Turnock* [1964] Crim LR 173, the accused struck at X, a private citizen, but accidentally hit V, a police officer acting in the execution of his duty. Although the accused had no intention of assaulting V, the doctrine of transferred malice applied and he was found guilty of this offence.

If Jack could bring evidence to show that as a result of gashing his head he was not in control of his faculties, he could raise the defence of automatism. However, for this defence to succeed there needs to be a total destruction of voluntary control; reduced or imperfect awareness is not sufficient (*Attorney-General's Reference (No. 2 of 1992)* (1993) 99 Cr App R 429). So the fact that Jack was able to pick up and throw the bottle would probably ensure that this defence failed.

Jack might also raise self-defence, on the basis that he had been attacked and believed that the attack was still continuing. Although the burden of proof is on the prosecution to prove that Jack was not acting in self-defence, and Jack's belief that he had to resort to violence to protect himself need not be based on reasonable grounds (*R* v *Williams* [1987] 3 All ER 411), it will still be very difficult for this defence to succeed, as the indiscriminate throwing of a beer bottle may not be held to be reasonable and proportionate to the push.

Q Question 6

Arthur is a troublesome pest who continually annoys people. For two years he had been pestering Monica. He had never previously threatened to hurt her, but has constantly followed and watched her come and go from her house. However, on one occasion she saw him standing outside her living room window and he said 'I'm going to get you Monica'. Monica was frightened and phoned the police before Arthur moved away.

Arthur had also been telephoning Violet at least twice a week for over 12 months. When she picked up the phone he would simply remain silent, until she put the phone down. This caused Violet great distress and she had to seek psychiatric help for anxiety and headaches.

However, the person who has suffered most from Arthur's actions has been Wendy. She has suffered a complete nervous breakdown as a result of his conduct involving constant telephoning, sending hate mail and persistently following her.

Discuss the criminal responsibility of Arthur.

Commentary

The criminal law has to adapt to cope with new social ills and many recent cases have demonstrated the extent of the problem of stalking.

There will inevitably be some time-delay between the advent of new kinds of conduct, and the time when a policy decision is subsequently made to re-examine whether existing offences encompass such new conduct — or whether new legislation is needed. Unfortunately the existing provisions of the notorious Offences Against the Person Act 1861 have to be considered in relation to this conduct and the reported stalking cases again highlight the difficulties in applying that troublesome Act.

The question requires an analysis of the offences of assault and battery and the aggravated assaults as well as the recent important Court of Appeal and House of Lords decisions.

Brief mention should also be made of the Protection from Harassment Act 1997.

* Words alone — assault

* *Constanza* [1997]

* s. 47, Offences Against the Person Act 1861 — *Ireland* [1997]

* s. 20, Offences Against the Person Act 1861 — *Burstow* [1997]

* s. 4, Protection from Harassment Act 1997

⚭ Suggested answer

The most serious offences that Arthur will be charged with are under the Offences Against the Person Act 1861. In particular s. 18 wounding or causing grievous bodily harm, s. 20 malicious wounding and s. 47 assault occasioning actual bodily harm. However, in the first incident with Monica candidates must first consider if an assault has taken place.

An assault is any act by which the defendant intentionally or recklessly causes the victim to apprehend immediate and unlawful personal violence whereas a battery is any act by which the defendant intentionally or recklessly inflicts unlawful personal violence upon the victim. The House of Lords in *R* v *Savage and Parmenter* [1991] 4 All ER 698 confirmed that intention or subjective recklessness is sufficient *mens rea*, Lord Ackner stating (at p. 711): 'It is common ground that the mental element of assault is an intention to cause the victim to apprehend immediate and unlawful violence or recklessness whether such apprehension be caused.' Common assault, a term covering both assault and battery, should be charged under s. 39 of the Criminal Justice Act 1988.

The prosecution would face two problems regarding the *actus reus* of assault in Monica's case. First, the fact that there was no threatening gesture from Arthur raises the question whether words alone can constitute an assault. For many years it was thought that they could not, the *dicta* of Holroyd J in *R v Meade and Belt* (1823) 1 LEW CC 184 being accepted: 'No words or singing are equivalent to an assault'. However, in *R v Wilson* [1955] 1 All ER 744, Lord Goddard stated that the words 'get out the knives' in themselves would constitute an assault even if they were not accompanied by a threatening gesture. Similarly in the recent case of *R v Constanza* [1997] Crim LR 576, the Court of Appeal in upholding the accused's conviction under s. 47 of the Offences Against the Person Act 1861 for assault occasioning actual bodily harm rejected the appellant's submission that an assault could not be committed by words alone without a physical action.

The second problem is that the victim must apprehend immediate violence and Arthur could argue that as he was outside Monica's house he was in no position to immediately carry out the threat. However, this condition has been liberally interpreted and in *Smith v Superintendent of Woking Police Station* [1983] 76 Cr App R 234, the accused was convicted of assault by looking through the window of the victim's bedsitting room with intent to frighten her. More recently in *R v Ireland* [1997] 4 All ER 225 the House of Lords upheld the accused's conviction under s. 47 of the Offences Against the Person Act 1861 where the accused had phoned the victim and remained silent. The court held that the accused had put himself in immediate contact with the victim and when she lifted the telephone she was placed in immediate fear and suffered psychological harm. This decision was applied in *R v Constanza* [1997] Crim LR 576, where the court held that the Crown must prove that the victim feared violence 'at some time not excluding the immediate future' and rejected the defence submission that a person cannot have a fear of immediate violence unless they can see the potential perpetrator.

It is therefore submitted that in view of these recent developments expanding the concept of assault and the fact that the appropriate *mens rea* of intention or subjective recklessness can be easily established, that Arthur will be guilty of assaulting Monica.

The House of Lords' decision in *R v Ireland* establishes that silence can amount to an assault and Arthur would therefore face a charge under s. 47 of the Offences Against the Person Act 1861 in respect of Violet. The main difficulty for the prosecution would be in establishing that Violet suffered actual bodily harm. It is hard to envisage that those who drafted this offence considered that this phrase covered any harm other than physical injury, but it is now recognised that the distinctions between physical and mental injury may often be manifested by physical symptoms. In *R* v *Mike Chan-Fook* [1994] 2 All ER 552 the Court of Appeal held that psychiatric injury was actual bodily harm provided that the prosecution could bring sufficient expert psychiatric evidence to establish it. Further, it does not cover mere emotion, fear or hysteria. Thus whether Arthur's conduct has occasioned actual bodily harm would very much depend on expert evidence.

It is submitted that again the prosecution would have little difficulty in establishing Arthur's *mens rea*. This is because the House of Lords in *R* v *Savage and Parmenter* [1991] 4 All ER 698, confirmed that the *mens rea* for s. 47 of the Offences Against the Person Act 1861 was the same as for common assault. It is therefore not necessary for the prosecution to prove that the accused intended to cause or foresaw the risk of causing actual bodily harm.

In *R* v *Burstow* [1997] 4 All ER 225 the House of Lords held that grievous bodily harm can include psychiatric injury and therefore in respect of Wendy, Arthur could be convicted under s. 18 or s. 20 of the Offences Against the Person Act 1861. Both these offences involve the consequence of the victim suffering a wound or grievous bodily harm but whereas s. 18 uses the word 'cause', s. 20 uses 'inflict'. The effect of the difference between these two words has troubled the judiciary and commentators for many years but in *R* v *Burstow* Lord Bingham referred to the House of Lords' decision in *R* v *Mandair* [1994] 99 Cr App R 250 where Lord Mackay stated 'In my opinion, as I have said, the word "cause" is wider or at least not narrower than the word "inflict" ' — to justify the conclusion that there is not any radical divergence between the meaning of the two words and that an accused could be guilty under s. 20 even though the psychiatric injury was not the result of physical violence.

The major difference between s. 18 and s. 20 is the *mens rea*. Section 18 requires an intention to do grievous bodily harm or an intent to resist or prevent the lawful apprehension or detention ('detainer' in the statute) of any person. *R* v *Bryson* [1985] Crim LR 669 decided that intention has the same meaning as in the law of murder and therefore in accordance with *R* v *Moloney* [1985] 1 All ER 1025 the trial judge should not give a complex direction on the meaning of intent as it is a word in common use easily understood by the jury. As this case involves psychiatric harm the judge might take the view that this complicates the issue and that a direction is required.

In *R* v *Ireland* and *Burstow* where the facts were very similar to this problem the persons accused were convicted under s. 20 of the Offences Against the Person Act 1861. It is often difficult for the prosecution to establish the necessary intent required for a s. 18 conviction, but s. 20 only requires proof of maliciousness. Although the prohibited consequence of s. 20 is wounding or grievous bodily harm the House of Lords in *R* v *Mowatt* [1967] 3 All ER 47 stated that this meant the accused foresaw the risk of some physical harm, not necessarily grievous bodily harm. This decision was followed by the House of Lords in *R* v *Savage and Parmenter* [1991] 4 All ER 698.

It is therefore submitted that Arthur would be convicted under s. 20 of the Offences Against the Person Act 1861 in respect of his activities towards Wendy. No doubt he could also face charges under s. 4 of the Protection from Harassment Act 1997 where to satisfy the *mens rea* the prosecution has only to prove that a reasonable person would realise that the effect of the accused's conduct would be a fear of violence or sense of harassment.

Q Question 7

Answer both parts ((a) and (b)),

(a) Steve is having a coffee with his friends Dave and Barry. They discuss women's attitudes to sex and Dave expresses the view that all women really mean 'yes' when they say 'no' to sexual intercourse. Steve invites Dave and Barry back to his house where Linda, Steve's wife, is asleep. Steve tells Barry that Linda loves to have sex with men other than her husband, but also likes to pretend that she is being raped. Steve reassures Barry that any resistance on the part of Linda will be part of her 'play-acting'. Dave visits the bathroom and, in error, enters the bedroom where Linda is asleep in bed. He goes into her bedroom and starts to have sexual intercourse with Linda who is still asleep. On waking, Linda tries to fight Dave off but he continues to have sex with her.

Linda runs downstairs in distress. Barry takes this as his cue to have sexual intercourse with her on the sofa in the living room. Linda begs Barry to leave her alone but he persists. Steve stands by watching the events unfold.

Discuss the criminal liability of Dave and Barry.

(b) One evening Rory walks past Lizzie's house and notices that the front door is not fully closed. He pushes the door open and has a look around inside the house. He discovers Lizzie asleep in her bed. Without waking Lizzie he pulls her bed-clothes aside and raises her nightclothes enabling him to see her naked body.

The next day Rory, seeking to impress, tells his friend Kasra how he went out on a blind date the previous evening with Lizzie. He tells Kasra that the evening culminated in them having sexual intercourse at her house. Rory concludes by telling Kasra that Lizzie is 'always dead keen for it'.

The following day Kasra visits Lizzie's house posing as a double-glazing salesman. Lizzie agrees to let Kasra in so that he can give her an estimate. Whilst they are in her bedroom Kasra suggests that she might like to have sex with him there and then. Lizzie is shocked and frightened but she remains calm, suggesting that Kasra gets himself ready whilst she visits the bathroom. Lizzie leaves the bedroom intending to call the police. Kasra, encouraged by her response, runs after Lizzie and, pushing her onto the hallway floor, proceeds to have sexual intercourse with her, despite her protestations that he should stop. Once Kasra leaves, Lizzie calls the police.

Advise the Crown Prosecution Service as to the criminal liability of Rory and Kasra. Do not consider Rory's liability as an accomplice to Kasra.

Commentary

The Sexual Offences Act 2003 only came into force in May 2004, hence there is no indication at present as to how its provisions will be dealt with by the courts. Similarly candidates may have little clue as to the type of question that will be set in an examination. Some examiners may decide not to examine the area until the operation of the law becomes clearer. Others may simply set essay questions asking candidates to compare the old law with the 2003 Act. For the purposes of this chapter some problem questions have been selected to attempt an examination of how the law might now apply to situations that proved problematic under the pre-2004 law.

It should be stressed that factual problems involving sexual offences often, of necessity, refer to unpleasant attitudes and activities. Simply because the facts of the question reflect reprehensible attitudes or offensive notions of sexuality do not assume that these in any way reflect the views of the examiner! Chauvinistic attitudes towards consent do exist in real life and can cause problems when cases come to trial. Note the rubric to part (a) does not require consideration of Steve's liability, hence the answer does not cover issues relating to accessorial liability.

(a) Steve, Dave and Barry

• Dave and *actus reus* of rape

• Rebuttable assumptions concerning consent under the 2003 Act

• *Mens rea* for rape — objective test

• Dave and offence of trespass with intent to commit a sexual offence

(b) Rory and Kasra

• Rory's liability, s. 4, Sexual Offences Act 2003

• Rory's liability, s. 3, Sexual Offences Act 2003

• Rory's liability, s. 63, Sexual Offences Act 2003

• Kasra's liability, s. 63, Sexual Offences Act 2003

• Kasra's liability, s. 1, Sexual Offences Act 2003

⚙ Suggested answer to part (a)

On the given facts it is likely that Dave would be convicted of rape contrary to s. 1 of the Sexual Offences Act 2003. In terms of *actus reus* the prosecution would first have to prove that Dave had penetrated the vagina, anus or mouth of another person with his penis. The fact that he started to have sexual intercourse with Linda would appear to satisfy this. There is no need to prove ejaculation. Section 79(2) of the 2003 Act specifies that penetration '. . . is a continuing act from entry to withdrawal . . .'. The prosecution would have to establish that, at some time during the penetration Dave had the necessary *mens rea*.

The second element of *actus reus* to be established is that Linda did not consent to the penetration. The issue of consent is now governed by the rather complex provisions of sections 74 to 76 of the 2003 Act. Under s. 74 a person consents if she agrees by choice, and has the freedom and capacity to make that choice. This on its own would appear to be enough to establish that Linda could not have been consenting at the time Dave started to have sexual intercourse with her. A person who is asleep does not have the capacity to make decisions.

The matter is further clarified by s. 75, which goes on to establish certain rebuttable assumptions as to consent. Where the defendant has:

(i)   committed the *actus reus* of rape as defined in s. 1(1)(a) (i.e., has penetrated the vagina, anus or mouth of another person), and;

(ii) the complainant was asleep at the time of the penetration, and;

(iii) the defendant knew that this was the case

— the complainant will be taken not to have consented to the sexual intercourse unless sufficient evidence is adduced to raise an issue as to whether the complainant consented. This effectively places Dave under a burden to provide evidence that Linda was consenting even though she was asleep — on the facts there would appear to be no such evidence.

Turning to *mens rea*, Dave's penetration of Linda is clearly intentional, hence the only live issue will be as to whether or not he reasonably believed that Linda was consenting. To this end, s. 1(2) of the 2003 Act provides that whether or not a belief is reasonable is to be determined having regard to all the circumstances, including any steps the defendant took to ascertain whether the complainant was consenting. There is no evidence of Dave having taken such steps, hence he will be guilty of raping Linda. Note that Steve has said nothing to Dave about Linda enjoying 'rape fantasies'.

It should be noted that Dave may also have committed the offence of trespass with intent to commit a sexual offence, contrary to s. 63 of the Sexual Offences Act 2003. The offence is made out where he is a trespasser on any premises; he intends to commit rape; and he knows that, or is reckless as to whether, he is a trespasser. Being in Linda's bedroom intending to have sexual intercourse with her could make him a trespasser in premises. Intention to have sexual intercourse whilst she is asleep would be evidence of his intention to rape her. This offence replaces the offence under s. 9(1)(a) of the Theft Act 1968 — entry as a trespasser with intent to commit rape.

Barry's situation is very similar, except that Linda was clearly conscious at the time of the sexual intercourse. Again the prosecution would have to prove that Barry penetrated the vagina, anus or mouth of Linda with his penis, and that at the time she was not consenting. The starting point again is s. 74 of the 2003 Act and the proposition that a person consents if he or she agrees by choice, and has the freedom and capacity to make that choice. The physical overpowering of Linda by Barry would seem to suggest there was no free choice on her part. Under s. 75, once it is proved that:

(i)   Barry had sexual intercourse with Linda;

(ii) Barry was, immediately before the sexual intercourse, using violence against Linda, or causing her to fear that immediate violence would be used against her; and

(iii) Barry knew that those circumstances existed,

— Linda will be presumed not to have consented to the sexual intercourse unless sufficient evidence is adduced to raise an issue as to whether she consented.

Barry is to be taken not to have reasonably believed that the complainant consented unless sufficient evidence is adduced to raise an issue as to whether he reasonably believed it.

The problem for the prosecution is that s. 1(2) goes on to provide that whether or not Barry's belief is reasonable is to be determined having regard to all the circumstances, including any steps Barry took to ascertain whether the complainant was consenting. Under the pre-Sexual Offences Act 2003 law, *DPP* v *Morgan* [1975] 2 All ER 347, would have required Barry to be judged on the facts as he honestly believed them to be. Hence he could have relied on Steve's assurances as to Linda's consent. Under the 2003 Act the onus instead is on Barry to obtain Linda's consent. On the one hand Barry will contend that he acted on Steve's reassurances. On the other hand the prosecution must argue that the Act requires the jury to have regard to the steps taken by Barry to ask Linda if she was consenting. In the absence of any case law it is unclear how the courts will interpret these provisions. The test is now objective, but the reassurances by Steve may be seen as making Barry's assumptions as to consent reasonable. It is not to be assumed that the Act will necessarily bring within the scope of the offence of rape every instance of non-consensual intercourse that proved problematic prior to its enactment.

⑳ Suggested answer to part (b)

When Rory enters Lizzie's house he does so as a trespasser as he has no permission to be there. He does not commit an offence under s. 9(1)(a) of the Theft Act 1968, however, as he does not enter with intent to steal, do grievous bodily harm, or criminal damage. Where he subsequently pulls her bedclothes aside and raises her nightclothes to see her naked body, he probably does commit an offence contrary to

s. 4 of the Sexual Offences Act 2003 — causing a person to engage in sexual activity without consent. The prosecution would have to prove that the activity was 'sexual' in nature. For these purposes this is defined by s. 78 as penetration, touching or any other activity that, whatever its circumstances or any person's purpose in relation to it, a reasonable person would consider of a sexual nature. Alternatively it can be penetration, touching or any other activity that, because of its nature may be sexual and, because of its circumstances or the purpose of any person in relation to it (or both) it is sexual. The test is clearly objective, although the court can take into account the defendant's purpose.

That Lizzie was not consenting to the activity is presumed from the fact that she was asleep — see s. 75(2)(d) of the 2003 Act, and the fact that Rory was aware of this. In terms of *mens rea*, Rory's actions are intentional in lifting the nightclothes. There is no need to prove that he was aware that the actions were sexual. The only argument he could raise would be as regards consent. Given the facts there appears to be no basis on which he could argue that he reasonably believed Lizzie to be consenting. The facts also raise the possibility of a charge of sexual assault contrary to s. 3 of the 2003 Act. This provides that a person commits an offence if he intentionally touches another person, the touching is sexual, the complainant does not consent to the touching, and the defendant does not reasonably believe that the complainant consents. Whether the defendant's belief in the complainant's consent is reasonable is to be determined having regard to all the circumstances, including any steps the defendant has taken to ascertain whether the complainant consents. The technical difficulty for the prosecution with a s. 3 charge lies in proving that Rory touched Lizzie. Section 79(8) defines 'touching' as including touching with any part of the body, with anything else, through anything, and in particular includes touching amounting to penetration. There is no evidence that Rory actually touches Lizzie, although he may have done so 'through' her nightclothes. If this technicality can be overcome, a s. 3 charge is possible.

Rory might also have incurred liability for trespassing with intent to commit a sexual offence, contrary to s. 63 of the Sexual Offences Act 2003. The offence is made out where he is a trespasser on any premises and intends to commit a 'relevant offence' — for these purposes 'relevant offence' encompasses both sexual assault and causing sexual activity without consent. One assumes that the prosecution can prove that Rory knew that, or was reckless as to whether he was, a trespasser.

When Kasra deceives Lizzie into letting him enter her house he may also have committed the offence of trespass with intent to commit a sexual offence, contrary to s. 63 of the Sexual Offences Act 2003. Liability would require proof that he was present intending to have sexual intercourse regardless of whether or not Lizzie consented. If he believed that, having tricked her into letting him in, he would be able to have consensual intercourse, there may not be any liability under s. 63.

Does Kasra commit rape when he has sexual intercourse with Lizzie? The facts make it quite clear that the *actus reus* of the offence under s. 1 of the 2003 Act is made out. Kasra has penile penetration of Lizzie and she was not consenting. The problem area for the prosecution will be *mens rea*. Kasra will contend that he honestly believed Lizzie was consenting. The 2003 Act requires the defendant's belief in consent to be both honest and reasonable. Section 1(2) requires the jury to have regard to all the circumstances, including any steps Kasra took to ascertain whether Lizzie consented. Note that he does ask her if she would like to have sex. As a ploy to buy time to telephone the police she gives him the impression that she would be willing. All of this is evidence that Kasra will rely on to contend that a reasonable person would have thought Lizzie was consenting, and that he checked to make sure that she was. More difficult for Kasra is the fact that Lizzie subsequently makes it plain that she does not want to have sex with Kasra but he persists. It is at this point that the reasonableness of his belief in consent comes into question.

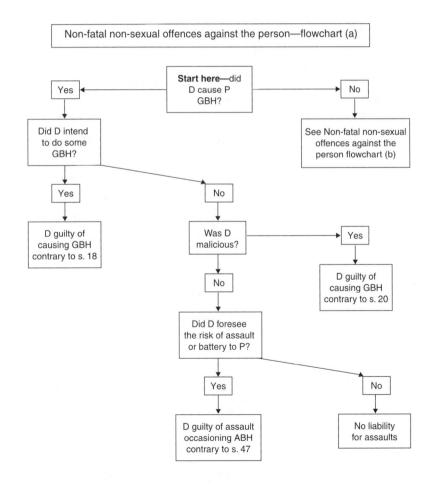

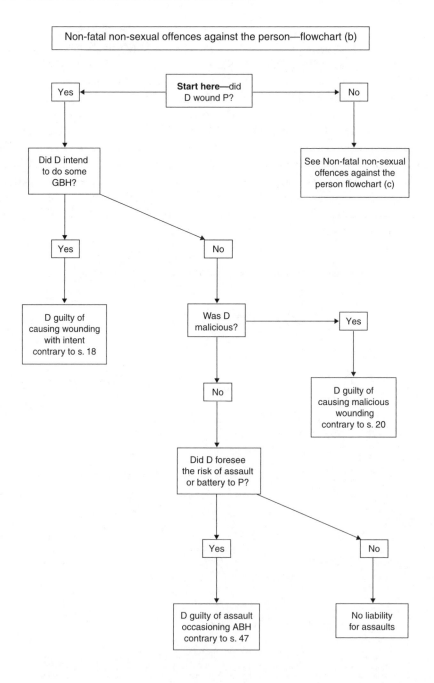

Non-fatal non-sexual offences against the person—flowchart (c)

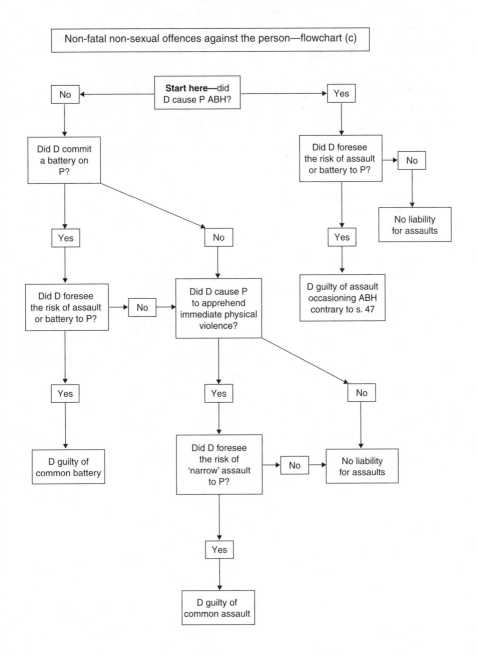

Further reading

Clarkson, C., 'Law Commission Report No. 218' [1994] Crim LR 324.

Lacey, N., 'Beset by Boundaries: The Home Office Review of Sex Offences' [2001] Crim LR 3.

Wells, C., 'Stalking: the Criminal Law's Response' [1997] Crim LR 463.

The defences I

Introduction

The general defences to criminal responsibility are a large and important part of the criminal law syllabus. An exam paper may well contain two questions on the general defences, or one full question with an additional one involving the specific defences which reduce murder to manslaughter. Therefore it is an area that you must know comprehensively, and because it contains a vast array of diverse material this is no easy task.

The defences have been divided between two chapters, the first dealing with the defences of automatism, insanity, diminished responsibility, and intoxication; and the second covering duress, necessity, mistake, and self-defence. In some textbooks you will find the material relating to automatism and mistake in chapters covering *actus reus* and *mens rea*, but as questions on insanity usually involve consideration of automatism (and often diminished responsibility) and questions on self-defence generally involve mistake, the questions in this chapter have been formed accordingly.

It must be appreciated that many people suffering from mental disorder who commit crimes never actually stand trial but will be detained under the Mental Health Act 1983 provisions. If they are tried and are deemed fit to plead, they have the difficult decision of whether to put their mental incapacity before the court. The risk in so doing is being found not guilty by reason of insanity on application of the *M'Naghten* Rules 1843, which (despite constant criticism) remain the test for insanity in the eyes of the law. That the concept of 'disease of the mind' is no longer a medical concept has long been recognised by the Butler Committee (1975) and the Law Commission, who recommended (Draft Code, cl. 35) that the concept of mental disorder was more appropriate (thus a mental disorder verdict would be returned if the defendant was suffering from severe mental illness or severe mental handicap).

It is clear that such a change is required, if only because many defendants are loath to risk the defence being put to the jury. So in *R* v *Sullivan* [1983] 2 All ER 673, the accused preferred to plead guilty to assault occasioning actual bodily harm, a crime which carries a maximum sentence of five years' imprisonment, when the trial judge suggested that his epilepsy constituted a disease of the mind and his relevant defence was therefore not automatism but insanity. This problem has to some extent been alleviated as far as murder is concerned by the Homicide Act 1957, which introduced the partial defence of diminished responsibility; and most mentally disordered defendants charged with murder would now plead this defence in the knowledge that it has succeeded in a wide variety of situations not covered by insanity.

As *Sullivan* indicates, the defences of insanity and automatism are closely linked, as for both defences the accused has acted while not in control of his or her mental faculties. If automatism succeeds the accused is found not guilty with no custodial repercussions; but although an accused found not guilty by reason of insanity will not inevitably be detained since the passing of the Criminal Procedure (Insanity and Unfitness to Plead) Act 1991, there is still the stigma of being labelled insane. There is a need for a clear boundary between the defences, but unfortunately this does not exist. This is aptly illustrated by the cases of *R* v *Quick* [1973] 3 All ER 347 and *R* v *Hennessey* [1989] 2 All ER 9, both involving defendants suffering from diabetes. In the first case, it was held by the Court of Appeal that a diabetic who was in a state of hypoglycaemia as a result of taking insulin and alcohol could not be deemed insane (within the *M'Naghten* Rules). In the second case, an accused in a state of hyperglycaemia because he hadn't taken his insulin was found to be insane! Only a criminal lawyer could explain the reasoning for this outcome.

The defence of intoxication has also undergone review by both the Law Commission (Consultation Paper No. 127 'Intoxication and Criminal Liability', 1993; Law Com. No. 229, 1995) and the House of Lords (*R* v *Kingston* [1994] 3 All ER 353). It can be a defence to certain crimes (those where the prosecution must prove intention) and it is also a factor in considering the availability of other defences. Accordingly two questions have been set on this important topic.

Q Question 1

Albert and John attend a party where they have some non-alcoholic drinks. It is known that Albert has recently been experiencing dizzy spells and fainting fits, but he has not sought medical treatment. At the party Albert becomes dizzy and is given six Valium tablets by an unknown person in an attempt to calm him down. Very shortly after taking the tablets Albert leaves the party with John. On the way home Albert repeatedly hits John over the head with a bottle, thereby killing him.

When arrested and charged with murder, Albert says: 'I cannot remember hitting him. I must have had a blackout.'

Discuss Albert's possible defences.

Commentary

Questions on mental abnormality are quite common in examinations. They are often in essay form, but this problem does require the student to take into account the alternative reasons why Albert acted as he did. If a murder has taken place and insanity is an obvious issue, a consideration of the related defences of automatism and diminished responsibility is required. The ingredients of all three defences must therefore be covered in detail with a clear demonstration of the differences between them. Sometimes voluntary intoxication must also be considered as it is easy to link relevant facts giving rise to this issue in a question of this nature.

For the sake of completeness, the non-availability of the defence of provocation is referred to briefly. However, this author would not deduct marks if this was not contained in a student's answer. Note that candidates are not asked to consider the liability of whoever supplied the drugs to Albert.

- **Diminished responsibility — s. 2, Homicide Act 1957**

- **Automatism —** *Bratty* **[1963]**

- **Insanity —** *M'Naghten* **Rules 1843**

- **Intoxication**

- **Provocation**

:Q: Suggested answer

Albert has caused the death of John in fact and in law. There is no evidence of anything that would suggest a *novus actus interveniens*. In order to support a charge of murder the prosecution will have to establish that Albert intended to kill John, or intended to do him some grievous bodily harm: see *R v Moloney* [1985] 1 All ER 1025 and *R v Woollin* [1998] 4 All ER 103. If Albert's evidence is plausible it may be that he will successfully defend a murder charge by relying on one of a number of defences involving a partial or complete denial of *mens rea*, such as automatism, insanity and diminished responsibility.

Diminished responsibility is only a partial defence that reduces murder to manslaughter. The defence was introduced by s. 2(1) of the Homicide Act 1957, which provides:

> Where a person kills or is a party to the killing of another, he shall not be convicted of murder if he was suffering from such abnormality of mind (whether arising from a condition of arrested or retarded development of mind or any inherent causes or induced by disease or injury) as substantially impaired his mental responsibility for his acts or omissions in doing or being a party to the killing.

Defendants charged with murder tend to rely on diminished responsibility rather than insanity, and it has succeeded in a wide variety of circumstances, including mercy killings, crimes of passion and killings as a result of irresistible impulse. Professor Andrew Ashworth has pointed out that in 80 per cent of cases where it is raised the prosecution are prepared to accept the plea. In two recent cases involving 'battered women's syndrome' — *R v Ahluwalia* [1992] 4 All ER 889 and *R v Thornton (No. 2)*

[1996] 1 WLR 1174 — although the juries had convicted the accused of murder, in the re-trials different juries found that the accused had established the defence of diminished responsibility on the balance of probability and were guilty of manslaughter.

Although the taking of Valium (unless there was evidence of uncontrollable addiction) could not constitute an abnormality of the mind, it is possible that the medical condition could be so regarded and that this defence could succeed in Albert's case. Albert would have to provide expert medical evidence establishing on the balance of probabilities that he was suffering from an abnormality of the mind.

Prima facie, the most attractive defence to Albert is automatism, as this is a complete defence to murder and the burden of proof is on the prosecution to disprove the existence of the defence. Automatism was defined by Lord Denning in *Bratty* v *Attorney-General for Northern Ireland* [1963] AC 386, as 'an act which is done by the muscles without any control by the mind such as a spasm, a reflex or a convulsion, or an act done by a person who is not conscious of what he is doing such as an act done whilst suffering from concussion or whilst sleep-walking'.

Albert will argue that he did not know what he was doing and therefore his act was involuntary. The prosecution must prove that the act was voluntary, but they are entitled to rely on the presumption that every man has sufficient mental capacity to be responsible for his act; and if the defence wishes to displace this presumption they must give some evidence from which the contrary may reasonably be inferred. Much will therefore depend on the expert medical evidence.

For automatism to succeed the court must accept that there was a total loss of control. In *Attorney-General's Reference (No. 2 of 1992)* [1993] 4 All ER 683, the Court of Appeal ruled that the trial judge was wrong to direct the jury that a syndrome known as 'driving without awareness' could amount to automatism. Impaired, reduced or partial control is not enough. So the prosecution could argue that as Albert had enough control to pick up a bottle and repeatedly hit John over the head, automatism should not apply.

A second problem concerns the fact that Albert had not sought medical treatment for his condition. The prosecution could argue that the automatism was therefore self-induced and that Albert was blameworthy in not seeking treatment. Further, if Albert had taken alcohol or non-prescribed hallucinatory drugs, automatism will not succeed (*R* v *Lipman* [1969] 3 All ER 410) — but see intoxication, below. Notwithstanding these two issues, if the Valium had the effect of completely destroying Albert's self-control, and he was unaware that this would be the consequence of taking the drug, he may succeed with the defence of automatism.

Where, however, there is evidence that Albert actually suffered from some inherent medical condition that, in conjunction with the Valium, had the effect of causing him to lose his self-control, the prosecution may seek to lead evidence suggesting that insanity is a more appropriate defence. Under the '*M'Naghten* rules' 1843, everyone is presumed sane until the contrary is proved. However, it is a defence for the accused to show that he was labouring under such defect of reason due to disease of the mind as either:

(a) not to know the nature and quality of his act; or

(b) if he did know this, not to know that what he was doing was wrong.

The trial judge must first decide if Albert was suffering from a disease of the mind, and if so, the jury will then decide if the other ingredients of the defence have been satisfied. The judicial pronouncements on insanity are certainly at variance with medical practice, and the question of public safety is a factor that the judiciary obviously takes into account. In *Bratty*, Lord Denning stated that 'any mental disorder which has manifested itself in violence and is prone to recur is a disease of the mind' and this was reiterated by Lord Diplock in *R v Sullivan*, where the House of Lords upheld the trial judge's decision to label epilepsy 'a disease of the mind', when he stated:

> if the effect of a disease is to impair these facilities [of reason, memory and understanding] so severely as to have either of these consequences referred to in the latter part of the rules, it matters not whether the aetiology of the impairment is organic, as in epilepsy, or functional, or whether the impairment itself is permanent or is transient and intermittent, provided that it subsisted at the time of the commission of the act.

Thus arteriosclerosis (*R v Kemp* [1956] 3 All ER 249); diabetes (*R v Hennessey* (1989) 89 Cr App R 10); and violent sleepwalking (*R v Burgess* [1991] 2 All ER 769) have all been deemed diseases of the mind. In the latter case the Court of Appeal held that many people sleepwalk, but that if an accused uses violence while sleepwalking, that must be due to a disease of the mind. So the accused, who while sleepwalking violently assaulted the victim, was found 'not guilty by reason of insanity' as he was plainly suffering from a defect of reason from some sort of failure of the mind causing him to act as he did without conscious motivation. The Court of Appeal upheld the trial judge's decision to label the condition as a disease of the mind, on the basis that it was due to an internal factor that manifested itself in violence.

If Albert is found 'not guilty by reason of insanity', he has the right to appeal under s. 1 of the Criminal Procedure (Insanity) Act 1964; and if the appeal succeeds because the judge wrongly directed the jury, the accused will be entitled to a 'not guilty' verdict with no custodial repercussions or attached conditions for treatment (Criminal Procedure (Insanity and Unfitness to Plead) Act 1991).

Albert may seek to rely on the common law defence of intoxication. There is little doubt that, if his loss of awareness was caused by the consumption of the Valium tablets, he could be regarded as a having been in a state of intoxication; see *R v Cole and Ors* [1993] Crim LR 300. Murder is a specific intent crime, hence on the basis of *DPP v Majewski* [1976] 2 All ER 142, self-induced intoxication can be raised as a defence. If it succeeds it will reduce Albert's liability to manslaughter.

There may be an argument that Albert might escape liability altogether on the basis of the intoxication. Even in respect of basic intent crimes such as manslaughter there must be evidence that the defendant was reckless in consuming the intoxicant. In the case of alcohol or Class A drugs this is rarely an issue. In the case of Valium there may be some debate as to whether Albert was aware of the risk of what side-effects there might be. *R* v *Hardie* [1984] 3 All ER 848, provides that if there is evidence that the self-administration of drugs may not have been reckless, the issue ought to be left to the jury. In short, if it was not Albert's fault that he lost consciousness he should be acquitted.

Finally, it is submitted that on the facts, as there is no evidence of it, provocation could not succeed as a partial defence. This has been illustrated by *R* v *Acott* [1997] 1 All ER 706, where the House of Lords confirmed that some evidence of provocation had to be raised for the judge to be under an obligation to put it to the jury.

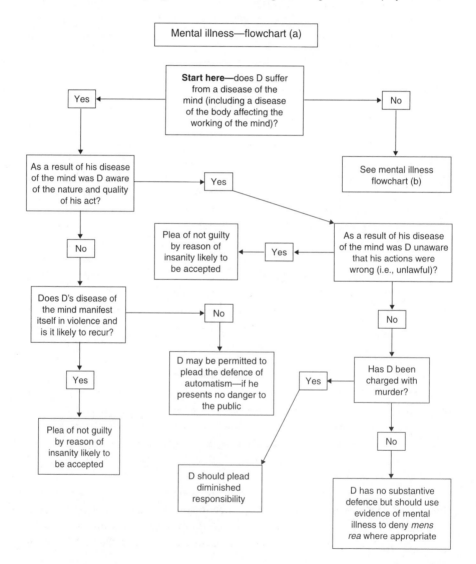

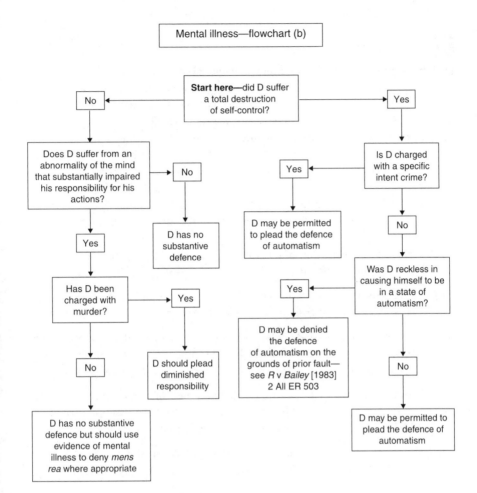

Mental illness—flowchart (b)

Q Question 2

Mark lives with Anita and James, Anita's two-year-old son from a previous relationship. Mark hates James and wishes the boy was dead. One day Anita loses her temper with James when he wets his bed. She attacks James with a poker striking him on the head. Mark, who is downstairs watching television when this happens, rushes upstairs to investigate the disturbance. He finds James bleeding profusely from a head wound. Mark tells Anita it is all her fault and goes out to the pub without summoning any help. By the time Anita calls an ambulance James has bled to death.

Advise the Crown Prosecution Service as to the possible criminal liability of Anita and Mark in respect of the death of James. Do not consider liability for non-fatal offences.

After fully considering the above, go on to consider how your answer would differ in each of these scenarios:

(i)   Anita had had an epileptic fit immediately prior to attacking James, the evidence being that she cannot recall attacking him.

(ii) Anita had been a diabetic who had taken insulin but had not eaten prior to the attack, the evidence being that the attack occurred whilst she was unaware of her actions because she had been in a hypoglycaemic state.

(iii) Anita had been a diabetic who had failed to take insulin prior to the attack, the evidence being that the attack occurred whilst she was unaware of her actions because she had been in a hyperglycaemic state.

(iv) When attacking James, Anita had honestly believed she was fighting off a nest of vipers because she voluntarily consumed LSD shortly beforehand.

Commentary

This rather bleak question provides a very effective run through of defences to murder based on provocation, automatism, insanity and intoxication. In particular it seeks to identify the borderline between sane and non-insane automatism, hence a good knowledge of the relevant authorities in that area is essential. Mark's liability also requires an effective examination of liability for failing to act where liability is based on membership of a household, rather than a clear duty relationship.

- Anita causes death — *mens rea* — provocation

- Mark's liability based on his failure to act

- Anita's liability and insanity

- Anita's liability and automatism — internal cause

- Anita's liability and automatism — external cause

- Anita's liability and intoxication

:ᄋ᷄: Suggested answer

(a) Anita's liability for the death of James

Anita causes the death of James in fact and in law. But for the attack James would not have died. There is no evidence of a *novus actus interveniens*. The evidence suggests that Anita acted with foresight as to the consequences of her actions. For murder the prosecution will have to show that she intended to kill or do some grievous bodily harm. On the basis of *R* v *Woollin* [1998] 4 All ER 103, the jury will be entitled to infer intent if there is evidence that Anita foresaw death or grievous bodily harm as virtually certain to result from her actions. It is hard to see how this evidence would not be present given that she has hit a young child on the head with a heavy metal object.

There is evidence that Anita lost her temper with the child, hence the defence of provocation ought to be left to the jury should she choose to raise it. *R* v *Doughty* (1986) 83 Cr App R 319 makes clear that anything can be provocation, even the actions of a small child. There are no issues here regarding 'cooling time' or cumulative provocation. Assuming that there is evidence that Anita was provoked to lose her self control, the question will then arise as to whether she acted in a manner that was reasonable. Following *R* v *Smith (Morgan)* [2000] 4 All ER 289, the courts will no longer apply a reasonable person test. No distinction is to be drawn between those characteristics of the accused that relate to the gravity of the provocation and those that relate to the accused's ability to exercise reasonable self-control. The approach now is simply to ask whether the accused, bearing in mind all the relevant evidence as to her circumstances and characteristics, exercised what was for her the degree of self-control it was reasonable to expect from her in the circumstances. Given that there is little evidence here of extenuating circumstances beyond possible social deprivation consequent upon single parenthood, the defence may not be made out.

If Anita did not have the *mens rea* for murder, she would be convicted of manslaughter based on her unlawful attack upon James. There are no contentious issues in this regard.

(b) Mark's liability for the death of James

Any attempt to impose liability on Mark in respect of the death of James would have to be based on his failure to help when he realised the harm that had been done to the child. Mark does not encourage or help in the attack, hence he cannot be an accomplice. His failure to act to help the child cannot raise any criminal liability unless he was under a legal duty to act at the time. A possible basis for that duty could be found under the Children and Young Persons Act 1933 if it is successfully argued that Mark has the role of parent or guardian in respect of James. Failing that, at common law, he may have incurred a duty towards James if he has chosen to live with the child's mother as a family unit; see *R* v *Gibbins and Proctor* (1918) 13 Cr App R 134. The court will examine the permanency and stability of the relationship, the involvement of Mark in the child's upbringing, and the degree of reliance on Mark. *R* v *Stone and Dobinson* [1977] QB 354, also stresses that a relationship of reliance can give rise to a positive legal duty of care. *R* v *Miller* [1983] 1 All ER 978 would not be relevant because the harm to James is not caused by Mark's accidental act.

Assuming Mark was under a common law duty to act, the prosecution would have to prove that his failure to act contributed to the death of James. Medical evidence would clearly show that James' condition worsened after Mark became aware of the injury. If Mark's omission was causative, he could be charged with murder if he had the necessary *mens rea* — see above. The evidence of his animosity towards the child, if available, would be cogent here. If Mark cannot be shown to have had the *mens rea* for murder it should be noted that he cannot be convicted of constructive manslaughter (unlawful act manslaughter) as this cannot be committed by omission: see *R* v *Lowe* [1973]. The prosecution would have to charge Mark with killing by gross negligence. Following *R* v *Adomako* [1994] 3 WLR 288, the jury would have to consider whether the extent to which Mark's conduct departed from the proper standard of care incumbent upon him (involving a risk of death to James) was such that it should be judged criminal. It is submitted that this would be made out on the facts.

(c) Variations on Anita's liability

(i) Anita had had an epileptic fit immediately prior to attacking James, the evidence being that she cannot recall attacking him

Anita would presumably argue that she had been in a state of automatism — *Attorney-General's Reference (No. 2 of 1992)* [1993] 3 WLR 982 — a total destruction of voluntary control on her part. Lord Denning in *Bratty* v *Attorney-General for Northern Ireland* [1963] AC 386, suggested that automatism could arise from a fit or spasm. If Anita succeeds with this argument she will be acquitted. Her problem is that the courts will look at what gave rise to the lack of awareness. In her case it is her epilepsy — an internal condition; a defect of the nervous system that affects the working of the brain. Her condition has the effect that she is unaware of her actions — the '*M'Naghten*'s rules' (1843) 10 C & F 200, clearly provide that a defendant can be regarded as criminally insane if she is (was) labouring under a defect of reason, from disease of the mind, as not to know the nature and quality of the act she was doing. Further, epilepsy is a condition that manifests itself in violence and is likely to recur. As such the courts will not allow her to plead automatism.

She can either plead guilty, or plead not guilty on the grounds of insanity; see the explanation of this in *R* v *Sullivan* [1983] 1 All ER 577. Rather than run the risk of the insanity defence, Anita might be better advised to rely on the defence of diminished responsibility under s. 2(1) of the Homicide Act 1957. She would have little difficulty in establishing medical evidence that she had been suffering from an abnormality of mind arising from a disease or injury such as substantially impaired her mental responsibility for her acts. If successful the defence would reduce her liability to manslaughter.

(ii) Anita had been a diabetic who had taken insulin but had not eaten prior to the attack, the evidence being that the attack occurred whilst she was unaware of her actions because she had been in a hypoglycaemic state

On the basis of *R* v *Quick* [1973] QB 910, diabetes resulting in hypoglycaemia is not regarded in law as a mental condition. As Lawton LJ observed, Quick's mental condition was not caused by his diabetes but by his use of the insulin prescribed by his doctor. The malfunctioning of Quick's mind was caused by an external factor and not a bodily disorder in the nature of a disease that disturbed the working of his mind. This would suggest that Anita would be permitted the defence of automatism, but it should be noted that in *R* v *Bailey* [1983] 2 All ER 503, the court ruled that the defence would not be available in cases where the state of automatism could be regarded as 'self-induced', i.e., there was evidence that the defendant was at fault in lapsing into the state of automatism. The test is whether or not Anita was aware of the consequences of taking insulin and not eating. If she was reckless in taking the insulin and not eating this will provide the basic intent for any offence she commits whilst in the subsequent state of automatism. On these facts that would mean she might incur liability for manslaughter (a basic intent crime), but not murder (a specific intent crime).

(iii) Anita had been a diabetic who had failed to take insulin prior to the attack, the evidence being that the attack occurred whilst she was unaware of her actions because she had been in a hyperglycaemic state

On the basis of *R* v *Hennessy* [1989] 1 WLR 287 (diabetic failing to take insulin resulting in hyperglycaemic state), the defence of automatism will not be available. The hyperglycaemia (high blood sugar), will be regarded as having been caused by an inherent defect (the diabetes), i.e., a disease. If that disease causes a malfunction of the mind that manifests itself in violence the courts will only allow Anita the defence of insanity.

(iv) When attacking James, Anita had honestly believed she was fighting off a nest of vipers because she voluntarily consumed LSD shortly beforehand

Anita might wish to raise the defence of automatism but, for reasons outlined above, she will be regarded as having brought about the condition through her own fault, hence the defence will not be available (*R* v *Bailey*). Intoxication can be raised as a defence to murder: *DPP* v *Majewski* [1976] — as murder is a regarded as a specific intent crime. Anita will thus be convicted of manslaughter on the grounds of intoxication. *R* v *Lipman* [1970] 1 QB 152 confirms this.

Q Question 3

Martin got so drunk that he did not know what he was doing. While in this state he killed Vernon, and held down Walter while he was killed by Oswald. He then hit Zoro over the head causing him serious injury, and took his wallet. Lastly, he broke into Ray's house, mistakenly believing it was his own house.

Discuss the criminal liability of Martin.

Commentary

This question requires knowledge of and an ability to apply the principles concerning the defence of intoxication. This question is slightly artificial because it informs the student that Martin is drunk and leaves little room for discussion about the ingredients of the offences that have been committed. Many exam questions will leave these issues in doubt, and they will therefore require much more consideration.

For this reason the author has abandoned the usual technique of dealing first with the offences in detail, and then considering possible defences.

- Consider relevant offences

- Intoxication and *Majewski*

- Specific and basic intent

- Aiding and abetting — *Powell and English* [1997]

- Robbery and burglary

- Criminal damage — *Jaggard* v *Dickinson* [1980]

:Ọ: Suggested answer

Martin could be charged with murder, aiding and abetting murder, robbery, aggravated assault, burglary and criminal damage, arising out of the incidents that have taken place. As he was drunk at the time he will be able to raise the issue of intoxication which can negative the *mens rea* of certain offences and therefore act as a defence.

Martin obviously causes the death of Vernon and will be charged with murder. The mens rea required is intention to kill or to do some grievous bodily harm; see *R v Woollin* [1998] 4 All ER 103. The main defence Martin will seek to rely on is self-induced intoxication.

The leading case on intoxication is *DPP v Majewski* [1976] 2 All ER 142, where the House of Lords decided that intoxication can be a defence to crimes of specific intent but not to those of basic intent. Not all judges and commentators agree on the precise definition of these terms, but it is generally considered that a crime of specific intent is one where the prosecution must prove actual intention on behalf of the accused, whereas recklessness is sufficient *mens rea* for a crime of basic intent. Thus if an accused is charged with murder, a crime of specific intent, his defence of intoxication could succeed as in *R v Lipman* [1969] 3 All ER 410, where the accused, 'on a bad trip' after taking a non-prescribed hallucinatory drug, wrongly believed he was being attacked by snakes and strangled his girlfriend. The prosecution in *Lipman* could not prove that the accused intended to kill or cause grievous bodily harm and therefore he could not be convicted of murder. However, he was convicted of manslaughter as — manslaughter being a crime of basic intent, where the prosecution do not have to prove intention — intoxication is no defence.

The rationale for this approach is questionable, but it appears to be that if you are reckless enough to get so drunk in the first place that you do not know what you are doing, this takes the place of the recklessness that would otherwise have to be established at the time of the *actus reus*. The Law Commission's Consultation Paper No. 127 ('Intoxication and Criminal Liability', 1993) pointed out that this approach is a rough form of justice and conflicts with many of the established principles of criminal responsibility. In particular, it conflicts with the general principle of contemporaneity, i.e., the fact that the *actus reus* and *mens rea* must be present at the same time, and is another example of constructive crime, as the deemed recklessness relates only to the risk of becoming drunk, not to the specific harm prohibited. Further, although traditionally the burden of proof remains on the prosecution if the offence is one of basic intent, an accused, by putting forward intoxication as a defence, is in reality pleading guilty.

However, despite recognising these anomalies, the Law Commission in their final report (No. 229, 1995) recommended following the approach adopted by the US Model Penal Code 1962, which is very similar to the approach in *Majewski*. This is another example of the criminal law applying principles not of strict logic, but of public policy. The House of Lords in *Majewski* recognised that if voluntary intoxication by drink or drugs can negative the special or specific intention necessary for the commission of crimes such as murder or theft, how can you justify in strict logic the view that it cannot negative a basic intent crime? The answer is that in strict logic this view cannot be justified. But this is the view that has been adopted by the common law which is founded on common sense and experience rather than strict logic.

Regarding Martin's liability in respect of Walter, unless Martin is charged as a co-principal, the relevant offence will be aiding and abetting murder. The *mens rea* requirement for this offence is an intention to assist, contemplating death or grievous bodily harm as a possible consequence (*Chan Wing Siu v R* [1984] 3 All ER 877), or a realisation that the primary party might kill with intent to do so, or with intent to cause grievous bodily harm — *R v Powell and English* [1997] 4 All ER 545. There is no binding authority as to whether intoxication is a defence to this crime, but it could be argued that as the *mens rea* requires more than recklessness it is not a crime of basic intent and therefore intoxication is a complete defence. However, it is submitted that as policy plays a major part in determining the applicable principles in this topic, the court would look first at the principal offence to decide if intoxication was a defence, and then apply this principle to determine the accomplice's responsibility. Thus as intoxication would reduce the murder charge to a manslaughter conviction, Martin would be guilty of aiding and abetting manslaughter. It would be most odd if Oswald was found guilty of manslaughter because of his drunkenness, whereas Martin was completely acquitted because of his.

The third incident involves both a crime against the person and a crime against property. Martin could be charged with offences under the Offences Against the Person Act 1861 as he has caused Zoro serious (i.e., grievous) bodily harm. The most serious offence is s. 18 (wounding or causing grievous bodily harm with intent), but as intention is required (*R v Belfon* [1976] 3 All ER 46) intoxication is a defence. However, the less serious offence under s. 20 (malicious wounding or inflicting grievous bodily harm) is a crime of basic intent (*Majewski*) and therefore intoxication would not succeed as a defence.

As Martin has taken Zoro's wallet he could be charged with robbery. This is defined under s. 8(1) of the Theft Act 1968: 'A person is guilty of robbery if he steals, and immediately before or at the time of doing so, and in order to do so, he uses force on any person or puts or seeks to put any person in fear of being then and there subjected to force'. However, Martin can be convicted of robbery only if he is guilty of theft, and as theft is an offence of specific intent, his defence of intoxication can succeed and he would therefore not be guilty.

When he broke into Ray's house, Martin could be committing the crimes of burglary and criminal damage. Burglary is defined by s. 9 of the Theft Act 1968 and requires the accused to enter a building or part of a building as a trespasser with intent to commit certain substantive offences, or to have actually committed or attempted to commit certain offences. However, even if the prosecution could prove that Martin had the necessary *mens rea* to be a trespasser (*R v Collins* [1972] 2 All ER 1105), there is no evidence of an intention to commit a substantive offence as Martin wrongly believes that he is entering his own house.

Lastly, Martin could be guilty of criminal damage under s. 1(1) of the Criminal Damage Act 1971:

> A person who without lawful excuse destroys or damages any property belonging to another intending to destroy or damage any such property or being reckless as to whether any such property would be destroyed or damaged shall be guilty of an offence.

Metropolitan Police Commissioner v *Caldwell* [1981] 1 All ER 961 clearly establishes that this is a crime of basic intent and therefore intoxication could not generally be a defence. However, in *Jaggard* v *Dickinson* [1980] 3 All ER 716, an accused who while drunk mistakenly broke into X's house, believing it to be Y's house, where Y had given him consent to break in, was held by the Court of Appeal to have the defence of lawful excuse under s. 5(2)(a) of the Criminal Damage Act 1971. Further in *R* v *Smith* [1974] 1 All ER 632, the Court of Appeal quashed the conviction of a tenant of a flat who had damaged his landlord's property in the mistaken belief that it was his own. The prosecution would argue, though, that following *R* v *O'Grady* [1987] 3 All ER 420, a mistake caused by drunkenness cannot negative *mens rea*, and as the principles applicable to intoxication are often governed by policy, this argument is likely to succeed and Martin's defence may fail.

Q Question 4

Alfred is an alcoholic. He has a grudge against Victor and decides that he is going to kill him. He then drinks 12 pints of strong beer and, while in a drunken stupor, mistakenly believing that Victor is about to attack him, stabs Victor with a knife causing his death.

Discuss Alfred's possible defences to a charge of murder.

Commentary

In many examination papers there will be a full question involving murder and man-slaughter in detail. In order to avoid duplication of answer material, another question in which a murder has taken place will simply require the student to discuss possible defences. This is such a question.

It is slightly unusual, because generally you would expect to cover two or three defences in detail. This question, however, requires the student to consider a number of defences, some of which are not always closely related to each other. In this sense it is similar to a mixed question (see Chapter 10). With the constraints of time, an in-depth analysis of all the relevant defences is not possible, so recognition of all the defences and conciseness are essential.

- Mistake and self-defence
  - *Williams* [1984]
  - *O'Grady* [1987]
- Provocation — *Thornton* [1996]
- Diminished responsibility — *Tandy* [1987]
- Insanity — *M'Naghten* Rules 1843
- Automatism — *Lipman* [1969]
- Intoxication
  - *Majewski* [1977]
  - *Gallagher* [1963]

⌖ Suggested answer

There are a number of possible defences available to Alfred, but *prima facie* the most favourable would be self-defence, as this is a complete defence to a murder charge. Alfred has the evidential duty to raise self-defence, but the burden of proof remains on the prosecution to prove that the force used was not necessary or reasonable. The fact that an accused has made a mistake will not necessarily rule out the defence, as in *R v Williams* (1984) 74 Cr App R 276, the court held that the accused is to be judged on the facts as the accused believed them to be. Therefore, if an unreasonable mistake as to the facts has been made, this will not in itself cause the defence to fail, provided the mistake was honestly made. However, according to *R v O'Grady* [1987] 3 All ER 420, a mistake arising from voluntary intoxication cannot be relied upon for self-defence. Therefore as Alfred was drunk this defence will fail.

Alfred might next turn to provocation which (if successful) would reduce murder to manslaughter under s. 3 of the Homicide Act 1957:

> Where on a charge of murder there is evidence on which the jury can find that the person charged was provoked (whether by things done or by things said or by both together) to lose his self-control, the question whether the provocation was enough to make a reasonable man do as he did shall be left to be determined by the jury; and in determining that question the jury shall take into account everything both done and said according to the effect which, in their opinion, it would have on a reasonable man.

Although the jury could take into account the fact that Alfred was an alcoholic when assessing whether a reasonable man with the accused's characteristics would have done as he did (*R v Morhall* [1995] 3 All ER 659), they cannot take into account the fact that he was drunk at the time. However, the main problem facing Alfred is convincing the judge that he did lose his self-control and that this is a case of provocation.

Despite cases such as *R* v *Ahluwalia* [1992] 4 All ER 889 and *R* v *Thornton* [1996] 2 Cr App R 108 recognising the fact that women suffering from 'battered women's syndrome' may react on a slower fuse, the courts still insist that there must be a sudden and temporary loss of self-control. As Alfred has a grudge against Victor, it is likely that his conduct will be regarded as a cold-blooded act of revenge, rather than retaliation in the heat of the moment to provocation.

However, Alfred might have more chance of success with another defence under the Homicide Act 1957 which reduces murder to manslaughter, i.e., diminished responsibility under s. 2:

> Where a person kills or is party to the killing of another, he shall not be convicted of murder if he was suffering from such abnormality of mind (whether arising from a condition of arrested or retarded development of mind or any inherent causes or induced by disease or injury) as substantially impaired his mental responsibility for his acts or omissions in doing or being a party to the killing.

For diminished responsibility, unlike provocation, Alfred would have to prove the existence of the defence on the balance of probabilities. If he killed because he was drunk, this in itself would not amount to an abnormality of the mind. On the other hand, several cases (including *R* v *Tandy* (1987) 87 Cr App R 45) make it clear that an alcoholic's craving for drink, if irresistible, can constitute such an abnormality. In *Tandy*, the accused, an alcoholic, after a heavy drinking session, killed her daughter. Medical evidence called on her behalf stated that when she awoke in the morning she had to have an alcoholic drink, and this triggered a mechanism which meant she carried on drinking. However, the prosecution medical evidence, while accepting that when she had taken one alcoholic drink she had to continue drinking, contended that the accused could on some days resist the first drink so that her urge to drink was *not* irresistible. The jury accepted the prosecution evidence and the defence of diminished responsibility failed, with the Court of Appeal ruling that the trial judge's direction to the jury was correct and dismissing the appeal.

It is therefore unlikely that, on the facts, this defence would succeed; and by raising diminished responsibility, Alfred runs the risk of being found 'not guilty by reason of insanity'. This is because once an accused puts his lack of mental capacity before the court in the form of a plea of automation or diminished responsi- bility, the trial judge can direct the jury to consider the defence of insanity under the *M'Naghten* Rules 1843, by reason of s. 6 of the Criminal Procedure (Insanity) Act 1954.

Under the rules, Alfred would have the defence of insanity if, at the time of commit- ting the act, he was labouring under such a defect of reason, from disease of the mind, as not to know the nature and quality of the act he was doing or, if he did know it, he did not know that what he was doing was wrong. In the unlikely event of Alfred wanting this defence to succeed, he would have the burden of proving it on the balance of probabilities; whereas if the prosecution were seeking a verdict of 'not guilty by reason of insanity' (from which, incidentally, the accused has a right of appeal under the Criminal Procedure (Insanity) Act 1964), they would have to establish it beyond reasonable doubt.

In *R v Quick and Paddison* [1973] QB 910, the Court of Appeal stated that a condition produced by the application of extraneous substances such as alcohol or drugs, could not be regarded as a disease of the mind if it was only a temporary or transient state. However, in *R v Inseal* [1992] Crim LR 35, it was recognised that heavy drinking over a long period of time could have had such an effect on the mind as to amount to a disease of the mind within the meaning of the *M'Naghten* Rules. Surprisingly, this is a question of law for the trial judge, and if the judge resolves that a disease of the mind exists then the jury must decide if the other elements of the defence have been made out.

It is submitted that Alfred would not raise the defence of insanity; and if the trial judge threatened to leave it to the jury, he might do the same thing as many accused in this position and change his plea to guilty, in the hope that the judge's conduct might be sufficient for a successful appeal (as was the case in *R v Quick*).

Alfred could also claim that as he was so drunk and did not know what he was doing, he has the defence of automatism, defined by Lord Denning in *Bratty v Attorney-General for Northern Ireland* [1963] AC 386 as 'an act which is done by the muscles without any control by the mind such as a spasm, a reflex or a convulsion; or an act done by a person who is not conscious of what he is doing such as an act done whilst suffering from concussion or whilst sleep-walking'. However, *R v Lipman* [1969] 3 All ER 410 makes it quite clear that this defence cannot succeed if the state has been induced by the accused voluntarily taking alcohol or non-prescribed hallucinatory drugs.

The related defence of intoxication would be Alfred's final argument, as it is accepted that intoxication can be a defence to crimes of specific but not basic intent (*DPP v Majewski* [1977] AC 443). Murder is a crime of specific intent and therefore, in theory, on the application of this principle, Alfred could only be guilty of manslaughter, a crime of basic intent. However, it would appear that Alfred would fall foul of the principle established in *Attorney-General for Northern Ireland v Gallagher* [1963] AC 349, that if you form the *mens rea* of the offence and then deliberately get drunk to give yourself 'Dutch courage', so that you do not know what you are doing when you perform the *actus reus*, the defence will fail.

In conclusion, one can see that there are serious weaknesses surrounding all the defences that Alfred would consider. His best hope of success would be diminished responsibility, reducing murder to manslaughter. Even on this defence, he could not be confident of success.

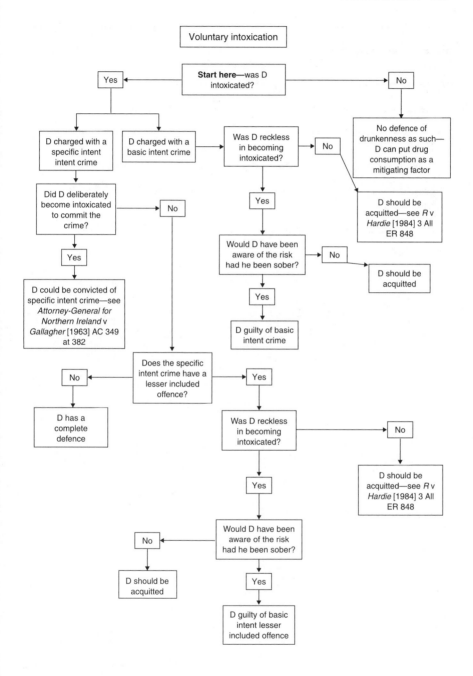

Voluntary intoxication

Start here—was D intoxicated?

Yes / No

D charged with a specific intent intent crime

D charged with a basic intent crime

Was D reckless in becoming intoxicated? — No

No defence of drunkenness as such—D can put drug consumption as a mitigating factor

Did D deliberately become intoxicated to commit the crime? — No

Yes

D should be acquitted—see *R* v *Hardie* [1984] 3 All ER 848

Yes

D could be convicted of specific intent crime—see *Attorney-General for Northern Ireland* v *Gallagher* [1963] AC 349 at 382

Would D have been aware of the risk had he been sober? — No

D should be acquitted

Yes

D guilty of basic intent crime

Does the specific intent crime have a lesser included offence? — Yes

No

D has a complete defence

Was D reckless in becoming intoxicated? — No

D should be acquitted—see *R* v *Hardie* [1984] 3 All ER 848

Yes

Would D have been aware of the risk had he been sober? — No

D should be acquitted

Yes

D guilty of basic intent lesser included offence

Further reading

Gough, S., 'Surviving Without Majewski' [2000] Crim LR 719.

Griew, E., 'The Future of Diminished Responsibility' [1988] Crim LR 75.

McKay, R.D., 'The Abnormality of Mind Factor in Diminished Responsibility' [1999] Crim LR 117.

Samiloff, J., 'Time of Change the Voluntary Intoxication Rule?' [2004] NLJ 154.

Virgo, G., 'The Law Commission Consultation Paper on Intoxication' [1993] Crim LR 415.

Ward, T., 'Magistrates, Insanity and the Common Law' [1997] Crim LR 796.

The defences II

Introduction

The questions in this chapter focus on the defences of compulsion — duress by threats (sometimes referred to as duress *per minas*), duress of circumstances, necessity and self-defence. Mistake is also considered in so far as a mistake of fact may lead a defendant to wrongly believe in the existence of circumstances that would give rise to a substantive defence. Candidates need to be prepared to tackle essay questions that focus primarily on compulsion defences and problem questions where compulsion arises as a defence — typically in relation to non-sexual offences against the person.

Although duress by threats has existed as a defence for many years, uncertainty regarding the correct principles to be applied has recently been highlighted by the Law Commission's Consultation Paper No. 122, which identified the following five questions as requiring discussion:

(a) Against whom must the threat be directed?

(b) If the actor might resort to police or other official protection, is it relevant that such resort is likely to prove, or that the actor thinks it is likely to prove, ineffective?

(c) Must the actor's belief in the existence or nature or seriousness of the threat, or in the impossibility of avoiding the threatened harm, be reasonably held?

(d) Is the defence to be denied to one who is incapable of mounting the resistance to the threat that would be put up by a person of 'reasonable firmness' or steadfastness?

(e) Should the defence be available on a charge of murder or attempted murder?

It is, of course, this last question which has demonstrated the difference of opinion between the Law Commission and the Law Lords. On two occasions the Law Commission have recommended that duress should be available as a defence to murder, but in both *R v Howe* [1987] 1 All ER 771 and *R v Gotts* [1992] 1 All ER 832, the House of Lords refused to so recognise it. This issue is fully explored in Question 4.

The development of the defence of necessity has always been hampered by the decision in *R v Dudley and Stephens* [1881–5] All ER Rep 61 that it was not available on a murder charge. The effect of this case for many years was that when a defendant chose the lesser of two evils, the defence would not be considered. The restrictive approach has been demonstrated by decisions such as *R v Kitson* (1955) 39 Cr App R 66. The defendant had fallen asleep whilst travelling as a passenger in a car. When he awoke he found that he had to suddenly take control of the car because the driver was no longer in control. Although the defendant was drunk he managed to steer the car to safety. The defence of necessity was not permitted and the conviction for driving under the influence of alcohol was upheld. The courts have now recognised that the defence of duress of circumstances may be available in the same way as duress by threats, see e.g., *R v Pommell* [1995] 2 Cr App R 607.

Many commentators believed that duress of circumstances was the defence of necessity in disguise, but the Law Commission have recognised that there is a difference between the two concepts, by recommending that, whereas duress by circumstances should be defined by statute, necessity should be allowed to develop through judicial decision (see cl. 43 of the Draft Code, and the Draft Criminal Law Bill). Necessity was recognised as a defence by the House of Lords in *F v West Berkshire Authority* [1989] 2 All ER 545, where Lord Brandon said that 'it will not only be lawful for doctors, on the ground of necessity to operate on or give other medical treatment to adult patients disabled from giving their consent, it will also be their common law duty to do so'.

Further recognition of the defence of necessity was made by the Court of Appeal in *Re A (Children) (Conjoined Twins: Surgical Separation)* [2000] 4 All ER 961, when the court authorised an operation to separate conjoined twins, which was necessary to save the life of the stronger twin, although it would inevitably cause the death of the weaker twin. Brooke LJ stated that the three necessary requirements for the application of the defence of necessity were satisfied; namely

(a) the act was needed to avoid inevitable and irreparable evil;

(b) no more should be done than was reasonably necessary for the purpose to be achieved; and

(c) the evil inflicted was not disproportionate to the evil avoided.

Dudley and Stephens was distinguished, and although *Re A* is a civil case, it is clear that the defence of necessity could be developed to apply to all offences.

An issue that often affects the defences of duress and self-defence is mistake. There may be situations where, in fact the conditions for the defence may not be in place but the defendant nevertheless honestly believes that they are. Should the court judge the defendant on the facts as she honestly believed them to be, or should the law only permit reliance on reasonable mistakes of fact? As far as self-defence is concerned the courts have followed the House of Lords' decision in *DPP v Morgan* [1975] 2 All ER 347 and applied the subjective test: see *R v Williams* (1983) 78 Cr App R 276. With duress the approach taken was initially to favour the objective test: see *R v Graham* [1982] 1 All ER 801, and *R* v *Abdul-Hussain & Ors* [1999] Crim LR 570. It is submitted that the preferable approach is that endorsed by the Court of Appeal in *R* v *Martin* [2000] Crim LR 615, where it was held that, as regards the defence of duress *per minas*, the accused should be judged on the facts as she believed them to be. This would accord with the general trend towards subjectivism in criminal law: see *B* v *DPP* [2000] 1 All ER 833. The matter requires clarification by the House of Lords, not least in light of the Court of Appeal decision in *R* v *Safi* [2003] Crim LR 721 (decided after *R* v *Martin*), where the court certified that the following point of law of general public importance was involved in the decision: 'May a defendant seek to rely on the defence of duress where he reasonably [or genuinely] may believe that he is subject to a threat of death or serious injury where there is in fact no evidence of any such threat or circumstances giving rise to such a threat?'

The other major controversy relating to self-defence is the House of Lords' decision in *R* v *Clegg* [1995] 1 All ER 334, concluding (against the recommendations of the Law Commission, 14th Report, Cmnd 7844) that a defendant entitled to use force in self-defence but who kills the attacker by using unreasonable force, will be guilty of murder instead of manslaughter. Perhaps the defendant in these circumstances lacks the culpability of a murderer, but as Australia recognised (*Zecevic* v *DPP (Victoria)* (1987) 162 CLR 645), in practical terms the defendant is generally in a better position if the prosecution's case is weak and the jury only have the options of murder or acquittal (as opposed to a third option of manslaughter). The problem of course for Clegg was that he was tried by a 'Diplock court' with no jury; but even if there is a jury, it is often difficult to predict the outcome.

Q Question 1

Mary, an unmarried mother aged 17, suffers from anxiety and panic attacks. She is a member of a protest group, 'Free West Country TV from Welsh Influence', and is told by Alan, the leader of the group, that unless she takes part in an attack on the local TV station her young daughter will be killed.

As a result, Mary takes part in the raid. She accosts Sid, a motorist, takes his car and causes him slight injuries. Then she collects Alan and drives him to the TV station where he murders a night-watchman, Bill.

Discuss the criminal liability of Mary.

Commentary

The question concerns the conditions surrounding the defence of duress. There have been many recent developments regarding this defence, and the debate as to whether duress should be a defence to murder is still on going (see Law Com. No. 83 and Working Paper No. 55). So it is always likely to crop up in an examination question.

As always with problem questions concerning defences, the facts disclose certain offences, which can generally be covered quite quickly, although this answer requires a fairly comprehensive discussion on aiding and abetting murder. Most of the marks however, are awarded for coverage of the defence of duress.

Note: you are not required to discuss Alan's criminal responsibility.

- **Consider offences**
  - assault; aggravated assault
  - theft: s. 12, Theft Act 1968
  - aiding and abetting murder
- **Duress — definition**
- **Conditions for the defence of duress**
- **Duress and murder**

:Ö: Suggested answer

Mary could be charged with a number of offences in connection with this event. When she accosts Sid, the motorist, she could be guilty of common assault under s. 39 of the Criminal Justice Act 1988. However, as she has caused him slight injuries the charge is more likely to be the more serious offence of assault occasioning actual bodily harm under s. 47 of the Offences Against the Person Act 1861. Actual bodily harm covers slight injuries such as bruising, or even psychiatric injury, which is established by expert evidence (*R v Mike Chan-Fook* [1994] 2 All ER 552). The *mens rea* for the s. 47 offence is the same as for assault and battery. There is no requirement for the prosecution to prove that Mary intended or foresaw the risk of actual bodily harm (*R v Savage and Parmenter* [1991] 4 All ER 698).

Further, when Mary takes Sid's car she could be committing theft under s. 1 of the Theft Act 1968, i.e., she 'dishonestly appropriates property belonging to another with the intention of permanently depriving the other of it'. However, when a car is taken it is often difficult to establish that the accused had an intention permanently to deprive, as the car is often dumped and traced back to its owner. Therefore, the more usual charge is under s. 12 of the Theft Act 1968, 'taking a conveyance without the owner's authority'. For this offence temporary deprivation is sufficient.

The most serious offence that Mary might face is aiding and abetting murder. An unlawful homicide has occurred and Alan is the principal offender. Mary was present at the scene of the crime, and it is clear that driving the principal offender to the murder scene satisfies the *actus reus* of being an accomplice to murder (*DPP for Northern Ireland v Lynch* [1975] AC 653; overruled on another point by *R v Howe* [1987] AC 417). Whether Mary would have the necessary *mens rea* for this offence will be discussed after consideration of the defence of duress.

Duress is a long-established general defence available when there have been 'threats of immediate death or serious personal violence so great as to overbear the ordinary powers of human resistance' (*Attorney-General* v *Whelan* [1934] IR 518). However in *R* v *Abdul-Hussain and others* [1999] Crim LR 570 the Court of Appeal in a detailed analysis decided that if there was a threat of imminent death or grievous bodily harm, as opposed to immediate, this would be sufficient for duress to succeed. Threats of lesser harm, such as false imprisonment or damage to property, are not sufficient (*R* v *Howe*) and the threat must be of immediate death or grievous bodily harm. So if an accused has an opportunity to nullify the threat by seeking police protection and fails to do so, the defence will probably fail (*R* v *Hudson and Taylor* [1971] 2 All ER 244).

The fact that the threats were to harm Mary's child, and not Mary herself, will not necessarily cause the defence to fail. The Australian case of *Hurley and Murray* [1967] VR 526, decided that threats to kill the accused's *de facto* wife amounted to duress; and threats against the life or safety of D's family and others to whom he owes a duty almost certainly will, and threats to a stranger probably will, be sufficient evidence of duress.

It is arguable whether there should be an objective requirement that the will of a reasonable person would have been overborne for the defence to succeed, since if the accused was too frightened to resist, then this should be sufficient. However, the relevance of the objective criterion was confirmed in *R* v *Graham* [1982] 1 All ER 801, where the House of Lords approved the following jury direction formulated by Lord Lane CJ:

> was (D) or may he have been, impelled to act as he did because, as a result of what he reasonably believed (E) had said or done, he had good cause to fear that if he did not so act (E) would kill him or . . . cause him serious physical injury? . . . If so, have the prosecution made the jury sure that a sober person of reasonable firmness, sharing the characteristics of (D), would not have responded to whatever he reasonably believed (E) said or did by taking part in the killing?

Note that the *R* v *Graham* formulation requires Mary's belief in the circumstances giving rise to the duress to have been reasonable. There is authority to the contrary: see *R* v *Martin* [2000] Crim LR 615, suggesting that the accused should be judged on the facts as she believed them to be. However, that view was subsequently doubted by the Court of Appeal in *R* v *Safi* [2003] Crim LR 721. On the facts of this case, however, nothing turns on the distinction. As regards the application of the test for duress, therefore, Mary can argue that the jury should take into account her age and medical condition when considering the objective test set out by Lord Lane CJ, in *R* v *Graham* above.

This is very similar to what was the objective condition in the defence of provocation, where many characteristics were held to be relevant, including disreputable ones such as glue-sniffing (*R* v *Morhall* [1995] 3 All ER 659). Thus, by analogy with provocation, the fact that Mary is aged 17 and arguably less resilient than an adult, and consequently less able to resist the threat, may be taken into account. However, the fact that she suffers from anxiety and panic attacks is less certain of being admitted. In *R v Hegarty* [1994] Crim LR 353, expert evidence to show that the accused was 'emotionally unstable or in a grossly elevated state' was held inadmissible; whereas in *R v Emery* (1993) 14 Cr App R (S) 394, the Court of Appeal stated *obiter* that it would be correct to allow expert evidence as to the causes and effects of learned helplessness. The traditional approach has always been that, as it is within the jury's experience as to how a reasonable person should react, there is no need to hear from experts. However, as Beldam LJ pointed out in *R v Hurst* [1995] 1 Cr App R 82: 'we find it hard to see how the person of reasonable firmness can be invested with the characteristics of a personality which lacks reasonable firmness'. It is therefore submitted that, unless there is expert psychiatric evidence to the effect that this is a recognised psychiatric illness (in which case, in accordance with *R v Bowen* [1996] 4 All ER 837, the jury should consider it), the anxiety and panic should not be taken into account when considering the objective condition.

A further difficulty that Mary faces regarding the availability of duress as a defence is the fact that she is an existing member of the protest group. In *R v Sharp* [1987] QB 853, Lord Lane CJ stated:

> Where a person has voluntarily, and with knowledge of its nature, joined a criminal organisation or gang which he knew might bring pressure on him to commit an offence and was an active member when he was put under such pressure, he cannot avail himself of the defence of duress.

Because the protection of society demands that people do not easily capitulate to the threat of violence, this principle has been strictly enforced in a number of cases, and in *R v Heath* [2000] Crim LR 109 the Court of Appeal held that the accused, a heroin user, could not rely on duress, because although he was not a member of any criminal organisation, he had voluntarily exposed himself to unlawful violence. Against this, in *R v Z* [2003] EWCA Crim 191, the Court of Appeal opted not to follow *R v Heath*, holding that anticipation of compulsion by threats, unconnected with a view to the commission of crime, did not deprive a defendant of the defence of duress. It was not enough for the prosecution to prove that Mary had voluntarily exposed herself to the risk of unlawful violence from other members of the protest group. It had to be proved that she had voluntarily exposed herself to the risk that she might be required, under threats of violence, to commit criminal offences. On the facts it seems unlikely that Mary would be prevented from raising duress on the grounds that she could have avoided the threats being made.

One factor in Mary's favour is that once she raises the issue of duress the prosecution have to disprove the existence of the defence. On the facts, there are weaknesses, as has been pointed out, but it is submitted that the defence of duress would have a good chance of succeeding with a sympathetic jury.

Duress has been recognised as a general defence to all crimes except treason and murder. Thus, if it succeeds, Mary could not be found guilty of the offences under the 1861 or 1968 Acts. However, she could be found guilty of being an accomplice to murder, as *DPP for Northern Ireland* v *Lynch* (where the House of Lords decided that duress was a defence to an accomplice to murder) was overruled in *R* v *Howe*. The House of Lords in *Howe* decided that there is no difference between the culpability of an accomplice and that of a principal offender. They applied the traditional approach that you are never justified in taking someone else's life simply because yours is threatened, so that duress would be no defence.

Although Mary has committed the *actus reus* of aiding and abetting murder, she can be found guilty of this offence only if the prosecution prove that she contemplated death or grievous bodily harm as a possible consequence (*Chan Wing Siu* v *R* [1984] 3 All ER 877) or she realised that the primary party, Alan, might kill with intent to do so, or with intent to cause grievous bodily harm — *R* v *Powell and English* [1997] 4 All ER 545. Mary will argue that violence against the person was clearly outside the scope of the agreement; but if she pleads duress to the other charges, she is in effect admitting that she did contemplate death or grievous bodily harm. She could point out that she contemplated this consequence in respect of another victim, her daughter, in a separate attack; but for accomplice liability there is no requirement for the prosecution to prove that the accomplice knew all the details of the principal offence (*R* v *Bainbridge* [1959] 3 All ER 200), and the prosecution could argue that by analogy with the doctrine of transferred malice, contemplation of such violence to anyone is sufficient.

If the court accepted the prosecution's contention, Mary could fall back on the weak argument that she did not intend to assist Alan, but simply intended to save her daughter. This submission was surprisingly accepted in *R* v *Steane* [1947] 1 All ER 813, where the accused's conviction for doing acts likely to assist the enemy with intent to assist the enemy, was quashed on the grounds that his participation in Nazi broadcasts during the war was done with the intention of saving his wife and family from a concentration camp and not with the intention of assisting the enemy.

It is submitted that Mary should not on these facts be found guilty of aiding and abetting murder; and in practice, as was pointed out by Lord Griffith in *R* v *Howe* [1987] 1 All ER 771, the Crown Prosecution Service would exercise its discretion in the public interest and not prosecute her for this offence, but instead call her as leading prosecution witness in the trial of Alan for murder.

Q Question 2

Anne, who was of a nervous disposition, was approached by John who wanted to kiss her. Anne, who knew that John had a reputation for violence, wrongly believed that he had a knife and wanted to rape her. She concluded that the only way to stop him was to kill him, and so she took out a gun and repeatedly shot him. He died instantly. John was unarmed.

Discuss the criminal liability of Anne.

Commentary

This is a relatively straightforward question as it involves only one major topic, self-defence. However, there are many important principles that need to be stated and analysed, and the question is further complicated by the issue of mistake.

There have been many important cases in this area in recent years and the decisions in *DPP* v *Morgan* [1976] AC 182, *R* v *Williams* [1987] 3 All ER 411 and *R* v *Clegg* [1995] 1 All ER 334 must be applied. Nevertheless, if you have mastered this topic this problem would give you a great opportunity to pick up high marks.

- Murder — definition

- Self-defence — definition
    - reasonable force
    - mistake — *Williams* [1987]
    - excessive force — *Clegg* [1995], *Martin* [2002]

Suggested answer

The prosecution will charge Anne with murder. She has caused John's death in fact and there is no evidence of any *novus actus interveniens*. The prosecution will be able to establish that Anne had the necessary *mens rea*, which is intention to kill or cause grievous bodily harm: see *R* v *Moloney* [1985] 1 All ER 1025. The focus of this answer, therefore, should be on the defences available to Anne. Foremost amongst these is self-defence at common law (i.e., the use of reasonable force), and the statutory version of self-defence under s. 3 of the Criminal Law Act 1967. Section 3 provides that a person may use such force as is reasonable in the circumstances in the prevention of crime, thus both defences allow persons to use reasonable force to defend themselves or others from an attack.

Traditionally, for the common law defence to succeed it would have to be established that the accused actually retreated from the offered violence. However, in *R* v *Julien* [1969] 2 All ER 856 it was stated that the accused need only demonstrate that he or she is prepared to temporise and disengage, and perhaps to make some physical withdrawal. In *R* v *Bird* [1985] 2 All ER 513 this *dictum* was disapproved, the Court of Appeal holding that in some circumstances this may be too heavy a responsibility on the accused, and the best way to deal with this issue was simply to leave it to the jury to determine whether the accused had acted reasonably.

The prosecution would argue that far from retreating, Anne was the aggressor. This in itself would not rule out self-defence succeeding, as in *Beckford* v *R* [1987] 3 All ER 425 Lord Griffith in the Privy Council stated (at p. 431): 'Furthermore a person about to be attacked does not have to wait for the assailant to strike the first blow or fire the first shot. Circumstances may justify a pre-emptive strike'. However, no jury is going to accept an accused's assertion that he or she believed he or she was about to be attacked without testing it against all the surrounding circumstances. Further, as the Court of Appeal stated in *R* v *Whyte* [1987] 3 All ER 416, the defence is not open to the accused if there was an obvious and easy way of avoiding the incident instead of using violence.

Although the courts have held that it is only in exceptional circumstances that the jury will conclude that the accused mistakenly believed an attack was impending, it is submitted that Anne on the facts might have held this belief as it is a subjective test. The jury would therefore consider whether the use of force was reasonable. The Criminal Law Revision Committee's 14th Report, *Offences Against the Person* (Cmnd. 7844 (1980)) stated that the court 'would take into account all the circumstances, including in particular the nature and degree of force used, the seriousness of the evil to be prevented and the possibility of preventing it by other means'. Clearly if Anne was being attacked by a person with a knife who wanted to rape her, she would be entitled to use force to defend herself. However, she still faces two problems: was it reasonable to kill to prevent rape; and is she entitled to be judged on the facts as she believed them to be?

The first question was considered by Lord Diplock in *Attorney-General for Northern Ireland Reference (No. 1 of 1975)* [1976] 2 All ER 937, where the accused had shot and killed the victim mistakenly believing that he was an escaping terrorist. The court held that where the only options open to the accused were either to let the deceased escape or to shoot at him knowing that death or grievous bodily harm was probable, it would be open to the jury to take the view that it would not be unreasonable to assess the kind of harm to be averted by preventing the escape as even greater. Thus the jury would ask themselves whether they were satisfied that no reasonable person with knowledge of such facts as were known to the accused or believed by him to exist, in the circumstances and time available for reflection, would have done as the accused did. Thus if a reasonable person might have done as Anne did, shooting to kill could be reasonable self-defence.

The second problem involves the issue of mistake. The House of Lords in *DPP* v *Morgan* [1976] AC 182, made it clear that a defendant pleading mistake of fact was effectively raising an issue as to *mens rea*. As such mistake was to be viewed subject-ively — i.e., the defendant was to be judged on the facts as he honestly believed them to be. Of course the effect of *DPP* v *Morgan* as regards mistake as to consent in rape cases has now been swept away by the provisions of the Sexual Offences Act 2003. The wider impact of the ruling stands, however. In *DPP* v *Morgan* the House of Lords was concerned with a defendant who had made a mistake as to an element of an offence (i.e., whether or not the victim was consenting to sexual intercourse). *R* v *Williams* [1987] 3 All ER 411, makes it clear that the same approach (i.e., judging the defendant on the facts as he honestly believes them to be) applies equally where the defendant makes a mistake of fact giving rise to the belief that he can act in self-defence. In *Williams*, M witnessed a youth snatching a woman's handbag, chased after him, caught him and knocked him to the ground. W, who came on the scene, was told by M that M was arresting the youth and that he was a police officer (which he was not). W asked M to produce his warrant card which he could not do. A struggle then ensued during which W punched M. In quashing W's conviction for assault occasioning actual bodily harm (s. 47 of the Offences Against the Person Act 1861), the Court of Appeal held that W would lack the necessary *mens rea* if, on the facts as he mistakenly believed them to be, he was entitled to use reasonable force either in self-defence or in the prevention of crime.

Thus the reasonableness of Anne's belief is theoretically irrelevant, although in practice the more unreasonable the mistake the more unlikely it is that the jury will accept that Anne made it. However, as Anne is of a nervous disposition and John has a reputation for violence, there is evidence to enable the jury to reach the conclusion that Anne honestly believed she was about to be attacked. Further, it is not for Anne to prove the defence. Once Anne has satisfied the evidential burden, the prosecution have the burden of proof. This is favourable for Anne as the jury has to judge her on the facts as she believed them to be, and as long as no more than reasonable force was used in those mistakenly perceived circumstances there is no criminal liability. As Lord Morris stated in *Palmer* v *R* [1977] 1 All ER 1077 (at p. 1088): 'if a jury thought that in a moment of unexpected anguish a person attacked had only done what he honestly and instinctively thought was necessary, that would be most potent evidence that only reasonable defensive action had been taken'.

If the jury concluded that Anne was entitled to use force in self-defence but had used unreasonable force, it would appear, following the House of Lords' decision in *R* v *Clegg* [1995] 1 All ER 334, that she would be convicted of murder. The Law Commission (cl. 59 of the Draft Code) have accepted the argument that a person in this situation lacks the culpability of a murderer. However, although the House of Lords agreed with this approach, their Lordships felt that it was for Parliament and not them to change the law, and Clegg's conviction for murder (as opposed to manslaughter) was upheld. This principle was recently followed by the Court of Appeal in *R* v *Martin* [2002] 2 WLR 1. Oddly the law in Australia has recently been changed (in *Zecevic* v *DPP (Victoria)* (1987) 61 ALJR 375); whereas for many years an accused who used unreasonable force in self-defence in killing the victim was guilty of manslaughter, now he would be guilty of murder.

Q Question 3

James was driving on a narrow mountain road. He came to a hairpin bend where he saw Norma sitting in her parked car. Because the road was narrow he could not go back or forward, or around the car. He saw a sign by the side of the road 'Danger — serious risk of avalanche' and noticed small rocks coming down the mountainside. Fearing an impending avalanche and believing he had no alternative, he drove into the car in front, knocking it over the mountainside. He realised that this course of action was dangerous, and it resulted in Norma (the occupant of the car) being killed and the car being badly damaged. There was in fact no avalanche.

Discuss the criminal liability (if any) of James.

Commentary

This question involves a detailed consideration of the defence of necessity/duress of circumstances. There are many uncertainties concerning the defence and this question should be attempted only if you are confident of dealing with these issues.

You must, however, guard against the risk of dealing only with this defence, as you must give due consideration to the ingredients of the offences with which James could be charged. Thus a full discussion of the concepts of intention and recklessness must be given in relation to murder, manslaughter, and criminal damage.

Note: road traffic offences have not been considered in detail.

- Murder — definition

- Intention — *Moloney* [1985], *Woollin* [1998]

- Involuntary manslaughter

- Criminal damage — s. 1(1) and s. 1(2), Criminal Damage Act 1971

- Necessity/duress of circumstances

    - conditions — *Graham* [1982]

    - availability — *Pommell* [1995]

:Q: Suggested answer

James could face charges involving unlawful homicide and criminal damage, but he would be able to raise the defence of necessity and/or duress of circumstances. The most serious offence to consider is murder. James has clearly caused Norma's death in fact — but for his actions she would not have died. There is no evidence to suggest that there has been any break in the chain of causation. The *mens rea* of murder is satisfied by the prosecution proving that James intended to kill or cause grievous bodily harm (*R* v *Moloney* [1985] 1 All ER 1025). This is a question of fact for the jury. Although the general rule is that intention is a word in common use, easily understood by the public, and therefore there is no need for the trial judge to embark on a detailed explanation of the concept, this case might require a further direction.

Whereas it is clear that foresight of consequence is some evidence of intention, it is not in itself conclusive evidence. Similarly, a judge cannot direct the jury that if James foresaw the consequence and the result was a natural consequence, James intended it. The trial judge would now probably use the direction suggested by the House of Lords in *R* v *Woollin* [1998] 4 All ER 103 that the jury would not be entitled to find the necessary intention unless they felt sure that death or serious bodily harm was a virtually certain result of D's actions (barring some unforeseen intervention), and that D had appreciated that fact.

James could argue that although he foresaw this possible consequence, death or grievous bodily harm was not his purpose as his motive was to save himself. Although this argument succeeded in *R* v *Steane* [1947] 1 All ER 813, this was not a murder case, and it is recognised that motive is not the same as intention. Motive is the reason why one acts, whereas intention is the state of mind present when the act is committed.

If the jury decided that James lacked the *mens rea* for murder, he could still be found guilty of involuntary (constructive) manslaughter, i.e., unlawful killing without intention to kill or do grievous bodily harm. For constructive manslaughter the prosecution must prove that James committed a dangerous criminal act that caused the victim's death. Traditionally there has been a reluctance to use a driving offence as the unlawful act in constructive manslaughter. Thus in *Andrews* v *DPP* [1937] AC 576, the House of Lords held that an accused would not automatically be guilty of manslaughter when he killed the victim as a result of careless driving. Lord Aitkin said: 'There is an obvious difference in the law of manslaughter between doing an unlawful act and doing a lawful act with a degree of carelessness which the legislature makes criminal'. However, in the present case James realised the risk, and it is submitted that this would be sufficient to constitute the unlawful act, i.e., causing death by dangerous driving under the Road Traffic Act 1991.

Alternatively the prosecution could rely on offences under the Criminal Damage Act 1971. It appears that James committed criminal damage under s. 1(1) of the Act when he damaged Norma's car. Liability could be based on 'simple' criminal damage contrary to s. 1(1) of the 1971 Act, or on aggravated criminal damage contrary to s. 1(2), i.e., damaging or destroying property either intending that or being reckless that the life of another would thereby be endangered.

The second ingredient of constructive manslaughter is that the act must be dangerous. It is enough that a sober and reasonable person at the scene of the unlawful act would have been aware of the possibility of some physical harm occurring as a result of James' actions: see *R* v *Church* [1965] 2 All ER 72, and *R* v *Dawson* (1985) 81 Cr App R 150. Given the facts, it is submitted that the prosecution would have no difficulty in satisfying this condition.

There has always been uncertainty as to what should be and what is the *mens rea* for unlawful act manslaughter. As Lord Hope explained in *Attorney-General's Reference (No. 3 of 1994)* [1997] 3 All ER 936, the prosecution must prove that the defendant intended to do what he did. It is not necessary to prove that he knew that his act was unlawful or dangerous. It is unnecessary to prove that he knew that his act was likely to injure the person who died as a result of it. All that need be proved is that he intentionally did what he did.

On this basis, liability for constructive manslaughter should be made out.

It is worth noting that James could also incur liability for causing death by dangerous driving contrary to s. 1 of the Road Traffic Act 1991. The fault element is 'dangerousness', and this is assessed objectively.

What defences might be available to James?

For many years the development of the defence was hindered by the decision in *R* v *Dudley and Stephens* [1881–5] All ER Rep 61, in which two shipwrecked seaman killed and ate a cabin boy in order to survive. The court ruled that necessity could be no defence to murder and the accused were found guilty, and many commentators believed that the case was authority for the principle that necessity was not available as a general defence to other charges. It was not until the mid-1980s that the argument was renewed in a number of cases involving road traffic offences (*R* v *Willer* (1987) 83 Cr App R 225; *R* v *Conway* [1988] 3 WLR 1338; and *R* v *Martin* [1989] 1 All ER 652) and the related defence of duress of circumstances was developed.

If the defence is raised the prosecution retains the burden of proof, and according to the House of Lords in *R* v *Graham* [1982] 1 All ER 801 the jury should be directed as follows:

(a) Was the defendant, or may he have been, impelled to act as he did because as a result of what he reasonably believed to be the situation he had good cause to fear that if he did not so act death or serious physical injury would result?

(b) If so, have the prosecution made the jury sure that a sober person of reasonable firmness sharing the characteristics of the defendant would not have responded to the situation by acting as the defendant did?

There is a surprising amount of reference to the objective element in this defence, and this could be a problem for James as, although he believed there was an impending avalanche, this was not in fact the case. Although in *R* v *Williams* [1987] 3 All ER 411 it was recognised that for the defence of self-defence, the accused should be judged on the facts as he believed them to be, and an honest but unreasonable mistake would not prevent the defence succeeding, *Graham* was approved by the House of Lords in *R* v *Howe* [1987] 1 All ER 771. James must therefore argue that the subjective approach should also apply to necessity and duress, but unless the jury believe that he had reasonable grounds to conclude there was an impending avalanche, the defence will fail.

Despite the recent recognition by the Court of Appeal (Civil Division) in *Re A (Children) (Conjoined Twins: Surgical Separation)* [2000] 4 All ER 961, that necessity could be a defence to murder in relation to medical treatment to separate conjoined twins, it is most unlikely that the defence could help James if he possessed the necessary *mens rea* for murder. Although in this case *R v Dudley and Stephens* was distinguished, it has been approved by the House of Lords in *R v Howe*. However, in *R v Pommell* [1995] 2 Cr App R 607 it was recognised that the defence, being closely related to the defence of duress by threats, appears to be general, applying to all crimes except murder, attempted murder and some forms of treason. Thus if the jury accepted that James lacked malice aforethought and he had reasonable grounds to believe that his life was in danger, he would be acquitted of all charges.

Q Question 4

The uncertainties surrounding the defence of duress by threats justify the House of Lords' decisions in *R v Howe* [1987] 1 All ER 771 and *R v Gotts* [1992] 1 All ER 832, rejecting duress as a defence to murder.
   Discuss.

Commentary

This is one of the most controversial topics within the criminal law, the Law Commission's views being the opposite of two recent House of Lords' decisions.

   The question requires an analysis of the defence of duress with reference to the uncertainties concerning its ingredients. There are many arguments justifying an extension of the defence to murder and these must be covered in detail, together with the counter-arguments of the House of Lords found mainly in *R v Howe* [1987] 1 All ER 771.

   Because there is so much to cover you must avoid the pitfall of covering the facts of the key cases in detail. They are not important and you simply do not have enough time.

- Duress — definition

- Threats against whom?

- Types of threats

- Subjective and objective tests

- Availability of *Howe* [1987]

- Gang membership — *Sharp* [1987]

- Law Commission No. 122

:Q̇: Suggested answer

The defence of duress is available when the accused has been forced to commit a crime against his will. This is because 'threats of immediate death or serious personal violence so great as to overbear the ordinary power of human resistance should be accepted as a justification for acts which would otherwise be criminal' (*Attorney-General* v *Whelan* [1934] IR 518, *per* Murnaghan J). However, despite the fact that the defence has been recognised for many years, Lord Keith stated in *R* v *Gotts* [1992] 1 All ER 832, that 'the complexities and anomalies involved in the whole matter of the defence of duress seem to me to be such that the issue is much better left to Parliament to deal with in the light of broad considerations of policy'.

Lord Mackay also referred to these uncertainties in the leading House of Lords' decision in *R* v *Howe* [1987] 1 All ER 771, and used this argument in refusing to extend this defence to murder: 'I question whether the law has reached a sufficiently precise definition of that defence to make it right for us sitting in our judicial capacity to introduce it as a defence for an actual killer for the first time in the law of England.' There are many such uncertainties as was recently demonstrated in *R* v *Abdul Hussain and Ors* [1999] Crim LR 570 where the Court of Appeal decided that if there was a threat of imminent death or grievous bodily harm as opposed to immediate, duress was established. Nevertheless it is submitted that they could have been easily clarified by the House of Lords.

First, must the threat be against the accused, or is it sufficient if it is directed against a third party? In *Hurley* v *Murray* [1967] VR 526, the Supreme Court of Victoria held that threats to kill or seriously injure D's *de facto* wife amounted to duress; and as self-defence is available as a defence if D uses force against an attacker of a third party (*R* v *Duffy* [1966] 1 All ER 62), it is submitted that following the Law Commission's Draft Code such threats against a member of D's family should be sufficient.

Secondly, will threats of harm less than death or grievous bodily harm be sufficient? In *R* v *Graham* [1982] 1 All ER 801 and in *R* v *Conway* [1988] 3 All ER 1025, the Court of Appeal required death or grievous bodily harm to be threatened; and more recently in *R* v *Baker and Wilkins* [1997] Crim LR 497, the Court of Appeal rejected serious psychological injury as being sufficient for duress of circumstances. The defence will not succeed if the threats are to damage property or cause financial loss.

Thirdly, as it was recognised in *R* v *Graham* that the defence fails if the prosecution prove that a person of reasonable firmness sharing the characteristics of the defendant would not have given way to the threats as did the defendant, what characteristics can the jury take into account? Although there is an analogy on this point with the defence of provocation, as both are recognitions of human frailty, with duress the courts have not been prepared to accept that characteristics of an accused are generally relevant for the jury to consider. Thus in *R* v *Hegarty* [1994] Crim LR 353, the Court of Appeal stated that 'as the test predicted a sober person of reasonable firmness, there was no scope for attributing to that hypothetical person as one of the characteristics of the accused a pre-existing mental condition of being emotionally unstable or in a grossly elevated neurotic state'. As Beldam LJ pointed out in *R* v *Hurst* [1995] 1 Cr App R 82, 'we find it hard to see how the person of reasonable firmness can be invested with the characteristics of a personality which lacks reasonable firmness'. However, more recently in *R* v *Bowen* [1996] 4 All ER 837, the Court of Appeal stated that if the accused was suffering from a recognised psychiatric illness, this characteristic could be taken into account.

Perhaps it is contrary to principle to require the fear to be a reasonable one. Because of the difficulties of applying the test (for example, in *R* v *Emery* [1993] 14 Cr App R(S) 394, where the test was a woman of reasonable firmness suffering from a condition of dependent helplessness), it is submitted that a purely subjective test is justified.

Traditionally, duress has never been recognised as a defence to murder, *Blackstone's Commentaries of the Law of England* (1857) stating that a man under duress 'ought rather to die himself than escape by the murder of an innocent'. However, in *DPP for Northern Ireland* v *Lynch* [1975] AC 653, the House of Lords made an inroad into this blanket rule by holding that duress was available as a defence to an accused charged as an accomplice to murder, and shortly afterwards Lords Wilberforce and Edmund-Davies, in a much acclaimed minority judgment in the Privy Council decision in *Abbott* v *R* [1976] 3 All ER 140, concluded that the decision in *Lynch* should be extended to cover a principal offender. The Law Commission (Law Com. No. 83) also recommended this approach, but this trend was abruptly halted by the House of Lords in *R* v *Howe* where their Lordships not only confirmed the traditional approach, but also, using the Lord Chancellor's Practice Note [1966] 3 All ER 77, overruled their earlier decision in *Lynch*.

A number of reasons were given for this decision, although there are equally strong reasons for recognising the defence. First, Lord Hailsham pointed out that following superior orders is not a defence to murder (Article 8 of the chapter of the International Military Treaty series no. 26 of 1946), and *R* v *Dudley and Stephens* [1881–5] All ER Rep 61 also ruled out the similar defence of necessity. It is submitted that both necessity and duress should be a defence to murder and that the analogy with superior orders is inappropriate.

Secondly, the principle underlying the denial of both defences (duress and necessity) is the special sanctity that the law attaches to human life and which denies a person the right to take an innocent life even at the price of his own or another's life. However, in more recent years the Suicide Act 1961 and the House of Lords' decision in *Airedale NHS Trust* v *Bland* [1993] 1 All ER 821 have recognised that life does not have to be preserved at all costs, and it is not beneficial simply to adopt a blanket rule without good reason. Thus an accused should have the defence of duress considered if he or she was forced to take one life but in doing so save more.

Thirdly, Lord Hailsham stated in *R* v *Howe* (at p. 579): 'I do not at all accept in relation to the defence of murder it is either good morals, good policy or good law . . . that the ordinary man of reasonable fortitude is not to be supposed to be capable of heroism if he is asked to take an innocent life rather than sacrifice his own'. However, as the Law Commission have recognised (Law Com. No. 122), it is not fair to expect the standard of the reasonable person to be one of heroism and it should be for the jury to decide if the threat was one which an accused could reasonably be expected to resist.

The fourth argument, one often raised by traditionalists, was put by Lord Griffith. Now is not an appropriate time for change. The law must stand firm against a rising tide of violence and terrorism, and terrorists should not be able to rely on a defence of duress, which would be easy to raise but difficult to resist. However, the defence is not available to a member of a criminal or terrorist organisation (*R* v *Sharp* [1987] 3 All ER 103), and the question of whether the accused was a terrorist or an innocent tool is a proper question for the jury.

Two other weak arguments were also advanced for maintaining the *status quo*: first, Parliament has made no attempt to change the law despite the recommendations of the Law Commission, and therefore Parliament must be taken to agree with the present principle; and, secondly, any injustice that might result from application of the present law would be alleviated by the exercise of executive discretion not to prosecute or to release on licence a person serving a life sentence. It is submitted that reliance on executive discretion is not an adequate response in principle or practice; and as no Bill has been introduced proposing that duress be available as a defence to murder, Parliament has never had the opportunity of expressing an opinion on the matter.

Although in *R* v *Kingston* [1994] 3 All ER 353, Lord Mustill in the House of Lords stated that 'the Court should when faced with a new problem acknowledge the justice of the case and boldly create a new common law defence', their Lordships again refused so to do in *R* v *Gotts* where duress was held to be not available as a defence to attempted murder. This approach continues to fly in the face of the Law Commission's recommendation (No. 122), the Commission believing that all uncertainties surrounding the defence could be removed by a clear statutory definition.

Shifting the burden of proof to the accused is another safeguard against unmeritorious pleas succeeding; but leaving the law as it is, it is submitted, is the least satisfactory solution. This has been recognised by the Law Commission, who state: 'If however it were decided that duress should not be available as a complete defence, we would regard its statutory recognition as a partial defence reducing murder to manslaughter as the second best option.' Unsurprisingly, this view had already been rejected by the House of Lords in *Howe*.

Further reading

Clarkson, C.M.V., 'Necessary Action: A new defence' [2004] Crim LR 81.

Douglas, G.R., *'Dudley and Stephens* — Revisited and Updated', Justice of the Peace (Vol. 166) 40.

Douglas, G.R., 'Self-defence in the Light of *R* v *Martin*', Justice of the Peace (Vol. 166) 368.

Elliott, D.W., 'Necessity, Duress and Self-defence' [1989] Crim LR 611.

Rogers, J., 'Necessity, Private Defence and the Killing of Mary' [2001] Crim LR 515.

Smith, K.J.M., 'Duress and Steadfastness' [1999] Crim LR 363.

Inchoate offences and accessories

Introduction

How far from the actual substantive offence should the criminal law go to protect the public from people disposed to commit crime? This is essentially the key question in deciding on the appropriate basis for the criminal responsibility required for commission of the inchoate offences of incitement, conspiracy and attempt. It is submitted that it is virtually impossible to formulate principles in this area that will satisfy the correct balance between nipping crime in the bud and simply punishing criminal thoughts. Thus in *R v Cromack* [1978] Crim LR 217, it was held that an accused who wrote to his friend in prison asking him to instruct his wife to commit perjury at the accused's trial could be guilty of an attempt to incite perjury (even though the prisoner took no further action). In *R v Geddes* [1996] Crim LR 894, however, the Court of Appeal quashed the conviction for attempted false imprisonment, where an accused was found lurking near a boys' school with a rucksack containing a kitchen knife, rope and masking tape. The court held that the entire evidence was not sufficient in law to support a finding that the accused had done an act that was more than merely preparatory to wrongfully imprisoning a person unknown. Once again we are faced with the lack of a uniform approach and a common starting point. Incitement is a common law offence, whereas conspiracy is largely statutory, governed by the Criminal Law Act 1977, although there remain the common law conspiracies to defraud, corrupt public morals and outrage public decency. Attempt is governed by the Criminal Attempts Act 1981, which rules out the defence of impossibility on charges of attempt and statutory conspiracy, but not on charges of common law conspiracy and incitement (see *R v Fitzmaurice* [1983] 1 All ER 189).

Similarly when we look at accomplice responsibility, although there is a foundation — an Act which applies to an accomplice's conduct before or at the time of the substantive offence — it is an Act dating back to 1861 (the Accessories and Abettors Act 1861); and the differences between counselling, procuring, aiding and abetting were only revealed by the Court of Appeal's decision in *Attorney-General's Reference (No. 1 of 1975)* [1975] 2 All ER 684.

To some extent problems have been hidden by the prosecution's policy of charging all accomplices as principal offenders; but more recently the uncertainty in the law has been recognised by the points of law of public importance certified by the Court of Appeal in many decisions. The need for reform has been recognised by the Law Commission (Law Com. No. 131 — 'Assisting and Encouraging Crime'), but it appears unlikely that these recommendations will be implemented.

Rather than spending hours searching for coherent principles, your time might be better employed seeking answers to the following questions:

(a) What is the *mens rea* of incitement?

(b) Is recklessness sufficient *mens rea* for conspiracy?

(c) Is impossibility a defence to a statutory conspiracy?

(d) Is intention to cause grievous bodily harm sufficient *mens rea* for attempted murder?

(e) Who decides, on a charge of attempt, if the accused has done more than a merely preparatory act?

(f) What is the *mens rea* required for an accomplice to murder?

(g) Can an accomplice be guilty of a more serious offence than the principal offender?

(h) Is the defence of withdrawal available to —

    (i) an accomplice,

    (ii) a conspirator?

The questions in this chapter cover all the problem areas of these topics, and are quite demanding. If you read the answers thoroughly you will find the answers to the questions posed above. Remember, it is very easy for an examination question that is based on another topic (e.g., unlawful homicide) to include reference to accomplices or related inchoate offences, so they are subjects which you must know well at exam time.

Q Question 1

Amy, Betty, Claire, and Debbie plan to break into X's warehouse in order to steal. Amy, Betty, and Claire know that there will be a nightwatchman on the premises, but Debbie does not know this fact. Amy gives Betty a loaded revolver, telling her not to hesitate to use it if the occasion should so require. When they set off to X's warehouse, Debbie knows that Betty has a revolver in her possession but Claire does not. The four are interrupted by the nightwatchman, Victor. As Betty is in the act of firing the revolver, Amy, recognising Victor as her cousin, knocks Betty's hand to one side crying out 'Don't shoot'. Amy's act causes the bullet to miss Victor, but it strikes and kills a police officer who is entering the room.

Discuss the criminal liability of the parties.

Commentary

There are many points to cover in the answer, and it is therefore important to plan and to concentrate your efforts on the most important topic, accomplice liability. It is best to dispose of the two minor offences, conspiracy and burglary, quickly and then to cover the most serious offence, murder. In a typical exam paper, in addition to this question you could expect a full question on murder, so this answer does not require a detailed analysis of all aspects of that crime. Most of your answer will be taken up dealing with the intricacies of accomplice liability. You must, after stating the principles clearly, emphasise the difference between Claire and Debbie, as Debbie's knowledge of the gun puts her in a much worse position. Full consideration of the possible defence of withdrawal is also required when considering Amy's responsibility.

- Conspiracy — s. 1, Criminal Law Act 1977

- Burglary — s. 9, Theft Act 1968

- Murder/manslaughter

- Accomplice liability
    - *mens rea*: *Powell and Daniels* [1997]
    - withdrawal: *Becerra* [1975]
    - scope of agreement

⚡ Suggested answer

Even before the four parties enter the warehouse, they would be guilty of the crime of conspiracy to burgle under s. 1 of the Criminal Law Act 1977, as they have agreed to pursue a course of conduct which would necessarily involve a criminal offence. Similarly, as soon as they enter the warehouse, they will be guilty of burglary under s. 9 of the Theft Act 1968, as they are entering a building or part of a building as trespassers with intent to steal. As Betty is in possession of a gun when she enters the building, she could be charged with aggravated burglary under s. 10 of the Theft Act 1968; and if Amy and Debbie are deemed to be in joint possession of it, they too will be guilty of this offence.

Betty would be charged with murder, the unlawful killing of a human being within the Queen's peace. Since the Law Reform (Year and a Day Rule) Act 1996, death does not have to follow the unlawful act within a year and a day. The *mens rea* of murder, is satisfied by the prosecution proving that Betty intended to kill or intended to cause grievous bodily harm (*R v Moloney* [1985] 1 All ER 1025). Betty may argue that she did not intend to harm the victim, but the court will apply the doctrine of transferred malice. Thus if the accused has the necessary *mens rea* of the offence, but the actual victim is different from the intended victim, the *mens rea* will be transferred and the accused will be guilty (*R v Mitchell* [1983] 2 All ER 427).

Betty may be able to argue that she was simply firing a warning shot and that it was Amy's act of hitting her arm which caused her aim to alter resulting in the victim's death. In the unlikely event of this argument being accepted, Betty would still be guilty of involuntary manslaughter on the constructive basis. The prosecution could prove that she intended to do an act which was unlawful and dangerous (*R v Newbury and Jones* [1976] 2 All ER 365). Simply drawing and pointing a gun at someone would be unlawful, i.e., assault; and as the test for dangerous is objective ('the unlawful act must be such as all sober and reasonable people would inevitably recognise must subject the other person to at least the risk of some physical harm resulting therefrom, albeit not serious harm' *per* Edmund Davies J in *R v Church* [1965] 2 All ER 72), this element of the offence would be made out.

The other three participants would face charges of abetting murder. While it is clear that the prosecution must prove that the accomplice intended to assist, there has always been controversy about what other mental awareness has to be established to satisfy the *mens rea* requirement. In *DPP for Northern Ireland v Maxwell* [1978] 3 All ER 1140, the House of Lords stated that it was enough for the accomplice to contemplate the type of crime committed; and in respect of murder, the Privy Council in *Chan Wing Siu v R* [1984] 3 All ER 877 confirmed that contemplation of death or grievous bodily harm as a possible consequence is sufficient. As Sir Robin Cooke stated in *Chan Wing Siu*, the principle of liability 'turns on contemplation. It meets the case of a crime foreseen as a possible incident of the common unlawful enterprise. The criminal culpability lies in participating in the venture with that foresight'. This principle has been applied in many subsequent cases, in particular *R v Hyde* (1991) 92 Cr App R 131 and *Hui Chi Ming v R* [1991] 3 All ER 897, although the House of Lords has recognised the severity of a principle which allows an accomplice to be guilty of murder on less *mens rea* than that required by a principal offender (in *R v Powell and Daniels* [1997] 4 All ER 545). Nevertheless, the court did apply *Chan Wing Siu* to uphold the accused's conviction, and rejected the argument that the House of Lords' decisions in *R v Moloney* and *R v Hancock and Shankland* [1986] AC 455, applied to accessories to murder. The House of Lords recognised that the criminal law exists to control crime and a prime function of that system must be to deal justly but effectively with those who join with others in criminal enterprises.

Thus the House applied *Chan Wing Siu* to uphold A's conviction stating that, to found a conviction for murder, it was sufficient for a secondary party to have realised, in the course of a joint enterprise, that the primary party might kill with intent to do so or with intent to cause grievous bodily harm. This principle was applied in *R v Uddin* [1998] 2 All ER 744 where the Court of Appeal took the opportunity to explain in detail the principles to be applied for accessory liability.

Initially, when Amy gives Betty the gun with the instructions 'not to hesitate to use it' she would be committing the crime of incitement to murder, mere encouragement to commit the crime with the appropriate contemplation being sufficient. However, as Betty has committed the offence this makes Amy an abettor. From the facts she cannot argue that the unlawful homicide was not contemplated or outside the scope of the agreement, but she could contend that she had effectively withdrawn before the murder took place. The key case on withdrawal is *R v Becerra and Cooper* (1975) 62 Cr App R 212, where before the principal offender in the course of a burglary killed the victim, the accomplice had said 'Come on let's go' and had left the building. The Court of Appeal, in upholding his conviction for murder, held that something vastly more substantial and effective was required to constitute a valid withdrawal, such as shouting a warning or physical intervention. Amy would argue that in shouting 'Don't shoot' and knocking Betty's hand, she had done all that she reasonably could to prevent the crime, but it is likely that the jury will conclude that her actions were too little too late. The prosecution could also argue that withdrawal should not be available as a defence as Amy does not have a good motive. However, in keeping with the general principle that motive is irrelevant in criminal law, this is not a requirement for the defence to succeed.

If Betty was found guilty of manslaughter, Amy might contend that she could not be found guilty of the more serious offence of abetting murder. This point arose in the Privy Council case of *Hui Chi Ming* v *R* [1991] 3 All ER 897, where the court upheld the conviction of the accused for murder even though the principal offenders had in an earlier trial been found guilty of manslaughter only. The principle is that if the *actus reus* has been committed, the court will look at the *mens rea* of the individual participants in order to ascertain their criminal responsibility.

Claire could argue that she cannot be guilty of abetting murder as she did not know that Betty had a gun, and therefore Betty's actions were outside the scope of the agreement. In *Davies* v *DPP* [1954] AC 378, the court stated that if there was a fight where the participants agreed to use fists only, but the principal offender stabbed the victim to death with a knife, the other gang members would not be guilty of abetting murder. Although they had agreed to use violence and may have contemplated death or serious injury, the court recognised that there was a difference between an agreement to use fists and an agreement to use weapons. Thus, if death was caused by the first blow, this would be an unforeseen consequence but within the scope of the agreement and the gang members would have been guilty of abetting murder. The scope of the agreement is all important, and if the prosecution cannot prove that Claire knew Betty had a gun, she cannot be guilty of abetting murder.

However, the prosecution could still contend that as Claire knew that there was a nightwatchman, she would have contemplated the risk of some physical violence; and that as there was an unlawful and dangerous act causing death, she should be found guilty of the lesser offence of abetting manslaughter. This is a point on which the authorities appear equally divided. In *R* v *Dunbar* [1995] 1 All ER 781, the Court of Appeal quashed an abettor's conviction for manslaughter on the basis that even though she contemplated some physical harm, she was exonerated of all criminal responsibility regarding the victim's death when the principal offender deliberately killed the victim. This decision followed a principle established in *R* v *Anderson and Morris* [1966] 2 All ER 644. However, in *R* v *Stewart and Schofield* [1995] 1 Cr App R 441 (following *R* v *Reid* (1975) 62 Cr App R 109) the Court of Appeal stated that in such circumstances the abettor could be guilty of abetting manslaughter, although this was certified as a point of law of public importance for the House of Lords to resolve. Unfortunately this point was not considered by the House in *Powell and English*, but the Court of Appeal in *R* v *Gilmour* [2000] 2 Cr App R 407, upheld the conviction of an accessory to manslaughter although the principal offender was guilty of murder.

Because Debbie knows that Betty has a gun she is in a much worse position than Claire, as it appears that Betty is acting within the scope of their agreement. Debbie would be forced to use the weak argument that although she knew that they had a gun, she did not contemplate that they would actually use it. In *R* v *Baldessare* (1930) 22 Cr App R 70, the court held that an accused who agreed to take and drive away a car was guilty of abetting manslaughter when the principal offender drove so negligently as to cause a pedestrian's death, as although this consequence was unforeseen it arose when the principal offender was acting within the scope of the agreement. It is submitted that Debbie will be found guilty of abetting murder.

Q Question 2

Alf planned to beat up Steve. Barry, Chris and Desmond told Alf that they would help him. On the appointed day, Barry failed to turn up, but Chris and Desmond held Steve while Alf hit him causing some minor bruising. Chris then said 'I can't do this anymore' and walked away to the other side of the room. Shortly after, Desmond said 'Come on let's go' and he left with Chris. Alf then hit Steve again, breaking his jaw.

Discuss the criminal responsibility of the parties.

Commentary

The criminal responsibility of accessories appears to be an area of the law that is in a state of transition. The Court of Appeal has certified many points of law of public importance on this topic which have remained unanswered, and the Law Commission have produced a consultation paper (No. 131) with proposals to change the nature of accomplice liability.

All this does not lead to certainty, and therefore this is a good area for an examination question. A good answer will deal with the *mens rea* required for an accomplice, but will then concentrate on the question of withdrawal, another topic where there has been a spate of cases. In addition you must deal with the criminal responsibility of Alf for offences under the Offences Against the Person Act 1861.

* **Conspiracy to assault**

* **s. 47, Offences Against the Person Act 1861**

* **s. 18, Offences Against the Person Act 1861**

* **Accomplice liability** — *Powell* [1997]
    - *Stewart and Schofield* [1995]
    - Withdrawal: *Rook* [1993], *Baker* [1994]

:Q: Suggested answer

Although there is a possibility that all four participants could be charged with conspiracy to assault under s. 1 of the Criminal Law Act 1977, as the court might consider that there is an agreement between them, it is more likely that Alf will be charged as a principal offender and the other three as accessories.

Alf, when he deliberately hits Steve causing him some bruising, would be guilty of assault occasioning actual bodily harm under s. 47 of the Offences Against the Person Act 1861. This offence is very easily established by the prosecution who only need to prove that an accused had the *mens rea* for common assault in order to satisfy the *mens rea* requirement under s. 47 (*R v Savage and Parmenter* [1991] 4 All ER 698). However, as Alf hit Steve again breaking his jaw, he would be charged under s. 18 of the 1861 Act with wounding or causing grievous bodily harm with intent. Whether this constitutes grievous bodily harm is a question of fact for the jury, but in *R v Wood* (1830) 1 Mood CC 278, a broken collar bone was held to constitute grievous bodily harm. The prosecution also must establish that Alf intended to cause grievous bodily harm, but it appears from the facts of the question that either this was Alf's purpose, or he knew that grievous bodily harm was a virtual certainty, and this would be sufficient. The House of Lords stated in *R v Moloney* [1985] 1 All ER 1025 that as 'intention' is a word in common use, the trial judge should simply leave it to the jury without giving them an involved direction unless the issue on the facts of the case is complicated. It is submitted that the jury would not require guidance on these facts and would be most likely to convict Alf under s. 18.

In the unlikely event of the prosecution not being able to establish intention, Alf would be convicted under s. 20 of the 1861 Act (wounding or inflicting grievous bodily harm maliciously); 'maliciously', the *mens rea*, can be satisfied by the prosecution proving that Alf intended or foresaw the risk of some physical harm (not necessarily grievous bodily harm: *R v Savage and Parmenter*).

Barry, Chris and Desmond could therefore be charged with abetting an offence under s. 18 of the Offences Against the Person Act 1861. The Accessories and Abettors

Act 1861, s. 8 provides: 'Whosoever shall aid, abet, counsel or procure the commission of any indictable offence shall be liable to be tried, indicted, and punished as a principal offender.' The prosecution must also prove that the accused intended to assist with knowledge of the type of crime intended (*DPP for Northern Ireland* v *Maxwell* [1978] 3 All ER 1140). However, difficulties arise when the crime committed by the principal offender is more serious than initially envisaged by the abettors. Thus if the principal offender deliberately exceeds the scope of the agreement, the accomplices may be exonerated (*Davies* v *DPP* [1954] 1 All ER 507). Nevertheless, if the court concludes that they were all acting with a common purpose and as part of a joint enterprise, the accomplices may be guilty if they contemplated the consequence (provided it was more than a fleeting thought) or gave tacit authorisation to the principal offender (*Chan Win Siu* v *R* [1984] 3 All ER 877). Thus accomplices would be guilty of murder if they realised that the primary party might kill with intent to do so or with intent to cause grievous bodily harm (*R* v *Powell and English* [1997] 4 All ER 545).

The difficulties are illustrated by the case of *R* v *Wan and Chan* [1995] Crim LR 295. D1 and D2 were alleged to have arranged for V to be beaten up. They were convicted of abetting an offence under s. 20, but were acquitted of abetting an offence under s. 18; and their appeal against conviction for abetting the s. 20 offence succeeded on the basis that the jury (in acquitting them of abetting the s. 18 offence) must have concluded that the principal offender exceeded the scope of the agreement and therefore D1 and D2 should be exonerated in respect of the charge of abetting an offence under s. 20. The Court of Appeal did, however, certify the following point of law of public importance: 'If two people have agreed to assault another, and in the course of the assault one of them causes grievous bodily harm and intends to do so, can the other be guilty of section 20 of the Offences Against the Person Act 1861 even if he was not present and did not intend to cause grievous bodily harm or contemplate that it might be used?'

However, in *R* v *Stewart and Schofield* [1995] 3 All ER 159, the Court of Appeal held that if the participant in a joint enterprise contemplates that the victim will suffer bodily harm, but the principal offender with the *mens rea* for murder kills the victim, the participant can still be convicted of manslaughter. This was also the outcome in the Court of Appeal decision in *R* v *Gilmour* [2000] 2 Cr App R 407, where the agreement was to post an incendiary bomb through a letterbox. The principal offender was guilty of murder, but as the accessory foresaw only minor physical harm, he was guilty of aiding and abetting manslaughter.

It is submitted that, on the facts, the jury would most likely decide that Barry, Chris and Desmond did contemplate some physical harm, and this would appear sufficient for a conviction of at least abetting a s. 20 offence. However, the accused may be able to use the defence of withdrawal. Barry would appear to have the strongest argument because he was not present when the crime was committed. Nevertheless, his earlier involvement is enough to constitute counselling (*Attorney-General's Reference (No. 1 of 1975)* [1975] QB 773); and in *R v Rook* [1993] 2 All ER 955, the Court of Appeal on similar facts stated that 'his absence on the day could not possibly amount to an unequivocal communication of his withdrawal'. As Rook knew that there was a real risk that the murder would take place, his conviction was upheld.

In order to constitute a valid withdrawal there must be evidence that the accomplice has taken all reasonable steps unequivocally to abandon the enterprise. This will depend on the accomplice's involvement. Thus in *R v Whitefield* (1984) 79 Cr App R 36, where the accomplice had given the principal offender information that would enable him to commit burglary, the Court of Appeal recognised that a valid withdrawal could be effected by the accomplice simply telling the principal offender that he was no longer prepared to assist. On the other hand, in *R v Becerra* (1975) 62 Cr App R 212, the leading case on withdrawal, the Court of Appeal stated that something vastly more substantial and effective was required than simply saying 'Come on let's go' and leaving, where the accomplice had given the principal offender a weapon, which he later used to kill a nightwatchman who interrupted their burglary. The court stated that to be an effective withdrawal, the accomplice should have tried to recover the weapon, shouted a warning to the victim, or physically intervened to prevent the attack. Similarly in *R v Baker* [1994] Crim LR 444, the Court of Appeal, in upholding a murder conviction, stated that an accomplice who had moved a few feet away from the spot where the victim was killed, uttering words 'I'm not doing it', had given far from unequivocal notice that he was wholly disassociating himself from the entire enterprise and had not effected a valid withdrawal.

Applying these principles, it appears that there is no difference between the responsibility of the three accomplices. Although they can argue that they were not actually present when the accused committed the s. 18 offence, it is submitted that they would all be found guilty of abetting this offence.

Q Question 3

Alvin contacted Bernard suggesting that they kill Zac because he had refused to pay them a debt. After hearing Alvin's proposals, Bernard secretly decided that he would not do anything to help Alvin, but he told Alvin that he would do anything he could to assist. Their conversation was overheard by Ceri and Desmond, who both agreed to help. Ceri obtained a loaded revolver and gave it to Alvin, and Desmond agreed to drive them in his car to Zac's house.

On the appointed day, Bernard failed to arrive; and after Desmond had taken them to their destination he telephoned the police in time to stop Alvin shooting at Zac.

Discuss the criminal responsibility of the parties.

Commentary

This is a relatively straightforward question concerning the inchoate offences and accomplice liability. The two areas often overlap, but in practice if the substantive offence was attempted or committed the Crown Prosecution Service would usually charge the participants as accomplices. If not, they will be charged with the inchoate offences.

This question requires you to consider incitement, conspiracy and attempt with regard to Alvin, although, as there is little factual information surrounding the attempted shooting, you cannot deal with this topic in great detail. The others could be guilty of conspiracy, and for Bernard you must consider the troublesome House of Lords' decision in *R v Anderson* [1985] 2 All ER 961 as interpreted by the Court of Appeal in *R v Siracusa* (1989) 90 Cr App R 340.

Lastly, the position of the parties' liability for abetting must be considered, in particular whether there is an offence of aiding and abetting an attempt.

* **Incitement**

* **Conspiracy to murder**
  * *Anderson* [1985], *Siracusa* [1989]

* **Attempted murder**
  * s. 1(1), Criminal Attempts Act 1981

* **Accomplice liability**

⚡ Suggested answer

There are a number of inchoate offences with which Alvin could be charged. His initial action in contacting Bernard suggesting that they kill Zac could amount to the crime of incitement to murder. An inciter is one who reaches and seeks to influence the mind of another by suggestion, request, proposal, argument, persuasion or inducement. Thus in *Invicta Plastics Ltd* v *Clare* [1976] Crim LR 131, a company who simply advertised the sale of a device 'Radatec' which could be used to detect police radar traps, was found guilty of incitement of an offence under s. 1(1) of the Wireless Telegraphy Act 1949. The prosecution must prove that Alvin knew of, or was wilfully blind to, the circumstances of the act incited that constituted the crime. This includes knowing that the person incited will act with the appropriate *mens rea* of the crime in question. It is submitted that Alvin's conduct clearly satisfies the *actus reus* of incitement, and the prosecution should be able to establish *mens rea*. The old common law offence of inciting a conspiracy was abolished by s. 5(7) of the Criminal Law Act 1977, but incitement to incite is still an offence (*R v Sirat* (1986) 83 Cr App R 41).

All four participants could be charged with conspiracy to murder under s. 1 of the

Criminal Law Act 1977. Formerly conspiracy was a common law offence, but since 1977 the only remaining common law conspiracies are conspiracy to defraud, conspiracy to corrupt public morals, and conspiracy to outrage public decency (see *Shaw* v *DPP* [1961] 2 All ER 446). In order to establish a statutory conspiracy, it must be shown that two or more persons agreed that a course of conduct should be pursued which, if the agreement were to be carried out in accordance with their intentions, either:

(a) would necessarily amount to or involve the commission of any offence or offences by one or more of the parties to the agreement; or

(b) would do so but for the existence of facts which render the commission of the offence or any of the offences impossible.

The prosecution must prove that an agreement existed between the parties, and if they are still in the course of negotiations this would not be sufficient. It is submitted that there is an agreement on the facts and, as they intend that death will result, the parties could be guilty of conspiracy to murder. However, Bernard will argue that as he had no intention to assist, and did nothing to assist, he cannot be guilty. The key case on this point is the House of Lords' decision in *R* v *Anderson* [1985] 2 All ER 961. In this case the accused was convicted of conspiring with a number of people to help one of them escape from jail. He had agreed to supply wire to cut the prison bars, but said he never intended the plan to be put into effect and believed that it could not possibly succeed. However, his conviction was upheld as he had agreed that the criminal course of conduct should be pursued, and it was not necessary to prove that he intended that the offence be committed. In this case Lord Bridge also stated (at p. 965) that the *mens rea* of conspiracy is established 'if and only if it is shown that the accused when he entered into the agreement, intended to play some part in the agreed course of conduct in furtherance of the criminal purpose which the agreed course of conduct was intended to achieve'. On this basis Bernard would have a defence, but unfortunately for him Lord Bridge's *dictum* was clarified by the Court of Appeal decision in *R* v *Siracusa* (1989) 90 Cr App R 340, where O'Connor J stated that 'participation in a conspiracy is infinitely variable: it can be active or passive. There is no need for the prosecution to prove an intention on each accused's part in the carrying out of the agreement'. It is submitted that Bernard would therefore be found guilty of conspiracy to murder.

Desmond may also be able to argue that he lacked the *mens rea* for conspiracy to murder, as his informing the police demonstrated that he had an intention to frustrate the intention of the conspiracy. In *R* v *McPhillips* [1990] 6 BNIL, Lord Lowry CJ in the Court of Appeal of Northern Ireland, held that an accused who had joined in a conspiracy to plant a bomb, timed to explode on the roof of a hall of a disco, was not a party to a conspiracy to murder because he intended to give a warning in time for the hall to be cleared. However, in *Yip Chiu Cheung* v *R* [1994] 2 All ER 924, the Privy Council held that an undercover police officer posing as a drug dealer would have the necessary *mens rea* for conspiracy, when he deliberately carried drugs to entrap other drug dealers. Neither his good motive nor the instructions of his superiors would have been a valid defence.

As withdrawal is recognised as a defence for an accomplice, it is submitted that a conspirator should have a similar defence, if only to provide an incentive for a conspirator to make efforts to stop the conspiracy succeeding. It is submitted that Desmond should not be found guilty of conspiracy. Perhaps the Crown Prosecution Service would decide it is not in the public interest to prosecute Desmond, and instead make him chief prosecution witness!

Alvin may also be guilty of attempted murder. Clearly he has the necessary *mens rea*, an intention to kill (*R* v *Whybrow* (1951) 35 Cr App R 141), but has he committed the *actus reus* of attempt? The test the prosecution must satisfy under s. 1(1) of the Criminal Attempts Act 1981 is that the accused has done an act that is more than merely preparatory to the offence. This is a question of fact for the jury after the trial judge has decided that there is sufficient evidence to be left to them to support such a finding. Thus in *R* v *Jones* (1990) 91 Cr App R 356, the Court of Appeal upheld the jury's decision that the accused had done more than a merely preparatory act for attempted murder in pointing a sawn-off shotgun at the victim, even though he had still to remove the safety catch. Whether Alvin would be guilty of attempted murder would therefore purely depend on what precise point the plan had reached before he was stopped.

Bernard, Ceri and Desmond may also face charges under the Accessories and Abettors Act 1861 of counselling, procuring, aiding and abetting. It is often difficult to identify precisely the specific involvement (see *R* v *Richards* [1974] 3 All ER 1088), but counselling and procuring are acts done before the principal offence whereas aiding and abetting take place at the time of its occurrence. Clearly, as they intended to assist and contemplated the type of crime (*Chan Wing Siu* v *R* [1984] 3 All ER 877) they appear to have the necessary *mens rea*. Desmond would argue that he had validly withdrawn by contacting the police in time for them to stop the murder (*R* v *Becerra* (1975) 62 Cr App R 212), and Bernard would contend that his failure to arrive constituted a withdrawal. It is submitted that whereas Desmond's argument would succeed, Bernard's would fail as in *R* v *Rook* [1993] 2 All ER 963, the Court of Appeal held merely not turning up to be insufficient, suggesting that a positive act may be required. Ceri does not appear to have any defence available, and his act of giving Alvin a loaded gun satisfies the ingredients of this offence.

Thus, Ceri and Bernard could be found guilty of abetting an attempted murder. Although the offence of attempt to aid and abet was abolished by s. 5 of the Criminal Law Act 1977, there is an offence of attempting to abet (see *R* v *Dunnington* [1984] 1 All ER 676).

Q Question 4

(a) Oliver and Pam, his wife, decide to remedy their financial problems by trying to obtain money fraudulently from Oliver's life assurance company. Oliver fakes his death by disappearing, while Pam (after informing the company that Oliver has died) asks for and receives a claims form to complete. However, before she returns the completed form Pam breaks down under the insurance company's agent's questioning.

Discuss the criminal responsibility of Oliver and Pam.

(b) Norman encouraged Ray to kill Violet. Norman gave Ray a substance which both believed to be a deadly poison capable of killing Violet. Ray went to Violet's house with a drink containing the poison, intending to make Violet drink it. However, when Ray knocked on the front door he was told that Violet had died one week earlier. Ray in a fit of remorse confessed to the police, who analysed the drink and discovered it was incapable of causing death.

Discuss the criminal responsibility of Norman and Ray.

Commentary

This two-part question concentrates on the inchoate offence of attempt, but also requires reference to conspiracy (in (a)) and incitement (in (b)). Both parts require consideration of whether the *actus reus* of attempt has been completed, and although the test is clearly stated in the Criminal Attempts Act 1981, the recent cases demonstrate that it is difficult to apply in practice. The most important of these decisions are covered in the answer.

The other troublesome aspect of attempt, impossibility, must also be covered in answering (b). Again, reference to the provisions of the Criminal Attempts Act 1981 must be made, together with the contrast for incitement. The two key cases on this point — R v *Fitzmaurice* [1983] 1 All ER 189 and R v *Shivpuri* [1985] 1 All ER 143 — must be covered.

(a)

- s. 15, Theft Act 1968 — consider

- Attempt — s. 1, Criminal Attempts Act 1981

  - *Campbell* [1990]

  - *Widdowson* [1985]

(b)

- Incitement to murder

- Impossibility — *Fitzmaurice* [1983]

- Attempted murder
  - s. 1(1), Criminal Attempts Act 1981
  - impossibility — *Shivpuri* [1985]

:Ợ: Suggested answer

(a) If Oliver and Pam had succeeded in obtaining the insurance money, they would have been guilty of obtaining property by deception under s. 15 of the Theft Act 1968. Although there was a clear agreement to defraud the company, they cannot be found guilty of conspiracy because s. 2 of the Criminal Law Act 1977 prevents husbands and wives conspiring with one another when there is no other person involved (*R v Chrastny* [1992] 1 All ER 189). This controversial rule has been criticised by the Law Commission, and its continued existence is surprising in view of the fact that spouses can conspire with one another for the tort of conspiracy. Oliver and Pam would therefore be charged with an attempt to obtain property by deception under s. 1 of the Criminal Attempts Act 1981. Although recklessness can suffice for the substantive offence, intention as to consequence (but not necessarily circumstances) must be established for attempt. In *R v Pearman* (1984) 80 Cr App R 259, this was defined as 'a decision to bring about, in so far as it lies within the accused's power, the commission of the offence which it is alleged the accused attempted to commit, no matter whether the accused desired that consequence of his act or not'. Clearly the prosecution will have no problem in establishing the parties' *mens rea*.

However, the situation is less clear in applying the test for *actus reus*. Under s. 1(1) of the Criminal Attempts Act 1981, it must be shown that the accused has done an act that is more than merely preparatory to the commission of the offence. This is a question to be determined by the jury after the trial judge has decided that there is sufficient evidence for them to consider (s. 4(3)). It can sometimes produce surprising results. Thus in *R v Campbell* (1990) 93 Cr App R 350, a jury convicted an accused of attempted robbery, when he was arrested on the entrance steps of a post office armed with an imitation gun and a ransom demand which he intended to give to the cashier. Nevertheless, the Court of Appeal quashed his conviction on the ground that there was insufficient evidence for the trial judge to leave the question of attempt to the jury!

Before the 1981 Act many different tests had been suggested for determining the *actus reus* of attempt. In *DPP v Stonehouse* [1977] 2 All ER 909, Lord Diplock, commenting on the proximity test, stated that only acts immediately connected with the offence could be attempts: 'In other words the offender must have crossed the Rubicon and burnt his boats'. However, this was rejected in *R* v *Gullefer* [1990] 3 All ER 882, where Lord Lane referred to an alternative test formulated by Stephen (*Digest of Criminal Law*, 5th edn, 1894): 'an attempt to commit a crime is an act done with intent to commit that crime and forming part of a series of acts which constitute its actual commission, if it were not interrupted'.

The pre-1981 Act tests no longer apply, but it is likely that juries in applying the statutory test are likely to reach the same decisions as their predecessors. Thus Oliver is likely to be found guilty on analogy with *DPP* v *Stonehouse*. In this case the House of Lords upheld the conviction of the accused in similar circumstances to Oliver's. Stonehouse had faked his death by appearing to drown off the coast of Miami, knowing his death would be reported and that his wife would make a claim on his life assurance policy. Although he argued that merely disappearing could not constitute the *actus reus* of attempt, the House of Lords stated that as he had done the last act he had to do, knowing that the ensuing chain of events (if successful) would result in the money being paid to his wife, this was enough.

On the other hand, on analogy with *R* v *Robinson* [1915] 2 KB 342, Pam might escape conviction. In this case a jeweller, who was insured against theft, faked a burglary intending to make a fraudulent insurance claim. However, before he submitted the claims form he broke down under police questioning and admitted his plan. His conviction was quashed. Similarly, the accused in *Comer* v *Bloomfield* (1970) 55 Cr App R 305, who in similar circumstances had actually obtained a claims form but had not submitted it, was acquitted. Both these cases are pre-1981, and although in *Stonehouse* the House of Lords suggested that they might be too favourable to the accused, the Court of Appeal in *R* v *Widdowson* (1985) 82 Cr App R 314 quashed a conviction of attempt to obtain services by deception, where an accused had written to a finance company, giving a false name and salary, requesting information on credit facilities. The court held that such conduct could amount to mere preparation only and was not sufficient to constitute an attempt.

It is therefore submitted, in the light of similar decisions, that Oliver would be found guilty of attempting to obtain property by deception; but Pam would not have committed more than a merely preparatory act and would therefore be not guilty.

(b) Norman, in encouraging Ray to kill Violet, could be committing the crime of incitement to murder; and Ray, in going to Violet's house in this way, could be guilty of attempted murder. The mere incitement of another to commit an offence is a crime, whether the incitement is successful or not. Clearly the *actus reus* of the offence has been committed, and as Norman intends to bring about Violet's unlawful death the *mens rea* is satisfied. However, Norman will argue that as Violet had already died, he has the defence of impossibility.

The House of Lords in *DPP* v *Nock* [1978] 2 All ER 654, decided that impossibility is a general defence at common law, and this was confirmed by the Court of Appeal decision in *R* v *Fitzmaurice* [1983] 1 All ER 189. In this case the defence failed, as it was possible on the facts for the actual crime incited to take place. However, Neill J said:

> If B and C agree to kill D and A, standing beside B and C, though not intending to take any active part whatever in the crime, encourages them to do so, we can see no satisfactory reason, if it turns out later that D was already dead, why A should be convicted of incitement to murder whereas B and C at common law would be entitled to an acquittal on a charge of conspiracy.

It is submitted, therefore, that if at the time when Norman encouraged Ray, Violet was actually dead, Norman could not be guilty of incitement; but if Violet was then alive but died later, impossibility would not succeed and Norman would be guilty.

Although Ray would have the same argument of impossibility, he will be in a worse position as he will be charged with attempted murder under s. 1(1) of the Criminal Attempts Act 1981. The prosecution must prove that he has done more than a merely preparatory act and that he had an intention to kill; an intention to cause grievous bodily harm is not sufficient for attempted murder (*R* v *Whybrow* (1951) 35 Cr App R 141). It is a question of fact for the jury whether the accused's acts are more than merely preparatory, but most juries given such evidence normally conclude that they are, even if the Court of Appeal later disagrees. See, for example, the surprising case of *R* v *Campbell* (1990) 93 Cr App R 350.

Ray has two arguments regarding impossibility, the first being that Violet could not have been killed even if she had taken the drink. This point on impossibility of means, arose in the case of *R* v *White* (1910) 4 Cr App R 257, where the accused put potassium cyanide into a drink with intent to murder his mother. Although medical evidence established that she died not as a result of taking the drink, but of heart failure, the accused was convicted of attempted murder. There was some dispute as to whether the quantity of poison in the drink was in fact capable of killing the victim, but the court suggested that even if this was the case the accused would still be found guilty.

Ray's second argument, that Violet was already dead, might well have succeeded under the old common law provisions (*Haughton* v *Smith* [1973] 3 All ER 1109), but the position is now governed by s. 1(2) and s. 1(3) of the 1981 Act. Section 1(2) states that 'a person may be guilty of attempting to commit an offence to which this section applies even though the facts are such that the commission of the offence is impossible'; and s. 1(3) has the effect that the accused is to be judged on the facts as the accused believed them to be.

These provisions were analysed in great detail by the House of Lords in *R* v *Shivpuri* [1985] 1 All ER 143, where the House overruled its earlier decision in *Anderton* v *Ryan* [1985] 2 All ER 355. In *Shivpuri* the House of Lords upheld the accused's conviction for attempt to import a controlled drug. He had believed that he was in possession of heroin, which proved on analysis to be a harmless substance akin to snuff. However, the fact that he believed it was a prohibited drug was sufficient for a conviction of attempt. Thus, on application of these provisions, Norman and Ray are guilty of conspiracy to murder and Ray of attempted murder.

In respect of Ray's criminal responsibility, it is therefore irrelevant whether Violet was already dead when he was incited by Norman, or whether she died afterwards. In either case, on application of the Criminal Attempts Act 1981 and the House of Lords' decision in *R* v *Shivpuri*, provided the jury are satisfied that Ray's conduct constitutes more than a merely preparatory act, he will be guilty of attempted murder.

Q Question 5

Fred decides to take his family and friends for a meal at an expensive restaurant. However, as he is penniless he informs them of a plan to enable them to leave without paying, and they agree to it.

Thus Fred, his wife Bonnie, their sons Clive (aged 13) and Dave (aged nine), together with Eric, their friend (who is, unknown to them, a police informer), go to a restaurant, consume a meal and tell their waitress they have already paid their bill, which is untrue. Then they all walk out without paying. Eric immediately contacts the police and they are all arrested.

Discuss the criminal liability of the parties.

Commentary

The question involves conspiracy and the Theft Act 1978. Both are difficult topics that are generally disliked by students, although questions involving these topics can usually yield high marks to the well-prepared candidate. You must consider statutory and common law conspiracy to defraud, and consider the status of the participants. This involves the question whether infants and police informers can be regarded as 'other persons' for the purpose of conspiracy.

There is some overlap between the three offences contained in the 1978 Theft Act, and the answer mentions them all: (i) obtaining services by deception under s. 1; (ii) evasion of liability by deception under s. 2; and (iii) making off without payment under s. 3. The cases of *R* v *Holt* [1981] 2 All ER 584 and *R* v *Brooks and Brooks* (1982) 76 Cr App R 66 are very relevant in this context. All three offences contain the ingredient of dishonesty which is a question of fact for the jury. The pressure of time prevents a detailed analysis of this important issue, but the test under *R* v *Ghosh* [1982] 2 All ER 689 should be stated.

- Conspiracy
  - s. 1, Criminal Law Act 1977

- s. 2, Criminal Law Act 1977
- *Anderson* [1985]
- *Yip Chiu* [1994]
- Entrapment — *Sang* [1979]

- Theft Act 1978

⚙ Suggested answer

At the outset the parties are clearly involved in a conspiracy, i.e., 'an agreement of two or more to do an unlawful act, or a lawful act by unlawful means' (Willis J in *Mulchay* v *R* (1868) LR 3 HL 306). Most charges of conspiracy are under s. 1 of the Criminal Law Act 1977, i.e., where a person agrees with any other person or persons that a course of conduct be pursued which, if their agreement is carried out in accordance with their intentions, will necessarily amount to or involve the commission of an offence, or would do so but for the existence of facts which render the commission of the offence impossible. However, three common law conspiracies still remain: corrupting public morals; outraging public decency; and (the one that might be charged in this situation) conspiracy to defraud. This last was widely defined in *Scott* v *Metropolitan Police Commissioner* [1974] 3 All ER 1032 as 'an agreement by one or more by dishonesty to deprive a person of something which is his or to which he is or might be entitled'.

After difficulties arising from the House of Lords' decision in *R* v *Ayres* [1984] 1 All ER 619, it is now clear that as a result of s. 12 of the Criminal Justice Act 1987, an agreement to commit a crime involving fraud is both a statutory conspiracy and a conspiracy to defraud. So it would be for the Crown Prosecution Service to decide with which type of conspiracy to charge the parties.

However, s. 2 of the Criminal Law Act 1977 states that a person will not be guilty of conspiracy if the only other person with whom he agrees is: (i) a spouse, (ii) a person under the age of criminal responsibility, or (iii) the intended victim of the offence. Fred could therefore argue that Bonnie, as his wife, would not be 'another person', nor would Dave as (being under 10) he is irrebutably presumed to be incapable of committing a crime. In the past, Fred would also have contended that Clive (who is between the ages of 10 and 14) is *doli incapax* and therefore cannot be 'another person'. The House of Lords in *C* v *DPP* [1995] 2 All ER 43 confirmed this principle, but it was abolished by s. 34 of the Crime and Disorder Act 1998. Thus Clive could be guilty of conspiracy.

Eric, the police informer, could be regarded as 'another person'. This is not free from doubt as Lord Bridge in *R* v *Anderson* [1985] 2 All ER 961, in an attempt to stop undercover police operatives and informers being charged with conspiracy, stated that the *mens rea* of conspiracy is established 'if and only if, it is shown that the accused when he entered into the agreement intended to play some part in the agreed course of conduct'. On the other hand, the Court of Appeal in *R* v *Siracusa* [1989] Crim LR 712, stated that participation in a conspiracy can be active or passive; and in *Yip Chiu Cheung* v *R* [1994] 2 All ER 924, the Privy Council held that an undercover police officer who, with his superior's authorisation, transported prohibited drugs in order to entrap other drug dealers, did have the *mens rea* for conspiracy and was 'another person' with whom a co-conspirator (whose conviction was upheld) agreed.

It is therefore submitted that Fred would be guilty of conspiracy as he has agreed with another person, and there is no defence of entrapment available in English law (*R* v *Sang* (1979) 69 Cr App R 282). The criminal responsibility of Eric (in the unlikely event of his being charged) is uncertain, but Betty would be guilty, even though she might have only agreed with her husband Fred, if she knew that there were other parties also involved in the conspiracy (*R* v *Chrastny* [1992] 1 All ER 189).

The parties would also face charges under the Theft Act 1978. Section 1 provides that a person who by any deception dishonestly obtains services from another shall be guilty of an offence. There has clearly been a deception as when Fred ordered a meal at a restaurant he impliedly represented that he would pay for it (*DPP* v *Ray* [1973] 3 All ER 131). However for s. 1, the prosecution must prove that the deception preceded the obtaining of services, and if the accused formed the intention to deceive after consuming the meal s. 1 will not apply. They may there-fore be charged under s. 2 (evasion of liability by deception). They are clearly liable to pay, and in representing to the waitress that they have already paid they are practising a deception. There are three subsections in s. 2 creating three separate (but overlapping) offences. In the identical case of *R* v *Holt* [1981] 2 All ER 854, the accused was convicted under s. 2(1)(b), i.e., 'with intent to make permanent default in whole or in part on any existing liability to make a payment or with intent to let another do so, dishonestly induces the creditor to wait for payment or forgo payment'.

Lastly, an offence under s. 3 would seem to have been committed as the parties have, knowing that payment on the spot for goods supplied or services done was required, dishonestly made off without having paid as required, with intent to avoid payment of the amount due. Whether or not the accused 'makes off' is a question of fact for the jury, but the words are to be given their ordinary meaning. Thus in *R* v *Brooks and Brooks* (1982) 76 Cr App R 66, the accused — who had left a restaurant without paying the bill, but who had voluntarily returned to the restaurant when requested by the manager — were deemed to have made off because they had passed the point where payment was expected.

All three offences require the prosecution to prove that the accused had acted dishonestly. Again, this is a word in common use and a question of fact for the jury (*R* v *Feely* [1973] 1 All ER 341). However, following *R* v *Ghosh* [1982] 2 All ER 689, the jury must consider two questions:

(a) Was what was done dishonest according to the ordinary standards of reasonable and honest people? If not, the accused is not guilty.

(b) If it was, did the accused realise that reasonable and honest people regard what he did as dishonest? If so, he is guilty; if not, he is not guilty.

It is submitted that Fred would be held to be dishonest, but both Betty and Clive could argue either that they were under no liability to make payment (the liability being Fred's) or that they honestly believed that Fred was treating them. Such belief does not have to be on reasonable grounds (*R v Small* [1987] Crim LR 777), although in view of their criminal agreement, it is submitted that this argument is unlikely to succeed. Dave, being under the age of criminal responsibility, will not be guilty.

Further reading

Clarkson, C., 'Complicity, Powell and Manslaughter' [1998] Crim LR 556.

Dennis, I.H., 'The Rationale of Criminal Conspiracy' [1997] 93 LQR 39.

Law Commission Consultation Paper No. 131 — 'Assisting and Encouraging Offenders'.

Smith, J.C. [1998] Crim LR 231.

Smith, K.J.M., 'Withdrawal in Complicity' [2001] Crim LR 769.

Theft and criminal damage

Introduction

Unlike other areas of the criminal law syllabus, both theft and criminal damage are governed by comparatively modern legislative measures: the Theft Act 1968 and the Criminal Damage Act 1971. The Theft Act 1968 was enacted to replace complex larceny laws. As Lord Diplock observed in *R v Treacey* [1971] AC 537: 'the Theft Act 1968 makes a welcome departure from the former style of drafting in criminal statutes. It is expressed in a simple language as used and understood by ordinary literate men and women. It avoids as far as possible those terms of art which have acquired a special meaning understood only by lawyers in which many of the final enactments which it supersedes were couched'.

Whatever Parliament's good intentions, however, the operation of the Theft Act 1968 in practice has thrown up many difficulties. Principal amongst these is the problem of consensual appropriation. Can a defendant steal property even though the 'victim' is giving it to her willingly? If the victim is deceived into parting with the property a deception charge should be brought. The problem cases have proved to be those where the defendant is seen to have behaved dishonestly in persuading the owner to transfer property, but no deception can be proved.

As a result of decisions such as *R v Hinks* [2000] 4 All ER 833, it is now possible for a defendant to be guilty of theft even though the victim validly transferred property to the defendant. The effect of this decision is that a civil court may declare that there was a valid gift of property from V to A, and therefore A has become the owner of that property, but this will not prevent a criminal court from holding that A had still dishonestly appropriated that property and is therefore guilty of stealing it. When you consider that theft is a property offence and ownership of property is a civil law issue, it is remarkable that the House of Lords has confirmed this approach.

This situation is partly the draftsmen's fault, but also stems from the fact that the law of theft is dependent on civil concepts of ownership, possession and passing of property — complicated topics which are constantly being analysed and altered by the civil courts (e.g., does a bribe received by an employee belong to the employer: *Attorney-General for Hong Kong v Reid* [1994] 1 All ER 1). As Lord Lane recognised in *Attorney-General's Reference (No. 1 of 1985)* [1986] 2 All ER 219: 'There are topics of conversation more popular in public houses than the finer points of the equitable doctrine of the constructive trust'. Yet knowledge of this topic is essential in determining if the accused is under a legal obligation to retain and deal with property in a particular way.

In approaching theft problems it pays to be methodical. Go through the five elements in turn. Some parts can be dealt with in a sentence without any reference to authority, others will require considerable coverage. Candidates often ask how they are to know which parts of the question require depth, and which can be dealt with quickly. The answer is really self-evident. If the point is an obvious one it will not provide many marks — state the obvious and move on. If the point is tricky and can be argued a number of ways — it requires depth (and will attract more marks). Deal with the *actus reus* first. If there is no property belonging to another there may be little need to consider *mens rea*. Bear in mind that the combined effects of the House of Lords' rulings on appropriation is that virtually anything can now be appropriation — hence this element will rarely be in doubt. Sections 5(3) and 5(4) of the Theft Act 1968 can raise tricky issues about when property passes, so be prepared to deal with these.

Because of the way the law of theft has developed, however, it is increasingly dishonesty that becomes the crucial issue. Candidates should remember that if they are considering liability for theft, s. 2(1)(a)–(c) of the 1968 Act should be considered first. If a defendant can show that he was not dishonest because he comes within one of the three exceptions there will be no need to consider *R* v *Ghosh* [1982] QB 1053. As regards intention to permanently deprive, remember that in most cases it will be self-evident. Resort should only be had to s. 6(1) and 6(2) in cases of difficulty where the defendant needs to be deemed to have intention to permanently deprive. Avoid a common mistake that candidates make. There is no need to prove that the owner was permanently deprived. The prosecution needs to prove the defendant's state of mind.

Criminal damage

Whilst theft questions nearly always appear on criminal law exam papers, criminal damage is more likely to arise as part of a question. Note in particular that it may be used as the unlawful act in cases of constructive manslaughter. Examiners also used to mix criminal damage in with assault questions in order to bring out the divergent approaches to reck-lessness depending on whether the defendant was charged with assault or criminal damage. However, now that *Metropolitan Police Commissioner* v *Caldwell* [1981] 1 All ER 961 no longer holds sway, the House of Lords' decision in *R* v *G* [2003] 4 All ER 765 marking a return to subjective recklessness under the Criminal Damage Act 1971 — that type of question may be less likely. Indeed questions dealing solely with criminal damage may become something of a rarity. That said, some examples are included at the end of this chapter for the purposes of exposition.

There are five offences under the Criminal Damage Act 1971, but by far the two most important for exam purposes are s. 1(1) ('simple' criminal damage) and s. 1(2) ('aggravated' criminal damage). An important point to remember regarding the offence of criminal damage under s. 1(1) is the fact that in addition to the general defences there are two specific defences contained in s. 5(2) and there are many interesting cases interpreting these provisions. Aggravated criminal damage is an odd offence as it is a combination of an offence against property and an offence against the person. It is very useful for the prosecution, as its ingredients are very easily satisfied.

Q Question 1

Brian visits his local store to complete his weekly shopping. He takes a bottle of wine from the shelf and places it in the store's wire container. He intends to find a lower price tag and substitute it for the price tag on the bottle of wine but fearing he is being watched by the store detective, puts the wine back on the shelf. He does, however, swap price tags on a bottle of brandy which he puts in the container; but when he comes to pay for it at the checkout point, the cashier Shirley notices the discrepancy and Brian pays the correct amount.

Shirley, instead of ringing up the money on her till as she is required to do, simply places it in her till, as she intends to take it for herself at the end of her shift.

Doris, another cashier, in breach of the store's instructions, had taken a £20 note from her till, as she needed the money to pay her hairdresser. She paid another £20 note into the till the day after.

Discuss the criminal responsibility of Brian, Doris and Shirley.

Commentary

This is a relatively straightforward theft question. Candidates should tackle the issues in the order in which they occur, looking methodically at the elements of theft. Try to avoid a lengthy explanation of the facts of cases — it is far better to show the examiner that you understand the gist of a decision and that you can apply it to the facts of the problem. You may have to deal with the same element of theft in a number of scenarios within the same question. You need to exercise judgement as to the need to repeat explanations already provided. Often, as for example with dishonesty, different parts of the problem deal with different facets of the concept. As a general point, note that the answer to this question does not require reference to a huge number of authorities. It is better to know a few key cases well and use them wisely, than to bombard the examiner with rafts of cases that add little to the solution of the problem.

* Theft — s. 1, Theft Act 1968

* s. 3, Theft Act 1968 — appropriation
    * *Lawrence* [1971]
    * *Morris* [1983]
    * *Gomez* [1993]

- s. 2, Theft Act 1968 — dishonesty
  - *Ghosh* [1982]

:Q: Suggested answer

Brian may have committed theft simply by placing the bottle of wine in the wire basket provided. At the time in question the bottle of wine is clearly property belonging to another by virtue of ss. 4(1) and 5(1) of the Theft Act 1968. Section 3(1) defines appropriation as any assumption by a person of the rights of an owner. In *R v Morris* [1983] 3 All ER 288, Lord Roskill enlarged upon this in stating that an appropriation could involve any assumption of any right of the owner. Thus simply placing the wine in the wire basket could amount to the *actus reus* of theft. The fact that supermarkets consent to such activity — indeed they invite their customers to use the wire baskets — is neither here nor there. In *Lawrence* v *Metropolitan Police Commissioner* [1970] 3 All ER 933, the House of Lords confirmed that, by omitting the phrase '. . . without the consent of the owner . . . ' from s. 3(1), Parliament had intended to relieve the prosecution of the burden of establishing that a taking of property belonging to another was without the owner's consent.

Assuming the *actus reus* of theft is made out, the prosecution will have to prove that Brian was dishonest when he placed the wine in the wire basket and that he had intention to permanently deprive. As to dishonesty, it is clear from the facts that he intended to swap price labels if he could. On this basis it is hard to see how Brian could claim not to have been dishonest by virtue of any of the 'escape routes' provided by s. 2(1)(a)–(c) of the 1968 Act. There is no evidence that he honestly believed he had the legal right to take the wine in order to swap labels, or that he honestly believed the owner would have consented. There seems little prospect that a jury, following a *R v Ghosh* [1982] QB 1053 direction, would conclude that he had acted dishonestly. At the time he first places the wine in the wire basket Brian does intend to permanently deprive the store of it. The practical difficulty clearly relates to the fact that he replaces the wine on the shelf. In legal terms this is of no importance, once the five elements of theft come together the offence is complete. Brian cannot 'unsteal' the wine by putting it back. In practical terms his replacement of the wine presents evidential difficulties. He will simply assert that he had not made up his mind to keep it. Indeed, unless he confesses, how will the prosecution ever determine that he intended to swap labels at all?

Swapping labels on the bottle of brandy clearly involves the *actus reus* of theft. The brandy is property belonging to another, and the label swapping is an obvious assumption of the rights of the owner; see *R v Morris* (above). Unless Brian claims that his label swapping was a prank designed to induce confusion, there seems little doubt that his appropriation will be found to have been dishonest. Referring again to s. 2(1)(a)–(c) of the 1968 Act, he is not asserting any legal right to swap labels, and cannot claim any belief in the owner's consent. It seems unlikely that any jury would condone such behaviour following a *R* v *Ghosh* (above) direction. If there were any argument as to intention to permanently deprive, the prosecution could rely on s. 6(1) of the 1968 Act, which provides that a defendant can be deemed to have had *means rea* where his intention is to treat the thing as his own to dispose of regardless of the other's rights. It is submitted that swapping price labels would come within the scope of this deeming section.

An alternative, but less obvious charge, would be attempting to obtain property by deception, contrary to s. 1(1) of the Criminal Attempts Act 1981. Presenting the brandy for purchase with the wrong label would be the deception. Brian has clearly taken steps more than merely preparatory to this; see *R* v *Gullefer* (1990) 91 Cr App R 356, and *R* v *Geddes* [1997] Crim LR 894. In fact by taking the brandy to the checkout he has done effectively all he can towards the commission of the offence. He also had the intention to commit the deception offence — hence he satisfies the requirement of the 1981 Act.

Without more evidence as to her state of mind, it appears to be the case that Shirley has committed theft. The money is property — see s. 4(1), and it belongs to her employer. There is no evidence that Brian intends to make Shirley the legal owner of the money. In any event, the prosecution could invoke s. 5(3) of the 1968 Act to assert that Shirley had been under a legal obligation (arising from her contract of employment) to retain and deal with the money in a particular way. Hence the money, throughout, remains property belonging to another. Although, for reasons explained above, appropriation does not require proof of an unauthorised act on the part of the defendant (it is that aspect of *R* v *Morris* that was doubted in subsequent decisions such as *R* v *Gomez* [1993] 1 All ER 1), failing to place the £20 in the cash register would be an obvious assumption of the rights of the owner. As to dishonesty, Shirley could argue that she honestly believed she had a legal right to the money (in lieu of wages?) — see s. 2(1)(a) — but there is no evidential basis for this. It is hard to see any other argument based on s. 2(1) of the 1968 Act, or indeed any argument that could exploit the residual common law *R* v *Ghosh* direction on dishonesty. Were Shirley's actions dishonest according to the ordinary standards of reasonable and honest people? Almost certainly yes. Did Shirley herself realise that what she was doing was by those standards dishonest? Again, there is no evidence to suggest this was not the case.

The evidence that Shirley intended to take the money for herself at the end of the shift is conclusive for the purposes of establishing intention to permanently deprive. No recourse to s. 6(1) of the 1968 Act would be necessary to resolve this issue.

In Doris's case, there clearly was an appropriation of property belonging to another when she took the £20. However, she would argue that she cannot be guilty of theft, because she lacked the necessary *mens rea*. First, the prosecution must prove that her appropriation was dishonest. Generally, returning the economic equivalent would be strong evidence of lack of dishonesty, but s. 2(2) of the 1968 Act states that a person's appropriation may be dishonest notwithstanding that she is willing to pay for the property. Doris might refer to s. 2(1)(b), which provides that D will not be dishonest if

D believes he has the consent of the owner. However, as Doris knows that cashiers are expressly prohibited from taking money from the till, the prosecution may succeed in establishing dishonesty.

If Doris cannot deny dishonesty by reliance on the s. 2(1) 'escape routes' the matter will be dealt with as one of fact for the jury who will decide the issue in accordance with the model direction from *R* v *Ghosh* (above):

(a) Was Doris' conduct dishonest according to the standards of ordinary reasonable people? If not, Doris must be acquitted.

(b) If it was, then was Doris aware that her conduct would be regarded as dishonest by ordinary reasonable people? If so, Doris is guilty; if not, she is not guilty.

The fact that Doris replaced the money may militate against her being found to have been dishonest according to the first limb of the *R* v *Ghosh* test.

Replacing one £20 note with another may not appear to be theft, not least because it appears to negate the element of intention to permanently deprive. However, as the store has been deprived permanently of its original property, the fact that the economic equivalent has been returned does not rule out theft (*R* v *Velumyl* [1989] Crim LR 299). This is recognised by the wording of s. 6(1) of the 1968 Act, which states a person's appropriation 'is nevertheless to be regarded as having the intention of permanently depriving the other of it if his intention is to treat the thing as his own to dispose of regardless of the other's rights; and a borrowing or lending of it may amount to so treating it'. Only if Doris returned exactly the same note could she deny an intention to permanently deprive.

▣ Question 2

Susan owns and runs a convenience store. Martina opens up a rival business in the same shopping precinct. Susan enters Martina's shop and, for fun, swaps price labels on two boxes of chocolates so that a £10 box is now priced at £2, and a £2 box is now priced at £10.

Stephen enters Martina's shop and, unaware of Susan's actions, selects the box of chocolates now (wrongly) priced at £2, knowing full well that it should be priced at £10. Stephen takes the box of chocolates to the counter and buys it for £2. The cashier, Gavin, does not realise that the item is wrongly priced.

Natasha goes to the delicatessen counter in Martina's shop and asks Joanne, the assistant, for six spicy sausages. The sausages cost 50p each. Joanne selects eight spicy sausages by mistake and wraps them up for Natasha. Joanne writes on the bag that it contains six sausages. Aware of Joanne's mistake, Natasha takes the bag to the counter where Gavin, unaware that the bag contains eight, not six, sausages, charges her £3.00.

The following day Martina visits Susan's store and removes a rental DVD without paying the £2.50 hire charge. She returns the DVD the next day having watched the film. At no time did Martina intend to keep the DVD.

Advise the CPS as to the criminal liability, if any, of:

(i)   Susan

(ii) Stephen

(iii) Natasha, and

(iv) Martina

Commentary

This question comprises four incidents, each of which can effectively be dealt with individually. As with all theft questions a methodical examination of each element is required. Candidates find that this sometimes throws up issues that were not immediately apparent. The facts of a problem like this can sometimes present candidates with a choice of advising as to liability for theft or deception. Often the sensible approach is to consider liability for deception first, although given the state of the law regarding appropriation, the distinction between theft and deception offences is often paper thin! Note the way in which civil law concepts come into play in determining criminal liability, for example the contract law of offer and acceptance as regards mis-priced goods. Be prepared to advise that the prosecution may not be able to establish criminal liability for some of these incidents, especially where dishonesty is an issue.

:Q: Suggested answer

Susan's liability

When Susan enters Martina's shop and, for fun, swaps price labels on two boxes of chocolates so that a £10 box is now priced at £2, and a £2 box is now priced at £10 she may have committed the offence of theft contrary to s. 1(1) of the Theft Act 1968. The two boxes of chocolates are clearly property (see s. 4(1)), and can be regarded as belonging to another as against Susan — see s. 5(1) of the 1968 Act. Swapping the price labels over would be regarded as an appropriation of property belonging to another. On the basis of s. 3(1) an appropriation is any assumption of the rights of the owner. In *R* v *Morris* [1983] 3 All ER 288, this was interpreted as any assumption of any right of the owner. There is no need to show an outright taking of the property. Swapping labels is effectively an assumption of the owner's right to determine the level of what contract lawyers would describe as the 'invitation to treat'. Hence the *actus reus* is made out. The live issue is dishonesty. As this was a practical joke it is unlikely that Susan can 'escape' under s. 2(1)(a)–(c) of the 1968 Act. There is no evidence that she honestly believed she had the right in law to play practical jokes, and no evidence that she honestly believed Martina would have consented had she known. Assuming s. 2(1)(a)–(c) does not avail her, the issue of dishonesty will be a question of fact for the jury, directed in accordance with *R* v *Ghosh* [1982] QB 1053:

(1) ... whether *according to the ordinary standards of reasonable and honest people what was done was dishonest*. If it was not dishonest by those standards, that is the end of the matter and the prosecution fails. If it was dishonest by those standards, then the jury must consider

(2) ... whether *the defendant himself must have realised that what he was doing was by those standards dishonest*.

It is hard to tell how a jury might regard Susan's actions. As the value involved is small, and given that there is no direct personal gain for her, a jury might be reluctant to conclude that she was dishonest.

Susan has no actual intention to permanently deprive. The issue is whether she can be deemed to have had this intent by virtue of s. 6(1) of the Theft Act 1968. Is it a situation where it was her intention to treat the property as her own to dispose of regardless of the other's rights? Compare and contrast *R* v *Cahill* [1993] Crim LR 141 and *DPP* v *Lavender* [1993] Crim LR 297 on this point. It could be argued that switching labels is evidence of her treating it as her own to dispose of, as she is creating the risk that someone might buy the goods at an undervalue. On the other hand, there is no disposal as such. This is very much a moot point. Any ambiguity under the statute should be resolved in the defendant's favour, but criminal courts often disregard this maxim.

There are two other possible offences to consider. The first is attempting to obtain property by deception (specifically attempting to enable another person to do so), contrary to s. 1(1) of the Criminal Attempts Act 1981. Susan has arguably taken (more than merely preparatory) steps to this by swapping labels; see *R* v *Gullefer* (1990) 91 Cr App R 356, and *R* v *Geddes* [1997] Crim LR 894. The problem lies with the *means rea* of attempt. The prosecution would have to prove that she intended that another person should obtain the goods by deception. If she was simply playing a joke, this may not be made out.

The second offence is burglary — although this would be a rather artificial charge. If she had the intention to swap labels before entering the store, and if this could be equated with an intention to steal (doubtful, see above), it might be possible to charge her with burglary contrary to s. 9(1)(a) of the Theft Act 1968 — entering a building as a trespasser with intent to steal. By entering intending to switch labels, even as a joke, she would be trespassing as she would be entering for a purpose in excess of the express or implied permission granted to the public at large as customers: see *R* v *Jones and Smith* [1976] 3 All ER 54. Similarly if she does commit theft in swapping labels she could be guilty of burglary under s. 9(1)(b) of the 1968 Act. Having entered a building as a trespasser she committed theft therein.

Stephen's liability

At the time Stephen selects the box of chocolates it is property belonging to another — see s. 4(1) and s. 5(1) of the Theft Act 1968.

Does he obtain the box of chocolates by deception, contrary to s. 15 of the Theft Act 1968, by offering to buy it for £2? It is doubtful whether he is making any representation as to price. He did not switch labels. To establish a deception the prosecution would have to prove that he was, by his conduct, implying that he was an honest customer who believed £2 to be the right price. There is no authority supporting such an extended concept of deception. Hence a deception charge is unlikely.

Turning to his possible liability for theft, did he appropriate the chocolates when he selected the box? As explained above, any assumption of the rights of the owner will suffice. Further, appropriation can be conduct to which the owner consents. In *Lawrence* v *Metropolitan Police Commissioner* [1970] 3 All ER 933, the House of Lords confirmed that, by omitting the phrase '. . . without the consent of the owner . . .' from s. 3(1), Parliament had intended to relieve the prosecution of the burden of establishing that a taking of property belonging to another was without the owner's consent. This has subsequently been reaffirmed in decisions such as *Dobson* v *General Accident (etc) plc* [1990] 3 WLR 1066, and *R* v *Gomez* [1993] 1 All ER 1. The *actus reus* of theft is therefore made out when Stephen selects the chocolates. Was he dishonest? Stephen will rely on s. 2(1)(a) of the 1968 Act, contending that he appropriated the property in the belief that he had, in law, the right to deprive the store of it. If he had studied any contract law he would argue that he believed he had the legal right to select the goods, even though wrongly priced, because the price tag was, in any event, only an invitation to treat. He will contend that anyone could pick up any item in a store and, regardless of the marked price, make an offer to buy it. It is up to the store to decide whether or not to accept the purchaser's offer. It is submitted that this provides a compelling basis from which he can refute dishonesty. The other provisions under s. 2(1)(b) and s. 2(1)(c) are less relevant. Again, if the s. 2(1)(a) argument does not succeed he could still rely on the jury. Directed as per *R* v *Ghosh* (above), the jury might not consider his actions as dishonest. Most people love a bargain and would try to buy an item at a lower price if given the chance.

Given that these facts seem to indicate a possible loophole in the law, the prosecution might seek to rely on the House of Lords' decision in *R* v *Hinks* [2000] 4 All ER 833. In a very questionable ruling, a majority of their Lordships held that a defendant could commit theft even where he acquired a valid title to property under a valid *inter vivos* transfer. In other words a defendant can steal property whilst becoming the owner of it. On this basis it could be argued that, notwithstanding that Stephen becomes the owner of the chocolates when he buys them, he nevertheless appropriates property belonging to another. The prosecution would still have the difficulties outlined above in relation to dishonesty, however.

If deception and theft charges fail, the prosecution might fall back on a charge of making off without payment, contrary to s. 3 of the Theft Act 1978. The offence requires proof that Stephen dishonestly made off without having paid as required or expected, that he knew payment was expected from him, and that he had intent to avoid payment of the amount due. The obvious problem is that he will argue that he did pay as required and expected — he paid the amount requested by the cashier. Even if this issue is surmounted there might still be difficulties in establishing dishonesty: see the *R* v *Ghosh* direction outlined above.

Natasha's liability

Does Natasha steal the sausages when she first takes possession of them? The sausages are property — see s. 4(1). Does property pass to her at the deli counter? Possibly not as she has not yet paid — hence she appropriates by taking them. Does she have *means rea* at this point? As to dishonesty see s. 2(1)(a)–(c) and *R* v *Ghosh* (above). She may believe that it is her good luck that she has been given the extra sausages and that she has the legal right to keep them (see s. 2(1)(a)). She has intention to permanently deprive. If property in the sausages does pass to Natasha at the deli counter, notwithstanding that she has not paid, s. 5(4) of the Theft Act 1968 (property got by mistake), cannot operate to prevent property passing here as she is not under any legal obligation to make restoration of the sausages.

Natasha may commit a deception offence at the checkout. She knows the bag is wrongly labelled but says nothing. She may be committing a deception by her silence accompanied by her conduct — implying that she believes the bag to be correctly marked-up — see *DPP* v *Ray* [1974] AC 370. The difficulty for the prosecution would be in proving that she was making any implied representations — e.g., that the bag is correctly labelled. If so, liability for obtaining property by deception contrary to s. 15 of the Theft Act 1968 could arise. The silence is the implied representation — a false one — hence a deception. The deception induces the cashier to pass property in the goods. *Mens rea* is apparent, subject to the proof of dishonesty as in *R* v *Ghosh*. As with Stephen, Natasha could be charged with making off contrary to s. 3 of the 1978 Act, and could also be charged with theft if *R* v *Hinks* (above) was relied upon by the prosecution. In each of these offences dishonesty might still prove the stumbling block for reasons outlined above.

Martina's liability

Martina cannot incur liability for theft or deception offences if she had no intention to permanently deprive Susan of the DVD. Under s. 6(1) Martina can be *regarded* as having the intention of permanently depriving Susan of the DVD if it was her intention to treat the thing as her own to dispose of regardless of Susan's rights — it is a question of fact whether taking the DVD for one night amounts to a disposal. The court may be persuaded by the argument that it was a borrowing for a period and in circumstances making it equivalent to an outright taking, given that Susan was deprived of the chance of hiring out the DVD whilst Martina had it: see by contrast

R v *Lloyd* [1985] QB 829. If intention to permanently deprive cannot be established the obvious charge is one of making off without payment contrary to s. 3 of the Theft Act 1978 — all elements are present, subject to proof of dishonesty.

Q Question 3

Alison visits her local library to borrow a book. The loan period is three weeks. On her way out of the library she stops at a vending machine to buy a bar of chocolate. She puts a £1 coin (the correct amount) into a vending machine to obtain a bar of chocolate. Because of a malfunctioning of the vending machine 10 bars of chocolate are dispensed. Alison takes all 10 bars.

Alison then visits Grace, her mother. Whilst Grace is busy making a cup of tea Alison takes a silver ornament from the mantelpiece and places it in her pocket intending to sell it later. Whilst they are having tea Grace tells Alison that she has bought her a silver ornament as a present. Grace searches for the ornament but is unable to find it. Alison says nothing about the fact that she has already taken it.

Alison telephones for a taxi to take her home from her mother's house. On arriving at her destination Alison tells the taxi driver that she has no money to pay for the ride. This is untrue. The taxi driver is furious and tells her to get out of his cab. He drives off without having been paid. Three months later Alison comes across the library book and realises that it is overdue. She has not received any reminders from the library so decides to keep the book.

Advise the Crown Prosecution Service as to the possible criminal liability of Alison.

Commentary

A number of discrete incidents here, the library book, the chocolate, the ornament and the taxi ride. Note the need to consider burglary in relation to the ornament. The question involves an issue regarding obtaining property by mistake. Candidates should resist the temptation to automatically bring in s. 5(4) of the 1968 Act. Remember that the subsection only applies where D is under a legal obligation to return the property, circumstances that normally only arise where money is received by mistake. Take care over the deception in relation to the taxi ride. Examiners often leave the issue open — liability depending on when D decided not to pay. If you are not given this information you may have to argue in the alternative, as demonstrated in the suggested answer that follows.

- Theft of library book — problems with intention to permanently deprive

- Subsequent appropriation of library book by keeping — dishonesty in issue

- Theft of chocolate bars — dishonesty problems

- Making off without payment
- Burglary and theft in relation to the ornament
- Deception offences in relation to the taxi ride

⋮Ọ̈⋮ Suggested answer

(a) Library book

When Alison borrowed the book she appropriated property belonging to another, as defined by ss. 4(1) and 5(1) of the Theft Act 1968. There is no liability for theft at this stage, however, as she does not appear to be dishonest — neither does she have any intention to permanently deprive at this point. Her decision several months later to keep the book could amount to theft. Under s. 3(1) she can appropriate property where she has come by it innocently, without stealing it, if she later assumes the rights of the owner by keeping it. Her intention to permanently deprive is self-evident when she decides to keep the book hence the only live issue is dishonesty. Consider first s. 2(1)(a)–(c) of the Theft Act 1968. Alison has not been asked to return the book. Might this cause her to believe that she has, in law, the right to deprive the library of it? The test is subjective. On the facts this seems like a weak argument. More promising is s. 2(1)(b) whereby Alison can argue that she honestly believed that the library would have consented had it known of the appropriation and the circumstances of it. Again the test is subjective. Alison might believe that the failure of the library to chase up the non-return of the book is evidence of the library not caring about her keeping it. Section 2(1)(c) is not relevant on the facts. If Alison cannot bring herself within s. 2(1)(a)–(c) she may have to rely on the jury, following a *R v Ghosh* [1982] QB 1053 direction. Under *Ghosh* the jury will be asked to consider two questions: whether according to the ordinary standards of reasonable and honest people Alison acted dishonestly in keeping the library book? If 'No', Alison must be acquitted. If 'Yes', the question will be whether or not Alison must have realised that what she was doing was by those standards dishonest. It seems unlikely that a jury would regard her behaviour as dishonest.

(b) Vending machine

Alison could be liable for theft of the additional bars of chocolate. The extra bars of chocolate are property — see s. 4(1) of the Theft Act 1968. There was no intention on the part of the owner that property should pass to Alison without her inserting the required amount of money. Hence the additional bars remain property belonging to another. There is no need to resort to s. 5(4) of the Theft Act 1968 here (property got by mistake), as s. 5(1) can be relied upon to establish that the property belongs to another. In any event it is doubtful that s. 5(4) could apply — was Alison under any legal obligation to make restoration of the additional bars of chocolate? Alison appropriates the bars of chocolate by taking them. Her intention to permanently deprive the owner is evident. Again dishonesty is the element that will provoke most argument. Referring again to s. 2(1)(a) of the Theft Act 1968, she might argue that she had the right in law to keep the chocolate. She does not have to establish any such legal right — merely provide evidence that she honestly thought she had such a right. She might well believe this. Section 2(1)(b) seems less compelling here, but s. 2(1)(c) might be worth considering. Did she believe the owner of the chocolate bars could not be found by taking reasonable steps? She could have alerted the library and returned them there and then, but she may have believed that the machine was nothing to do with the library. The subjective nature of the s. 2(1)(c) provision should be stressed here. If Alison cannot avoid a finding of dishonesty under s. 2(1) of the Theft Act 1968, she may still escape liability on the basis that she was not dishonest according to the common law approach to that concept, see *R* v *Ghosh* (above). Was Alison dishonest in keeping the chocolate according to the ordinary standards of reasonable and honest people? If 'No', Alison must be acquitted. If 'Yes', the question will be whether or not Alison must have realised that what she was doing was by those standards dishonest. It is very hard to predict what view a jury might take on applying this test.

As a last resort the prosecution might consider liability for making off without payment contrary to s. 3 of the Theft Act 1978. Having obtained the chocolate bars, however, how is Alison meant to make the additional payment? Dishonesty would also be a problem as outlined above.

(c) Silver ornament

In taking the silver ornament Alison appears to appropriate property belonging to another with intention to permanently deprive. It subsequently transpires that her mother intended to give her the ornament as a gift but at the time it was taken it was still property belonging to another as against Alison. The only issue that Alison can argue to avoid liability is dishonesty. Under s. 2(1)(b) of the Theft Act 1968, she can argue that she honestly believed her mother would have consented to the taking had she known of it. Alison will rely on the fact that her mother intended to give her the ornament as a present. The problem for Alison is that she did not know this when she took the ornament. Alternatively Alison might argue that if her mother had known how desperate she was for money she would have agreed to her taking the ornament to sell. This is a weak argument — if that was the case why did she not ask her mother outright?

Again, if an argument under s. 2(1) of the Theft Act 1968 fails, Alison will have to rely on the jury determining that she was not dishonest following a direction under *R* v *Ghosh* (above). It is submitted that this is unlikely to avail her.

Alison's silence when the issue of the missing ornament is raised is not legally significant. She cannot be charged with obtaining the ornament by deception as she obtains it prior to her silence as to its whereabouts.

If it can be shown that Alison intended to steal the ornament (or indeed anything) before she entered the house, she could be charged with burglary contrary to s. 9(1)(a) of the Theft Act 1968 — entry as a trespasser with intent to steal; or s. 9(1)(b) — having entered as a trespasser she therein stole.

Alison might try to argue that she could not be a trespasser in her mother's house, but see *R* v *Jones and Smith* [1976] 3 All ER 54 — if she enters intending to steal she enters for a purpose in excess of her express or implied permission — her mother does not give her permission to enter in order to steal.

(d) Taxi ride

Alison's liability depends on when she decided not to pay — if she never intended to pay she obtained services by deception contrary to s. 1(1) of the Theft Act 1978. Calling the taxi not intending to pay was the deception. The taxi ride was a service provided on the understanding that it had been or would be paid for. The deception is operative — the taxi driver would not have provided the service had he known he was not going to be paid. The *means rea* is evident — dishonesty and an intention to deceive. If Alison decided not to pay on arriving at her destination she could be charged with making off without payment contrary to s. 3(1) Theft Act 1978. She clearly fails to pay as required and as expected for services provided, and she knows that payment is required on the spot. The only argument might be as to whether she makes off — it is the taxi driver who throws her out of the taxi. It is submitted that Alison's behaviour is the type of 'mischief' the s. 3 offence was intended to cover — hence she should be liable. An alternative charge might be s. 2(1)(b) Theft Act 1978 — Alison dishonestly, by deception, induces the taxi driver to forgo payment in respect of an existing liability, and she has intent to make permanent default. The deception relates to her ability to pay. Whether or not the taxi driver is actually deceived is a moot point. He may have just given up any prospect of receiving payment — in which case a charge of attempting to evade a liability under s. 2(1)(b) of the 1978 Act would be in order.

Q Question 4

Dave entered a betting shop and placed a £10 bet on a horse to finish in the first three. His horse came second, but the bookmaker, mistakenly believing that Dave had bet on the winner, instructed his cashier to pay Dave £100, which was £40 more than he was entitled to. In Dave's excitement, he forcibly grabbed the money from the cashier's grasp and then, realising that he had been overpaid, pushed over a security guard standing by the exit.

On his way home, Dave was asked by a charity worker to make a contribution to famine relief and, taking the view that they needed the money more than his bookmaker or himself, gave the charity the £100.

Discuss the criminal liability of Dave.

Commentary

This question concentrates on two offences under the Theft Act 1968: theft and robbery. Theft is a vast topic, but your answer must concentrate on the concepts of property belonging to another, with reference to s. 5 of the 1968 Act and *R v Gilks* [1972] 3 All ER 280, and dishonesty, negatively defined under s. 2 of the Act. On the other hand, as robbery is aggravated theft, there is not nearly as much material to consider. However, a key point is whether Dave has used force immediately before or at the time of the theft, and the cases of *R v Dawson* (1976) 64 Cr App R 170 and *R v Hale* (1978) 68 Cr App R 415 must be applied.

This is not a difficult question as the cases and principles should be very familiar to a well-prepared student. It is a question that should yield high marks.

- Theft — s. 1, Theft Act 1968
  - *Gomez* [1993]
- s. 5(4), Theft Act 1968 — belonging to another
  - *Gilks* [1972]
- s. 2, Theft Act 1968 — dishonesty
  - *Ghosh* [1982]
- Robbery — s. 8, Theft Act 1968
  - *Dawson* [1976]
  - *Hale* [1978]

:Q: Suggested answer

Dave could be charged with theft and robbery under the Theft Act 1968. Theft is defined under s. 1, and Dave will be found guilty if he dishonestly appropriates property belonging to another with the intention of permanently depriving the other of it.

The first element of the *actus reus* to consider is whether Dave has appropriated the money, as initially he does have the bookmaker's consent. Although appropriation is defined under s. 3 as any assumption by a person of the rights of an owner, and this includes the assumption of any one right (*R v Morris, Anderson v Burnside* [1983] 3 All ER 288), the courts have experienced great difficulty with this concept when the owner has consented to the property being taken. However, the House of Lords' decision in *DPP v Gomez* [1993] 1 All ER 1 makes it clear that anyone doing anything to property belonging to another with or without the consent of the owner appropriates it. So Dave has appropriated the money.

The second difficulty is whether this is property belonging to another, as Dave could argue that it becomes his property when he obtains it from the cashier. Clearly the money is property, as s. 4(1) provides that ' "property" includes money and all other property, real or personal, including things in action and other intangible property'. 'Belonging to another' is governed by s. 5, and at first sight it appears the prosecution would have to resort to s. 5(4), which provides: 'Where a person gets property by another's mistake, and is under an obligation to make restoration . . . then to the extent of that obligation the property or proceeds shall be regarded (as against him) as belonging to the person entitled to restoration'. However, for the subsection to apply there must be a legal obligation to make restoration, and on similar facts in *R* v *Gilks* [1972] 3 All ER 280, the Court of Appeal held that there was no legal obligation as the transaction between a bookmaker and punter was a betting and wagering contract and therefore illegal. In *Gilks*, the accused's conviction was upheld, as the court used s. 5(1) to decide that the punter had appropriated property belonging to another. Section 5(1) states that property shall be regarded as belonging to any person having possession or control of it, or having in it any proprietary right or interest; and in *Lawrence* v *Metropolitan Police Commissioner* [1971] 2 All ER 1253, the House of Lords decided that an owner of property who mistakenly parts with possession or ownership of it, may still have a proprietary interest in it. On application of this principle, the prosecution here can establish that Dave committed the *actus reus* of theft.

The first and most difficult element of the *mens rea* of theft is dishonesty. This is partially defined in a negative sense by s. 2 of the 1968 Act, which provides that a person's appropriation is not to be regarded as dishonest if the person:

(a)   believes that he or she has in law the right to deprive the other of it; or

(b)   believes he or she would have the other's consent; or

(c)   believes that the person to whom the property belongs cannot be discovered by taking reasonable steps.

Dave might argue that he honestly believed that the charity had a better moral right to the money than the bookmaker, but a moral right is not the same as a legal right. It would therefore be difficult for s. 2(1)(a) to be satisfied. However, the question of dishonesty is one of fact for the jury, and the Court of Appeal in *R* v *Feely* [1973] 1 All ER 341 held that it is for the jury to decide not only what the defendant's state of mind was, but also whether that state of mind was dishonest.

Feely also decided that as dishonesty is a word in common use, the jury do not need the help of the judge to tell them what amounts to dishonesty. However, conflict emerged as to whether the jury had to ascertain if the accused considered the conduct dishonest (the subjective approach favoured in *Boggeln* v *Williams* [1978] 2 All ER 1061), or if it was sufficient if the jury considered the conduct dishonest regardless of the accused's belief (the objective approach favoured in *R* v *Gilks*). The uncertainty has now been resolved by the Court of Appeal decision in *R* v *Ghosh* [1982] 2 All ER 689, which gives a twofold test. Thus the jury must ask themselves:

(a) Was what was done dishonest according to the ordinary standards of reasonable and honest people? If not, D is not guilty.

(b) If it was, did D realise that reasonable and honest people regard what he did as dishonest? If so, he is guilty; if not, he is not guilty.

Although the test has been criticised as it may allow a 'Robin Hood' defence (and has not been applied in Australia), it does seem to operate fairly and Dave could not escape simply because in his opinion bookmakers were fair game. He would have to bring some evidence to show that he honestly believed that other people would not consider his conduct dishonest.

The second element of the *mens rea*, intention permanently to deprive, is satisfied when Dave gives the money to charity, and s. 5(4) provides that an intention not to make restoration shall be regarded as an intention to deprive.

It is submitted that Dave could not be charged under s. 15 of the Theft Act 1968 with obtaining property by deception, as there has been no operative deception on his behalf. If Dave had represented that he had bet on the winner the position would be different. However, if he is held dishonest and guilty of theft, he could also be convicted of robbery. This offence is defined by s. 8 of the 1968 Act: 'A person is guilty of robbery if he steals, and immediately before or at the time of doing so, and in order to do so, he uses force on any person or puts or seeks to put any person in fear of being then and there subjected to force.'

The key issue here would be, has Dave used force at the time of the theft in order to steal? Force is not defined in the Theft Act, and in *R v Dawson* (1976) 64 Cr App R 170, the Court of Appeal held that it is an ordinary English word and that its meaning is for the jury to decide. Thus in *Dawson*, a nudge in the back was force; and in *Corcoran v Anderton* (1980) 71 Cr App R 104, snatching a handbag was sufficient for the accused to be guilty of robbery. In this case, however, the victim had such a strong grip on the bag that D's act of pulling it caused her to fall to the ground, whereas Dave's grab has no such effect on the cashier. Further, if Dave has not formed the *mens rea* of theft at this time, even if the jury concluded that his action constituted force, it may not be deemed 'in order to steal'.

Quite clearly, pushing over the security guard would constitute force, and as Dave then realised that he had been overpaid, this would seem to constitute robbery. However, the courts have drawn a distinction between force used at the time of and in order to steal (robbery), and force used in order to escape (not robbery). The key question, therefore, is whether Dave was still in the act of appropriating the property when he pushed the security guard. This was also the problem before the court in *R v Hale* (1978) 68 Cr App R 415, where D, in the victim's bedroom, put some jewellery into his pocket shortly before his accomplice downstairs tied up the victim. The Court of Appeal, in upholding the conviction, decided that it was open to the jury to conclude that the appropriation was still continuing. Thus as the guard is in the shop, it is likely that this condition will be satisfied and Dave will be found guilty of robbery. If it was deemed to be force after the theft had taken place, Dave would not be guilty of robbery; but in addition to theft, he could be convicted of common assault under s. 39 of the Criminal Justice Act 1988.

Q Question 5(a)

Jerry is the managing director of, and majority shareholder in, Barnham Ltd, a company that owns an old people's home. Mike is an employee of Barnham who works at the home. The business is going badly and the home is deteriorating rapidly. This fact has been noted by Ben, an eccentric resident, who has complained on many occasions that the fire-fighting equipment is totally inadequate and that the residents and the adjoining local church are in danger from the risk of fire. Jerry instructs Mike to start a fire, so that Barnham Ltd will be able to make a claim for damage to the home on their insurance policy. Mike starts a small fire.

At the same time, and independently of Mike, Ben decides to test his theory and also starts a fire. Both fires spread, the home is badly damaged and, although nobody is injured, the residents have to be evacuated.

Before Jerry submits an insurance claims form, the police arrest Jerry, Mike and Ben.

Discuss the criminal liability of the parties.

Commentary

This question involves a detailed analysis of a number of issues under the Criminal Damage Act 1971. In particular, the offences under s. 1 and the two specific defences to s. 1(1) contained in s. 5(2) must be analysed in detail. These principles have been applied in a number of recent decisions which have emphasised the peculiarities of the law on this topic.

The advice on the *mens rea* required will need to reflect the fact that *Metropolitan Police Commissioner* v *Caldwell* [1981] 1 All ER 961, no longer determines the definition of recklessness in relation to the offence of criminal damage, *R* v *G* [2003] 4 All ER 765, reasserting the subjective approach to this type of fault. In addition, there are the two inchoate offences to consider briefly: incitement and attempt. The question has been framed in such a way so as to avoid considering the other inchoate crime, conspiracy.

- Incitement

- Criminal damage
    - s. 1(1), Criminal Damage Act 1971
    - s. 5(2), Criminal Damage Act 1971
    - *Denton* [1982]
    - *Appleyard* [1985]

- Aggravated criminal damage
  - s. 1(2), Criminal Damage Act 1971
- Recklessness — *Caldwell* [1981]
- Attempt — Criminal Attempts Act 1981
  - *Widdowson* [1985]
- *Ben*
  - Criminal damage
  - s. 1(1), Criminal Damage Act 1971
  - s. 5(2), Criminal Damage Act 1971 — *Hunt* [1977]

:Q̇: Suggested answer

When Jerry instructs Mike to start a fire, he is probably guilty of the crime of incitement. An inciter 'is one who reaches and seeks to influence the mind of another to the commission of a crime'. The machinations of criminal ingenuity being legion, the approach to the other's mind may take various forms, such as suggestion, proposal, request, exhortation, gesture, argument, persuasion or inducement.

Thus, although Jerry could be charged with inciting Mike to commit criminal damage under s. 1(1) of the Criminal Damage Act 1971, it is more likely that they will both be charged as principal offenders under that section: 'A person who without lawful excuse destroys or damages any property belonging to another intending to destroy or damage any such property or being reckless as to whether any such property would be destroyed or damaged shall be guilty of an offence.' As they have used fire, the charge may be arson under s. 1(3) of the 1971 Act as the maximum sentence is greater (life as opposed to 10 years).

Clearly, both Jerry and Mike have the necessary *mens rea* for these offences as they intend to damage the property. However, they may have a defence under s. 5(2) of the Act:

> A person charged with an offence to which this section applies shall, whether or not he would be treated for the purposes of this Act as having a lawful excuse apart from this subsection, be treated for those purposes as having a lawful excuse —
>
> > (a) if at the time of the act or acts alleged to constitute the offence he believed that the person or persons whom he believed to be entitled to consent to the destruction of or damage to the property in question had so consented, or would have so consented to it if he or they had known of the destruction or damage and its circumstances. . . .

Although their positions may seem identical, on analysis of the two leading cases on this section (*R v Denton* [1982] 1 All ER 65, *R v Appleyard* (1985) 81 Cr App R 319) there may be a difference in Jerry's and Mike's criminal responsibility. In *R v Denton*, an employee (D), had been instructed by his employer (X), to damage X's property by fire, so that X could make a fraudulent insurance claim. At D's trial, the judge ruled that s. 5(2) of the 1971 Act could not provide D with a lawful excuse, as he knew that his employer had consented to his starting the fire and damaging the property for fraudulent purposes only. The consent, ruled the trial judge, was therefore invalid. However, D's conviction was quashed on appeal, the court holding that no offence was committed under s. 1(1) or s. 1(3) of the Act by a person who burnt down his own premises; neither could that act become unlawful because of the intent to defraud the insurers.

On application of *Denton*, Mike would have a defence; and it would appear that Jerry could use the same argument. However, his responsibility appears to be governed by the decision in *R* v *Appleyard*. In this case, A, the managing director and majority shareholder of a company, X Ltd, set fire to X Ltd's property, with a view to making a fraudulent insurance claim. A argued on the authority of *Denton* that he could not be guilty of damaging his own property, but this argument was rejected on the basis that the company is a separate legal entity and, as the building was owned by the company, A was damaging property belonging to another. A also contended that, as he was in control of the company and could make decisions on the company's behalf, he had the defence under s. 5(2) as he had the consent of the company. Again, the court rejected the argument on the basis that company decisions must be made for a proper purpose and in the company's best interests. As this was clearly not the case, there was no consent or belief in the owner's consent. A's conviction was upheld by the Court of Appeal.

It is therefore submitted on authority of these cases that whereas Mike would be acquitted of these charges, Jerry would be convicted.

Jerry and Mike would also be charged under s. 1(2) of the 1971 Act:

> A person who without lawful excuse destroys or damages any property whether belonging to himself or another—
>
> (a) intending to destroy or damage any property or being reckless as to whether any property would be destroyed or damaged; and
>
> (b) intending by the destruction or damage to endanger the life of another or being reckless as to whether the life of another would be thereby endangered;
>
> shall be guilty of an offence.

The facts demonstrate that as the home was evacuated, life may have been endangered; it is only necessary that the prosecution show that life could have been (not actually was) endangered (*R* v *Dudley* [1989] Crim LR 57).

Jerry and Mike may argue that they lacked the *mens rea* for this offence because they did not foresee this consequence. Abandoning the objective approach to reckless-ness under the Criminal Damage Act 1971 that had been established in *Metropolitan Police Commissioner* v *Caldwell* [1981] 1 All ER 961, the House of Lords in *R* v *G* [2003] 4 All ER 765, confirmed that a defendant could not be guilty unless he had foreseen the risk of criminal damage (or the endangerment of life thereby) and had gone on to take that risk.

Lastly, Jerry may be charged under s. 1(1) of the Criminal Attempts Act 1981 with an attempt to obtain property by deception. Had Jerry's plan succeeded, this would have been a clear case of the full offence under s. 15 of the Theft Act 1968, as the money paid by the insurance company is regarded as property and they would have been deceived if Jerry had stated that the fire was an accident. However, for the prosecution to establish the offence of attempt, it must be shown that Jerry did more than a merely preparatory act with the appropriate *mens rea*; and whether an act is more than merely preparatory is a question of fact for the jury (Criminal Attempts Act 1981, s. 4(3)). Each case depends on its own particular facts, but in the similar case of *R v Robinson* [1915] 2 KB 341, D's conviction for attempting to obtain money by false pretences was quashed on the basis that as D had not actually submitted the fraudulent claims form, his conduct had not amounted to the *actus reus* of attempt. Although this case was before 1981 and therefore did not apply the present test, *R v Widdowson* (1985) 82 Cr App R 314 was decided in the same way, and it is therefore submitted that Jerry has not done more than a merely preparatory act and could not be found guilty of attempted deception.

Provided the prosecution can prove that he was aware of the risk of harm, Ben would appear to be guilty of criminal damage under s. 1(1) of the 1971 Act. He may, however, be able to argue that the defence of lawful excuse is available under s. 5(2)(b), i.e., if he destroyed or damaged the property in question . . . in order to protect property belonging to himself or another, and at the time of the act he believed:

(a) that the property was in immediate need of protection; and

(b) that the means of protection adopted or proposed to be adopted were or would be reasonable having regard to all the circumstances.

At first sight, this subsection appears to offer a defence in many circumstances, as it is written in subjective terms. However, an objective element has been imported by the cases, and in *R v Hill and Hall* (1988) 89 Cr App R 74, the Court of Appeal ruled that the trial judge has to decide whether the evidence submitted by D is sufficient to enable this defence to be left to the jury; see also *R v Kelleher* [2003] EWCA Crim 2846, where D was convicted of 'decapitating a statue of Margaret Thatcher claiming that he was doing so to save the world from the consequences of materialism'. In *R v Hunt* (1977) 66 Cr App R 105, the court, on similar facts to the problem, held that D's act in setting fire to property was not done in order to protect the property — which was not in any case in immediate need of protection, until D started the fire! Further, in *Blake* v *DPP* [1993] Crim LR 586, it was held that s. 5(2) is not satisfied by D's belief that God is the owner of all property and that God consents to the damage.

Consequently, Ben would also be guilty under s. 1(2) of the 1971 Act on the same basis as Jerry and Mike.

Q Question 5(b)

Tracey, aged 14, often played in a small wood above concealed waste ground. She and her friends were in the habit of throwing stones down on to the waste ground, in the knowledge that as nobody ever went on that ground there was no risk of injury.

One day a sign was erected by the woods: 'New greenhouses, do not throw stones'. Although she saw the sign, Tracey was of low intelligence and could not read. Unaware of the warning, she threw a stone to the waste ground. The stone smashed a pane of glass in a greenhouse and narrowly missed Bill the gardener. Bill was so shocked by the incident that he became depressed and suffered headaches for a month.

Discuss the criminal responsibility (if any) of Tracey.

Commentary

There are many interesting areas within the Criminal Damage Act 1971, a statute that has also attracted a number of odd cases (*Jaggard v Dickinson* [1980] 3 All ER 716, for example). It is difficult to set a question exclusively related to criminal damage, and examiners will often involve an offence against the person to test the students' awareness of the different offences. Again the answer to this question should reflect the shift from objective reckless-ness, as determined by *Metropolitan Police Commissioner v Caldwell* [1981] 1 All ER 961, towards subjective recklessness as laid down in *R v G* [2003] 4 All ER 765. Section 47 of the Offences Against the Person Act 1861 must also be considered; in particular, can psychiatric injury constitute actual bodily harm?

- Criminal damage — s. 1(1), Criminal Damage Act 1971
- Recklessness
  - *R v G* [2003]
- Aggravated criminal damage — s. 1(2), Criminal Damage Act 1971
  - *Steer* [1987]
  - *Webster and Warwick* [1995]
- s. 47, Offences Against the Person Act 1861
  - *Chan Fook* [1994]
  - *Savage and Parmenter* [1991]

:Q: Suggested answer

Tracey could face charges under the Criminal Damage Act 1971 and the Offences Against the Person Act 1861, although she will be able to contend that she did not possess the necessary *mens rea* for these offences.

Under s. 1(1) of the Criminal Damage Act 1971, a person who without lawful excuse destroys or damages any property belonging to another, intending to destroy or damage any such property or being reckless as to whether any such property would be destroyed or damaged, shall be guilty of an offence. There are specific defences to s. 1(1) in s. 5 of the Act, but as they relate either to a belief in the owner's consent, or to a necessary and reasonable act to prevent further damage to property, Tracey will be unable to use them. However, although she has clearly committed the *actus reus* of the offence, she can argue that she lacked the *mens rea*, on the basis that as she did not foresee the consequence, she neither intended it nor was reckless as to its occurrence.

Following the House of Lords' decision in *R v G* [2003] 4 All ER 765, where the objective approach to recklessness laid down in *Metropolitan Police Commissioner* v *Caldwell* [1981] 1 All ER 961, was abandoned, the prosecution will have to prove that Tracey was at least aware of the risk of harm and consciously took that risk.

Section 1(2) of the Criminal Damage Act 1971 is the most serious offence facing Tracey; and although there is the possibility of a life sentence if the accused is found guilty, the ingredients of the offence can be easily satisfied by the prosecution. It is not necessary to show that someone's life was actually endangered, simply that it could have been endangered (*R v Dudley* [1989] Crim LR 57); and *mens rea* can be satisfied by proof of (subjective) recklessness. Hence Tracey could incur liability if she foresaw the risk of criminal damage endangering life. It should be noted, however, that the endangerment to life must arise as a result of the criminal damage. This was confirmed by the House of Lords in *R v Steer* [1987] 2 All ER 833, where the accused fired bullets, which narrowly missed V, through the window of a house. The prosecution contended that as the accused had caused criminal damage and V's life had been endangered, the offence under s. 1(2) had been established. However, the House of Lords stated that this offence was committed only if the life had been or could have been endangered by the criminal damage.

It will sometimes be difficult on the facts to make this key distinction. Thus in *R v Webster and Warwick* [1995] 2 All ER 168, where the accused threw bricks at a moving police car, smashing a window and causing glass to fall over the officers, the court held that this ingredient for s. 1(2) could be satisfied, as the driver might lose control as a result of being showered with glass. Thus, if the gardener was endangered by the stone thrown by Tracey, she would not be guilty; but if endangerment was caused by the splintering glass, she would be!

Tracey might also be charged under s. 47 of the Offences Against the Person Act 1861: 'Whosoever shall be convicted upon an indictment of any assault occasioning actual bodily harm shall be liable . . . to [imprisonment for five years]'. Although Bill has not suffered direct physical injury, psychiatric injury can amount to actual bodily harm (*R v Mike Chan-Fook* [1994] 2 All ER 552); and in *R v Ireland* [1997] 4 All ER 225, the Court of Appeal and the House of Lords held that psychiatric injury can amount to grievous bodily harm for the purpose of s. 20 of the 1861 Act. However, minor emotional harm (e.g., fear or mild hysteria) will not be sufficient, and the prosecution must call expert psychiatric evidence to establish that Bill's depression and headaches constitute actual bodily harm.

Assault can be defined as intentionally or recklessly putting a person in fear of being then and there subjected to unlawful force (*Fagan* v *Metropolitan Police Commissioner* [1968] 3 All ER 442). It is quite clear that objective recklessness does not apply to common assault or s. 47 of the 1861 Act (*R* v *Savage and Parmenter* [1991] 4 All ER 698); and although the *mens rea* for s. 47 is satisfied by proving the *mens rea* of common assault (i.e., the prosecution does not have to prove that the accused foresaw the risk of actual bodily harm: *R* v *Roberts* (1971) 56 Cr App R 95) — it is submitted that as Tracey was unaware of any danger to the person, she could not be found guilty of this offence.

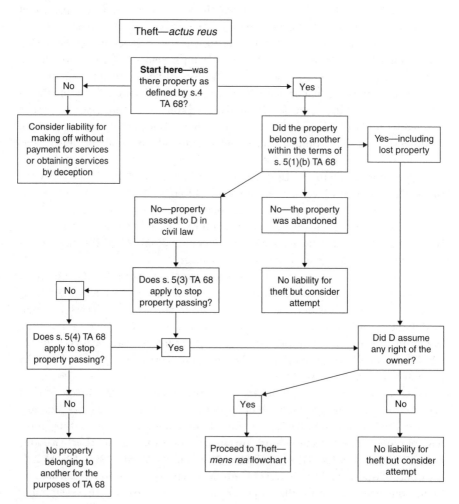

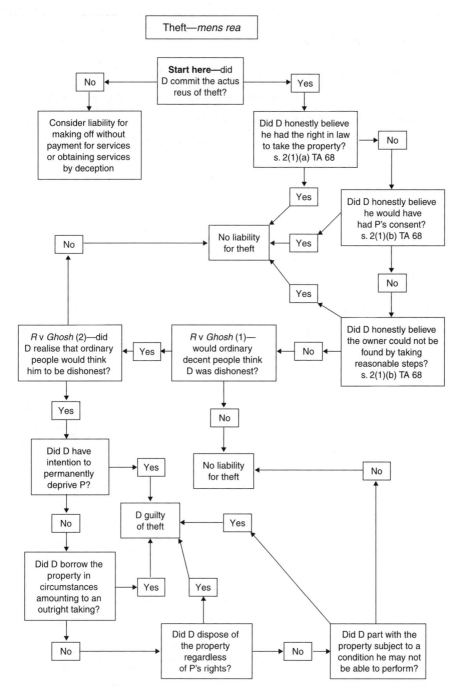

Theft—*mens rea*

Start here—did D commit the actus reus of theft?

No → Consider liability for making off without payment for services or obtaining services by deception

Yes → Did D honestly believe he had the right in law to take the property? s. 2(1)(a) TA 68

No → Did D honestly believe he would have had P's consent? s. 2(1)(b) TA 68

Yes → No liability for theft

Yes → No liability for theft

No → Did D honestly believe the owner could not be found by taking reasonable steps? s. 2(1)(b) TA 68

Yes → No liability for theft

No → *R v Ghosh* (1)— would ordinary decent people think D was dishonest?

Yes → *R v Ghosh* (2)—did D realise that ordinary people would think him to be dishonest?

No → No liability for theft

No → No liability for theft

Yes → Did D have intention to permanently deprive P?

Yes → D guilty of theft

No → Did D borrow the property in circumstances amounting to an outright taking?

Yes → D guilty of theft

No → Did D dispose of the property regardless of P's rights?

Yes → D guilty of theft

No → Did D part with the property subject to a condition he may not be able to perform?

Yes → D guilty of theft

No → No liability for theft

Further reading

Elliott, D.W., 'Directors' Thefts and Dishonesty' [1991] Crim LR 732.

Griew, E., 'Dishonesty — the Objections to Feely and Ghosh' [1985] Crim LR 341.

Heaton, R., 'Deceiving Without Thieving' [2001] Crim LR 712.

Shute, S., 'Appropriation and the Law of Theft' [2002] Crim LR 445.

Smith, J.C., 'Stealing Tickets' [1998] Crim LR 723.

Other Theft Act offences

Introduction

Many criminal law syllabuses will cover only a few other theft-related offences, such as robbery, burglary and deception. Professional courses (e.g., the Common Professional Exam) will also set questions on blackmail, handling, taking a conveyance and going equipped. There are many other offences under the Theft Act 1968, such as forgery and false accounting, but only specialist bodies would set questions on these crimes.

The questions included in this chapter are typical examination problems. It is rare that essay questions are set on these offences, as the rationale of the criminal law is best explored in other areas of the syllabus, such as *actus reus* and *mens rea*. Because there is not such a vast amount of material to cover on these offences as, for example, on causation or recklessness, the questions will often involve consideration of three or four offences. Some questions are set simply to test a student's ability to differentiate between closely related offences (for example, Question 2 concerning deception). Others may require detailed analysis of cases and concepts on one crime only — burglary and handling stolen goods lend themselves to this type of question.

Because of the diverse material, and the fact that studying theft and theft-related offences almost seems like studying a separate subject from criminal law, many students are very apprehensive about tackling questions on these topics. You should not be intimidated, however, as questions tend to be set on the well-known areas of difficulty which have been discussed in leading cases. A well-prepared student should be confident of scoring high marks on these questions, which may often be easier to answer than those from other parts of the syllabus.

Q Question 1

Ken is employed by Infinity plc and has his petrol paid for by his employer. The arrangement is that when he fills his tank at his local petrol station, owned and operated by Randy, the account held there by Infinity plc is debited to the extent of the amount due. Following a downsizing of Infinity plc Ken is made redundant on

1 March, but he continues to obtain his petrol from Randy's petrol station, telling him to charge the amount due to the Infinity plc account.

On one of these visits to the petrol station Ken sees a car stereo for sale priced at £9.99. A number of identical models are displayed for sale priced £99.99, and Ken realises that this one item has been mispriced. Ken, who notices that Randy's 12-year-old son Fred is minding the counter whilst Randy is dealing with another customer, takes the stereo to the counter where Fred sells it to him for £9.99.

A week later, Ken visits Randy's petrol station and fills his petrol tank as usual, but, on attempting to charge the amount due to the Infinity plc account, he is challenged by Randy who tells him that he will have to pay, and that he owes Randy for all the petrol he has obtained since 1 March. As Ken moves to run away, Randy grabs his car keys to stop him making off. Ken punches Randy in the face causing him to become concussed. Ken takes his car keys, and grabs a bag of sweets from the counter. Ken's actions are captured on Randy's security video and he is later apprehended.

Advise the Crown Prosecution Service as to the criminal liability of Ken.

Commentary

This is a good example of a Theft Act question that covers a wide range of offences. Note how one incident, such as the non-payment for the petrol, raises the possibility of a number of different charges. The task for candidates is to determine which might be the most appropriate. As a general rule concentrate on the offence that most accurately reflects the defendant's criminality. For example, technically Ken may have stolen the petrol, but to prove this involves a rather difficult argument on appropriation. It may be much better to proceed with a deception charge if possible. Dishonesty arises many times in a question such as this and it is often impossible to do more than hazard a guess as to how a jury might view the defendant's actions. Where you are given relevant facts, such as the circumstances of the victim, or the value of the property, you should bring these in to inform your advice — see for example the advice regarding the mispriced stereo.

- Obtaining petrol by deception

- Theft of petrol

- Making off without paying for the petrol

- Evasion of a liability by deception — various modes

- Selection of mis-priced goods — theft and deception

- Assault and robbery

:Ọ: **Suggested answer**

(a) Deception

The facts indicate that Ken continues to charge the cost of petrol to the Infinity plc account despite the fact that he is no longer employed by the company. Each time he did this he may have committed the offence of obtaining the petrol by deception contrary to s. 15 of the Theft Act 1968. The petrol is property belonging to another, at least whilst it is in the petrol station tanks and pumps. Ken obtains the petrol by filling his tank. Under s. 15(4) a deception can be by conduct. Ken exercises a deception by purporting to be a person who is going to use a valid means for payment. In effect his failure to advise the petrol station as to his changed status will be the deception: see *DPP v Ray* [1974] AC 370. Is the deception operative? Does the cashier activate the pump allowing him to serve himself with petrol on the basis that he is an honest person who is going to pay? Deception must operate so as to cause the obtaining of the petrol: see *Coady* [1996] Crim LR 518. If there is no evidence that the cashier forms an assessment of Ken's *bona fides* there will be difficulties for the prosecution. Assuming an operative deception is made out, *mens rea* appears to be evident, provided Ken realised that his line of credit had been terminated with his job. He intends to deceive, or is at least reckless as to whether or not he does so, and clearly has intention to permanently deprive the petrol station of the petrol. The only live issue would then be dishonesty. As this is a deception offence there is no statutory definition of dishonesty. The jury would be directed according to *R* v *Ghosh* [1982] QB 1053. According to the ordinary standards of reasonable and honest people was what Ken did dishonest? If it was dishonest by those standards, did Ken himself realise that what he was doing was by those standards dishonest? It is submitted that a jury would regard Ken's actions as dishonest.

(b) Theft

Theft of the petrol is problematic as property in it passes to Ken as it fills his tank. The prosecution could argue that he appropriates it by pouring it into his tank, but this would be a little artificial. The prosecution might seek to rely on *R* v *Hinks* [2000] 4 All ER 833, to contend that Ken steals the petrol even though property in it has passed to him, but this involves a strained use of the Theft Act 1968 that seems unnecessary given the more obvious deception charge.

(c) Making off without payment

In failing to pay for the petrol Ken may have committed the offence of making off without payment contrary to s. 3 of the Theft Act 1978. Ken knew that payment on the spot for goods supplied was required or expected from him. He made off without having paid as required or expected. He clearly had intent to permanently avoid payment: see *Allen* [1985] 2 All ER 641. Dishonesty, following a *Ghosh* direction as outlined above, would appear to be evident.

(d) Evasion of a liability by deception

In not paying for the petrol Ken could be charged under s. 2 of the Theft Act 1978. Under s. 2(1)(a) he could be charged with dishonestly securing the remission of the whole or part of an existing liability: see e.g., *Jackson* [1983] Crim LR 617. He had an existing liability to pay for the petrol, and he exercised a deception in claiming that he was entitled to charge it to the company account. The query is as to whether he really did secure the remission of the liability. In one sense he does as he shifts liability to Infinity plc, but would the company be bound to pay? Is it the fault of the petrol station in not checking? Much would turn upon the nature of the agreement between the company and the retailer. As to *mens rea*, Ken intended to deceive and would presumably be found to have been dishonest.

A charge under s. 2(1)(b) of the 1978 Act might be more appropriate, i.e., that with intent to make permanent default in whole or in part on an existing liability to make a payment, Ken dishonestly induced Randy to wait for payment . . . or to forgo payment. The charge here would have to be on the basis of making Randy wait for payment, but does Ken have intent to make permanent default if he thinks Infinity plc might pay? He might even try to argue that he was not dishonest in relation to Randy because he believed Infinity plc would pay — but this is not an attractive argument. Finally, Ken could be charged under s. 2(1)(c), in that he dishonestly obtained an exemption from or abatement of liability to make a payment.

(e) Liability for the mispriced item

The prosecution may allege that Ken committed theft in relation to the mispriced stereo. The stereo was property belonging to another: see s. 4(1) and s. 5(1) of the Theft Act 1968. Ken appropriates it simply by selecting it, even if the owner consents: see *Lawrence* v *Metropolitan Police Commissioner* [1970] 3 All ER 933, and *R* v *Gomez* [1993] 1 All ER 1. Ken evidently had intention to permanently deprive, hence the live issue is dishonesty, especially s. 2(1)(a). Ken will argue that he honestly believed he had the right in law to select the item and try to buy it at the lower price. The price tag is, in law, nothing more than an invitation to treat. A shopper who selects an item offers to buy it at the marked price. It is up to the retailer to decide whether or not to accept the offer. If the nuances of contract law prove to be beyond the average juror, Ken will seek to rely on the common law approach to dishonesty based on the *Ghosh* direction. According to the ordinary standards of reasonable and honest people was the selection of the mispriced item dishonest? If it was dishonest by those standards, did Ken himself realise that what he was doing was by those standards dishonest? Much depends on the extent to which the average juror would be prepared to take advantage of a mistake by a retailer. Some will see large companies as 'fair game' but may take a different view where family-run businesses are concerned. Also, the difference between the correct price and the erroneous price will be a factor. Here the difference is considerable, and the jurors might view Ken's actions as exploitative. The fact that he decides to buy the item when Randy's son is serving at the counter is suggestive of this. The prosecution might prefer to charge theft on the basis that Ken appropriates the stereo when he leaves the petrol station. One obvious problem with this approach is the argument that property has passed to Ken, hence he cannot steal the stereo. Even though there is a mistake as to price it is almost certainly the case that Ken acquires voidable title to the goods. The prosecution might seek to rely on *R* v *Hinks* (above), where the House of Lords, by a majority, held that a defendant could be guilty of theft even where he acquired title to property under a valid *inter vivos* transfer. Their Lordships were at a loss to explain how the property could still be regarded as property belonging to another if property in the goods had passed, but it provides an answer for the prosecution as regards Ken. Again, dishonesty would be an issue, as to which see above.

It might be possible to argue that Ken obtains the stereo by deception, contrary to s. 15 of the Theft Act 1968. The problem is in establishing that he makes any representation as to price. On the facts such a representation could only be implied from his conduct, i.e., he was impliedly representing that he honestly believed the item to be correctly priced. It seems very unlikely that this will work. It is the price tag that induced Fred to charge £9.99.

(f) Assault/robbery

Ken punches Randy in the face causing him to become concussed. Concussion is likely to amount to actual bodily harm — see *T* v *DPP* [2003] All ER (D) 20 — the harm caused involved an injurious impairment of the victim's sensory functions. The punch is clearly an assault and it causes the actual bodily harm. *Mens rea* is evident. A more serious charge would be robbery, contrary to s. 8 of the Theft Act 1968. Ken steals the sweets. His taking of the bag of sweets involves the dishonest appropriation of property belonging to another with intention to permanently deprive. Immediately before or at the time of stealing he uses force on Randy. The problem lies in whether or not he can be shown to have used the force in order to steal. The facts suggest that he used the force in order to recover his car keys. This in turn throws up the possibility that a charge of theft could be based on Ken using force to recover his keys. The problem then becomes one of whether or not he stole his keys when he grabbed them from Randy. The keys are property under s. 4(1). They could be regarded as property belonging to another as against Ken because they were in Randy's possession at the time — see s. 5(1). The problem for the prosecution is that Randy's possession may not have been lawful, however *R* v *Kelly* [1998] 3 All ER 741, confirms that it is possible to steal from one whose possession is unlawful. The taking of the keys would be the appropriation, and there is clearly intention to permanently deprive. The only remaining issue is dishonesty. Ken will rely on s. 2(1)(a) — he honestly believed he had the right in law to recover his keys — but given the context in which this occurs he is unlikely to engage the sympathy of the jury. Hence a conviction for robbery is technically possible.

Finally, in relation to the sweets, a charge of making off without payment contrary to s. 3 of the Theft Act 1978 would be sustainable.

Q Question 2

Peter owed £100 in bank charges and was short of money. He went to his bank and told the manager that he would soon be inheriting £50,000 under his uncle's will and that he would pay that money into his account. This was untrue but the bank manager believed him, and as a result he offered Peter the following, which he accepted:

(a)   £250 in cash to be repaid from the £50,000;

(b)   overdraft facilities of up to £10,000;

(c)   the removal of the £100 bank charges;

(d)   free investment advice, which customers had to pay for unless they had £10,000 in their account.

There was only £10 in his account and Peter never paid any more money into it. Discuss the criminal liability of Peter.

Commentary

This is a relatively straightforward question concerning deception. There is a range of offences under ss. 15 and 16 of the Theft Act 1968, and ss. 1 and 2 of the Theft Act 1978. Answers must make it clear that you know which offence covers the different consequences of the deception. In addition, as a result of the House of Lords' decision in *DPP* v *Gomez* [1993] 1 All ER 1, candidates must also cover theft, as this offence may now be charged in virtually every occasion (except when land is involved) where property has been obtained by deception.

Questions such as this simply require a knowledge of the relevant offences and an ability to apply them in a practical context. Given the range of issues there is not enough time to go into the intricacies of deception and the offences, and the facts of the question do not warrant such an approach.

- Deception

- s. 15, Theft Act 1968

- s. 16, Theft Act 1968

- *Watkins* [1976]

• s. 2, Theft Act 1978

• s. 1, Theft Act 1978

• Dishonesty — *Ghosh* [1982]

:Q: Suggested answer

Peter could be charged with a number of offences under the Theft Acts 1968 and 1978, as he has clearly deceived his bank manager. When Peter receives the £250, he could be guilty of obtaining property by deception under s. 15 of the 1968 Act. The money is property belonging to another and Peter clearly obtains it. The deception relates to his statement concerning the inheritance. Deception is defined under s. 15(4) of the Theft Act 1968: ' "deception" means any deception (whether deliberate or reckless) by words or conduct as to fact or as to law, including a deception as to the present intentions of the person using the deception or any other person'. The deception appears to be operative — had he known the truth the bank manager would not have given him the money. As to *mens rea*, in *Dip Kaur* v *Chief Constable for Hampshire* [1981] 2 All ER 430, the Court of Appeal confirmed that a deception is intentional if D knows that his statement is false and will or may be accepted as true by V; and a deception is reckless if D is aware that his statement may be false and will or may be accepted as true by V, or if he is aware that it is ambiguous and may be understood by V in a false sense. Assuming Peter knows the statement about the inheritance to be untrue this element of the *mens rea* will be made out. Peter clearly has intention to permanently deprive. Dishonesty will be determined by the jury following a direction based on *R* v *Ghosh* [1982] QB 1053. According to the ordinary standards of reasonable and honest people was what Peter did dishonest? If it was dishonest by those standards, did Peter himself realise that what he was doing was by those standards dishonest?

One problem for the prosecution relates to who gives Peter the money. If the bank manager personally hands the money to Peter a s. 15 charge may be straightforward. If, however, Peter goes to a cashier and is given the money he may argue that the deception is too remote from the obtaining of the money. The cashier provides Peter with the money because of the authorised overdraft, not because of any deception relating to the overdraft. If this were the case a charge under s. 16 of the Theft Act 1968 would be more appropriate, as to which see below.

As a result of the House of Lords' decision in *DPP* v *Gomez* [1993] 1 All ER 1, Peter may also be guilty of theft under s. 1 of the Theft Act 1968, on the basis that he dishonestly appropriates property belonging to another with the intention of permanently depriving the other of it. Before *Gomez* it was difficult to say that there had been an appropriation of property when the owner had consented to the accused taking it. However, in this case their Lordships, following their earlier decision in *Lawrence* v *Metropolitan Police Commissioner* [1971] 2 All ER 1253, confirmed that appropriation simply meant assuming any of the rights of an owner and need not necessarily involve an adverse interference with or usurpation of those rights. Further, *R* v *Hinks* [2000] 4 All ER 833, confirms that Peter can be guilty of stealing the money even where he acquires valid title to it under a valid transfer. The remaining issue would be dishonesty. Peter may argue that, under s. 2(1)(a) of the Theft Act 1968, he honestly believed he had the right to take the money because of the bank manager's agreement. He might also rely on s. 2(1)(b) by contending that he honestly believed the bank manager would have consented had he known of the circumstances. This is a less compelling argument. Failing these two arguments, dishonesty would be an issue for the jury following a *Ghosh* direction as explained above.

Although Peter may not actually use the overdraft facilities, the mere fact that he obtains them means that he might be guilty of the full offence under s. 16 of the Theft Act 1968 — by any deception dishonestly obtaining for himself or another any pecuniary advantage. Although the term 'pecuniary advantage' is potentially very wide, s. 16 is in fact very limited, covering certain specific consequences only. Thus under s. 16(2)(b), a pecuniary advantage will be obtained when Peter is allowed to borrow by way of overdraft or to take out any policy of insurance or annuity contract or obtain any improvement of the terms on which he is allowed to do so. In *R* v *Watkins* [1976] 1 All ER 578, where a bank agreed to grant credit facilities to the accused, he was convicted of the full offence even though he did not use those facilities. Liability depends upon proof that the deception was operative — would the bank manager have sanctioned the overdraft had he known the truth? Dishonesty, as per *R* v *Ghosh* (above) would also have to be established.

Section 2 of the Theft Act 1978 may apply to the cancellation of Peter's bank charges. This is the offence of evasion of liability by deception, and it can be committed under three separate (but overlapping) subsections of s. 2. Section 2(1)(a) would seem to be the most appropriate, as this makes it an offence for a person, by deception, dishonestly to secure the remission of the whole or any part of any existing liability to make a payment, whether his own liability or another's. Arguably s. 2(1)(b) would also apply. This covers an accused who:

> with intent to make permanent default in whole or in part on any existing liability to make a payment, or with intent to let another do so, dishonestly induces the creditor or any person claiming payment on behalf of the creditor to wait for payment (whether or not the due date for payment is deferred) or to forgo payment.

The main difficulty in securing a conviction under s. 2(1)(b) is that the prosecution must show that when Peter made the misrepresentation he had 'intent to make permanent default'. Section 2(1)(a) merely uses the phrase 'secures the remission', and it is submitted that a charge under this subsection would be the more appropriate. (Although in *R* v *Holt* [1981] 2 All ER 854, the Court of Appeal was not prepared to entertain detailed defence arguments concerning the differences between the subsections. Provided that it could be established that an offence under s. 2 had been committed, the court was not concerned if the charge was brought under s. 2(1)(a) or s. 2(1)(b).)

The final relevant offence is s. 1 of the Theft Act 1978, and this could apply as Peter is given free investment advice for which he would normally have to pay. This could constitute the offence of obtaining services by deception, which under s. 1(2) involves the obtaining of services where the other is induced to confer a benefit by doing some act or permitting some act to be done, on the understanding that the benefit has been or will be paid for. Certainly the investment advice is a service, and as it is normally paid for the offence would appear to be made out. However, commentators maintain that where D induces P by deception to render for nothing a service for which P would normally charge, D commits no offences under s. 1. The essence of s. 1 is that someone has been or will be paid, and the deception has to be directly related to this consequence: see further *R* v *Sofroniou* [2003] EWCA Crim 3681, where it was held that a 'putative mutual understanding as to payment' was required.

Thus the more appropriate charge would again be under s. 2, as s. 2(1)(c) provides that Peter would be evading liability, if he 'dishonestly obtains any exemption from or abatement of liability to make a payment'. Thus in *R* v *Firth* (1990) 91 Cr App R 217, a surgeon who evaded liability by failing to disclose that certain of his patients were private patients for whom he would otherwise have had to pay hospital fees, was found guilty under this provision.

In relation to the offences under ss. 1 and 2 of the Theft Act 1978 the prosecution would have to prove that Peter was dishonest. This should not present a problem on the facts of this case, but on authority of *R* v *Ghosh* [1982] 2 All ER 689 the jury must consider two questions:

(a) Were Peter's actions dishonest according to the ordinary standards of reasonable and honest people? If not, Peter is not guilty.

(b) If they were, did Peter realise that reasonable and honest people would regard what he did as dishonest? If so, he is guilty; if not, he is not guilty.

Q Question 3

Paul is very short of money and decides to remedy the situation. He sees an open window of a house and enters with a view to stealing anything inside which he might find of value. However, after examining the contents he decides that there is nothing worth anything to him and he leaves without taking anything.

He then meets Steve, who is having an affair with a secretary. Paul tells Steve that unless Steve gives him £500 he will tell Steve's wife about the affair. Steve replies that, as his wife already knows, he will give Paul nothing.

While driving home, Paul is stopped by the police who find a crow bar and other items which could be used for burglary, and Paul admits that he intended to use them to gain access if he found an unoccupied property.

Discuss the criminal liability of Paul.

Commentary

At first glance this appears to be a question on attempt, as Paul has not succeeded in his criminal ventures. Although this topic should be mentioned briefly, the answer must concentrate on three substantive offences under the Theft Act 1968, namely: burglary (s. 9), blackmail (s. 21), and going equipped (s. 25). They do to some extent resemble the inchoate offences, as they do not require the accused to obtain anything in order to be guilty; but your answer must state that Paul will be guilty of the full offence, not merely attempt.

If you can avoid the pitfalls you should be able to obtain a high mark, as all you are required to do is demonstrate a knowledge of the basic ingredients of the three offences.

- s. 9, Theft Act 1968
  - *Attorney-General's References (Nos 1 and 2 of 1979)* [1979]
- s. 21, Theft Act 1968 — blackmail
  - *Clear* [1968]
  - *Lambert* [1972]
- s. 25, Theft Act 1968 — going equipped
  - *Rashid* [1977]
  - *Hargreaves* [1985]

:Q: Suggested answer

As a result of entering another's property with intent to steal, Paul will be charged with burglary. This is defined under s. 9 of the Theft Act 1968, and the relevant part in this case is s. 9(1)(a), whereby a person is guilty of burglary if he enters any building or part of a building as a trespasser with intent to commit any such offence as is mentioned in s. 9(2), which includes stealing or attempting to steal anything therein. Thus it is not necessary for the prosecution to prove that Paul actually stole something, only that when he entered he intended to steal something. This will be sufficient for the full offence of burglary, not simply an attempt.

Paul has clearly entered a building as a trespasser with the requisite *mens rea* for these ingredients of the offence (*R* v *Collins* [1972] 2 All ER 1105), and therefore the only doubtful issue is whether his conditional intent to steal is sufficient. This particular question has caused difficulties. In *R* v *Easom* [1971] 2 All ER 945, where the accused had taken and then (after rifling through its contents) abandoned a ladies handbag, because there was nothing of value to him which he wanted to steal, his conviction for theft was quashed on the basis that his conditional intent was not regarded as an intention permanently to deprive for the purposes of theft. However, the position is different with burglary, as the law recognises the fact that most burglars do not intend to steal a specific thing, but will take anything they may find of value. The indictment should therefore state that Paul intended to steal 'some or all of the contents of the house'. On this basis, the Court of Appeal confirmed in *Attorney-General's References (Nos 1 and 2 of 1979)* [1979] 3 All ER 143, that the accused would be guilty of burglary. The fact that there is nothing in the building worth stealing is no bar to Paul's conviction.

Paul could also be charged with the offence of blackmail under s. 21 of the Theft Act 1968. Section 21(1) provides that a person is guilty of blackmail if:

> with a view to gain for himself or another or with intent to cause loss to another, he makes any unwarranted demand with menaces; and for this purpose a demand with menaces is unwarranted unless the person making it does so in the belief —
>
> (a) that he has reasonable grounds for making the demand; and
>
> (b) that the use of the menaces is a proper means of reinforcing the demand.

Paul has clearly made a demand, but this was not accompanied by the threat of physical violence, so can it be said that it was a demand with menaces? 'Menaces' was chosen by the Law Commission in preference to 'threats', as being the most appropriate term for blackmail, and was defined in *Thorne* v *Motor Trade Association* [1937] AC 397 as 'not limited to threats of violence but . . . including threats of any action detrimental to or unpleasant to the person addressed'. Further, it is not necessary for the prosecution to prove that the victim was affected by the demand, merely that it was of such a nature and extent that the mind of an ordinary person of normal stability and courage might be so influenced or made apprehensive as to accede unwillingly to the demand. Thus in *R* v *Clear* [1968] 1 All ER 74, an accused who demanded money from a litigant (for giving evidence) in a civil case was convicted of blackmail, although the victim was unaffected by the demand as his insurance company had agreed to settle any damages award.

A threat to tell Steve's wife could therefore be deemed a menace by the jury. Whether or not it is unwarranted depends on the accused's ability to convince the jury that he believed that he had reasonable grounds for making the demand and that the use of menaces was a proper means of reinforcing it. This is a subjective test, and in *R* v *Lambert* [1972] Crim LR 422 the trial judge directed the jury that they would find the menaces 'proper' if the accused honestly believed that they were proper. This again was a case where the accused demanded money as compensation for keeping quiet about a sexual liaison. If, on the other hand, the accused threatens to kill or harm the victim, he cannot claim that he thought this was 'proper' (*R* v *Harvey, Uylett and Plummer* (1981) 72 Cr App R 139). On the facts, it appears that Paul could not succeed with this argument; and as he has clearly made an unwarranted demand with menaces, it is submitted he will be found guilty of blackmail.

As Paul has equipment that could be used for burglary in his car, he could be charged under s. 25 of the Theft Act 1968 with 'going equipped'. Section 25 provides that a person shall be guilty of an offence if, when not at his place of abode, he has with him any article for use in the course of or in connection with any burglary, theft or cheat. From the prosecution's viewpoint, s. 25 has a great advantage over a charge of attempted burglary as for that offence the prosecution must prove that the accused has done more than a merely preparatory act (under s. 1(1) of the Criminal Attempts Act 1981). In practical terms this would require Paul to be on the very point of entering a particular property. Even this may not be sufficient, as in *R* v *Campbell* (1991) 93 Cr App R 350, the Court of Appeal quashed a conviction of attempted robbery where the accused was arrested on the entrance steps of a post office armed with an imitation gun and ransom demand, on the basis that as he was still outside the building his act was still only merely preparatory. No such difficulty arises under s. 25, and there have been convictions of British Rail stewards arrested on the way to their trains armed with sandwiches and coffee which they intended to pass off as British Rail products to passengers on the train (*R* v *Rashid* [1977] 2 All ER 237; *R* v *Corboz* [1984] Crim LR 302).

Paul would be able to argue that he lacked the necessary *mens rea* as he had not specifically formed the intention to use the equipment on a particular property. However, s. 25(3) provides that proof that the accused had with him any article made or adapted for use in committing burglary shall be evidence that he had it with him for such use; and in *R* v *Hargreaves* [1985] Crim LR 243, the Court of Appeal held that the prosecution had to prove only that the accused had formed the intention to use the article if a suitable opportunity arose.

Although it was recognised in *R* v *Bundy* [1977] 2 All ER 382 that a motor vehicle could in certain circumstances be a place of abode, it is submitted that it could not be in Paul's case as he was driving around in it at the time he was stopped. It is submitted that Paul has therefore committed all three offences: burglary, blackmail, and 'going equipped'.

Q Question 4

Ron knew that X had recently committed a serious criminal offence. He threatened to tell the police unless X gave him some property. As a result X gave Ron a watch, a ring and a lighter. Ron then gave the ring to Steve as a birthday present. He sold the watch at an undervalue to Trevor and asked William to look after the lighter for him until he wanted it returned. Steve, Trevor and William took these articles in good faith, not knowing how they had been obtained by Ron. However, three days later Ron told them the full story. Nevertheless, all three kept possession of the articles.

Discuss the criminal responsibility of Ron, Steve, Trevor and William.

Commentary

This is a difficult question requiring detailed knowledge of, and an ability to apply, the principles relating to handling stolen goods under s. 22 of the Theft Act 1968. In addition you need to be able to demonstrate an understanding of the relationship between s. 22 and theft (s. 1), with particular reference to the important protection for a bona fide purchaser for value contained in s. 3(2) of the 1968 Act. There are many important cases on these points which must be used to illustrate the application of the principles.

In addition you must also cover blackmail (Theft Act 1968, s. 21) and compounding (Criminal Law Act 1967, s. 5).

- Blackmail — s. 21, Theft Act 1968

- Compounding — s. 5(1), Criminal Law Act 1967

- Handling stolen goods — s. 22, Theft Act 1968
    - *Bloxham* [1982]
    - *Pitchley* [1972]
- Theft
    - s. 1, Theft Act 1968
    - s. 3(2), Theft Act 1968

:Q: Suggested answer

As a result of his dealings with X, Ron may have committed blackmail (Theft Act 1968, s. 21) and compounding (Criminal Law Act 1967, s. 5). Ron is guilty of blackmail if, with a view to gain for himself or another or with intent to cause loss to another, he makes any unwarranted demand with menaces; and for this purpose a demand with menaces is unwarranted unless the person making it does so in the belief:

    (a)   that he has reasonable grounds for making the demand; and

    (b)   that the use of menaces is a proper means of reinforcing the demand.

It is clear on the facts that Ron will have no defence to this charge and it appears he will also be guilty of compounding. Under s. 5(1) of the Criminal Law Act 1967:

> Where a person has committed an arrestable offence, any other person who, knowing or believing that the offence or some other arrestable offence has been committed, and that he has information which might be of material assistance in securing the prosecution or conviction of an offender for it, accepts or agrees to accept for not disclosing that information any consideration other than the making good of loss or injury caused by the offence, or the making of reasonable compensation for that loss or injury, shall be liable on conviction on indictment to imprisonment for not more than two years . . .

However, it is the possibility of charges under s. 22 of the Theft Act 1968 for handling stolen goods that will provoke the most argument. All four parties could be charged with this offence since, under s. 22(1), a person handles stolen goods 'if (otherwise than in the course of the stealing) knowing or believing them to be stolen goods he dishonestly receives the goods, or dishonestly undertakes or assists in their retention, removal, disposal or realisation by or for the benefit of another person, or if he arranges to do so'. Further, although the goods have been obtained by blackmail they are still regarded as stolen goods as a result of s. 24(4) of the 1968 Act.

Ron could be charged on the basis that he has assisted in the goods' disposal or realisation, by or for the benefit of another. As he has given the lighter to William only temporarily, to look after for Ron's benefit, this cannot constitute the offence; but his dealings with Steve and Trevor may satisfy this condition. The key case on this point is the House of Lords' decision in *R v Bloxham* [1982] 1 All ER 582. D had bought a car in good faith and later discovered that it had been stolen. He then sold it at an undervalue to V. As he had purchased in good faith he could not be guilty of theft, as a result of s. 3(2) of the Theft Act 1968 (the protection given to a bona fide purchaser), or of handling on the basis of dishonest receipt. But he was found guilty of handling on the basis that when he sold the car at an undervalue, he was assisting in its disposal for the benefit of another, namely the purchaser. However, their Lordships, in quashing his conviction and reversing the decision of the Court of Appeal, held that a purchaser of stolen goods is not 'another person' within the meaning of s. 22. So, although the sale was at an undervalue it was not deemed to be for the benefit of another. Thus Ron would not be guilty of handling as a result of the sale of the watch to Trevor.

Ron could use this argument if he was charged with handling as a result of giving the ring to Steve. However, in *Bloxham* their Lordships were clearly influenced by the fact that as D had bought in good faith and could not therefore be guilty of theft, it would be going against the spirit of the Theft Act 1968 to convict him of handling, where the maximum sentence is greater. Ron's position differs in this respect, and also in the fact that it is hard to argue that an outright gift benefits the donor and is not for another's benefit (i.e., the donee). It is therefore submitted that *Bloxham* can be distinguished and that Ron could be found guilty of handling in this instance.

Neither Steve, nor Trevor or William could be guilty of handling on the basis that they had dishonestly received the goods, but they may be found guilty on the alternative ground involving acting by or for the benefit of another. However, as Steve is given the ring as a present and keeps it for his own use, he is not doing an act for the benefit of another and cannot be found guilty of handling.

William, on the other hand, in keeping the lighter in custody for Ron, is clearly assisting in its retention for the benefit of another. Thus as soon as he knows the true position he has the necessary *mens rea* and would therefore be guilty. This was the case in *R v Pitchley* (1972) 57 Cr App R 30, one of the few cases where an omission to act was sufficient for the *actus reus* of the offence. There the accused had been given a sum of money to look after for his son. He received it in good faith and placed it in his bank account, where he allowed it to remain after discovering that his son had acquired it dishonestly. The court held that this was sufficient to constitute handling, on the basis that he assisted in its retention by or for the benefit of another.

As far as the crime of handling is concerned, Trevor would appear to be in the same position as Steve as he has not done an act by or for the benefit of another. However, there is a marked difference in their criminal responsibility for theft. This is because Trevor has the protection of s. 3(2) of the 1968 Act, which provides:

> Where property or a right or interest in property is or purports to be transferred for value to a person acting in good faith, no later assumption by him of rights which he believed himself to be acquiring shall, by reason of any defect in the transferor's title, amount to theft of the property.

The only way in which Trevor could be guilty is if the jury decided that as he bought the watch at an undervalue he was not acting in good faith and that s. 3(2) of the 1968 Act therefore does not apply.

Because Steve is not a purchaser he does not have the protection of s. 3(2). Further, under s. 3(1), 'appropriation' includes, where D has come by the property (innocently or not) 'without stealing it, any later assumption of a right to it by keeping or dealing with it as owner'. As the other ingredients of theft appear to be satisfied, it is therefore submitted that Steve will be guilty of theft.

Q Question 5

Alf is a general dealer who specialises in buying and selling secondhand watches. He does not have a house but eats, sleeps and lives in his dormobile while moving around the country. Bert is a rogue, who has obtained a gold watch worth £500 by giving Victor a stolen cheque which he knew would bounce.

Bert met Alf in a pub and sold him the watch for £25, no questions asked. Later, when Bert discovered the true value of the watch, he broke into Alf's dormobile and recovered it. When the police were investigating the incident they discovered safe-breaking equipment in the dormobile.

Discuss the criminal liability of Alf and Bert.

Commentary

This question tests general knowledge of several Theft Act offences. It does not require you to cover all aspects of the relevant offences in depth, but it does require an ability to deal thoroughly with specific principles.

You must cover s. 15 of the Theft Act 1968 (obtaining property by deception) and consider whether Alf could be committing the offence by deliberately paying Bert a sum which is much lower than the true value of the watch. Certainly Alf's expertise raises the possibility of handling stolen goods under s. 22 of the 1968 Act.

The precise status of Alf's dormobile must also be considered in relation to the offences of burglary (s. 9) and going equipped (s. 25). In this context the important case of *R* v *Bundy* [1977] 2 All ER 382 must be discussed.

- Deception — s. 15, Theft Act 1968
- Handling — s. 22, Theft Act 1968
  - *Bloxham* [1982]
  - *Silverman* [1987]
- Burglary — s. 9, Theft Act 1968
  - building — *B and S* v *Leathley* [1979]
- Going equipped — s. 25, Theft Act 1968

֎ Suggested answer

When Bert obtained the watch from Victor by giving him a cheque which he knew would bounce, he was committing the offence of obtaining property by deception. Under s. 15 of the Theft Act 1968: 'A person who by any deception dishonestly obtains property belonging to another, with the intention of permanently depriving the other of it, shall on conviction on indictment be liable to imprisonment . . .'. Since *R* v *Hazelton* (1874) LR 2 CCR 134, it has been recognised that by giving a cheque the accused represents that it will be met on presentation. As this did not happen there is a clear deception, and it also appears that Bert has acted dishonestly. This is a question of fact for the jury (*R* v *Feely* [1973] 1 All ER 341), but there is nothing to suggest that the prosecution would not be able to satisfy the test laid down by the Court of Appeal in *R* v *Ghosh* [1982] 2 All ER 689:

  (a) Was what was done dishonest according to the ordinary standards of honest and reasonable people? If not, D is not guilty.

(b)   If it was, did D realise that reasonable and honest people regard what he did as dishonest? If so, he is guilty; if not, he is not guilty.

Further, since the House of Lords' decision in *DPP* v *Gomez* [1993] 1 All ER 1, stating that D can appropriate property even when the owner has consented to D taking it, Bert would also be guilty of theft under s. 1 of the Theft Act 1968.

When Bert sold the watch to Alf, he may again have committed the offence under s. 15 of the 1968 Act. This is because a seller of goods impliedly represents that he has the right to sell the goods and can pass on a good title to the buyer (Sale of Goods Act 1979). As the watch is stolen, Bert cannot give a good title to Alf and there is therefore a deception. The only argument that Bert may have is that, Alf being a general dealer, he would have known from the low price that the goods were in fact stolen and therefore he was not deceived. However, even if this argument were to succeed, Bert could still be found guilty of an attempt to obtain property by deception under s. 1 of the Criminal Attempts Act 1981 as he has clearly done more than a merely preparatory act with the intention of committing the deception offence.

The fact that the watch is stolen property also raises the possibility of both parties committing offences under s. 22 of the 1968 Act:

> A person handles stolen goods if (otherwise than in the course of the stealing) knowing or believing them to be stolen goods he dishonestly receives the goods, or dishonestly under-takes or assists in their retention, removal, disposal or realisation by or for the benefit of another person, or if he arranges to do so.

Thus when Bert sold the watch, he was acting otherwise than in the course of the stealing (as this had already taken place when he obtained it from Victor), and it could be argued that he was assisting in its disposal for the benefit of another (Alf) when he sold it to Alf. This was the point of law for consideration in *R* v *Bloxham* [1982] 1 All ER 582, where the House of Lords decided that the seller of a stolen car, sold at an undervalue, was not acting for the benefit of another (the buyer) and could not therefore be guilty of handling. Therefore Bert will not be guilty as Alf, the purchaser, is not deemed to be 'another person' within s. 22 of the Act.

However, Alf may be guilty of handling under s. 22 if the prosecution can prove that he has the necessary *mens rea*. They must establish that he knew or believed the goods to be stolen; suspicion is not enough (*R* v *Grange* [1974] 1 All ER 928). This is a subjective test, but according to *R* v *Hall* (1985) 81 Cr App R 260:

> a man may be said to know that goods are stolen when he is told by someone with first-hand knowledge (someone such as the thief or burglar) that such is the case. Belief of course, is something short of knowledge. It may be the state of mind of a person who says to him-self 'I cannot say I know for certain that these goods are stolen, but there can be no other reasonable conclusion in the light of all the circumstances, in the light of all that I have heard and seen'.

As Alf is a general dealer with specialist knowledge of the value of secondhand watches, the jury may well conclude that in view of the low price agreed for the watch, he did know or believe the watch to be stolen, and that he dishonestly received it. In which case he would be guilty under s. 22. His expert knowledge could also mean that he was charged under s. 15 of the 1968 Act. It is difficult to envisage both parties being charged with deception arising out of the same transaction, but in *R v Silverman* (1987) 86 Cr App R 213, it was held that there was a deception by a builder who, knowing that he was being relied on to quote a fair price, deliberately obtained an extortionate sum from the victim. The prosecution could argue that as an 'expert' in this field, Alf knew that Bert was relying on him to offer him a fair price. However, it is submitted that in view of the nature of this business — buying and selling second-hand goods — it is unlikely that such an implied representation could be established.

When Bert breaks into Alf's dormobile and takes the watch, in addition to committing theft under s. 1 (dishonestly appropriating property belonging to another with the intention of permanently depriving the other of it) he may be committing burglary under s. 9. The prosecution will argue that he has entered a building or part of a building as a trespasser and has stolen something therein (in contravention of s. 9(1)(b) of the 1968 Act). It is submitted that Bert could not argue that he honestly believed that he had a claim of right in law to the watch and is therefore not dishonest (because of s. 2(1)(a)), and his only defence to burglary would be that the dormobile cannot be regarded as a building. There is no definition of 'building' under the Theft Act 1968, but it is generally taken to mean a structure of some substance and permanence. This could certainly include a dormobile, as in *B and S v Leathley* [1979] Crim LR 314 it was held that a freezer container detached from its chassis resting on railway sleepers and used to store frozen foods was a building. However, in practice the prosecution will not need to rely on this provision as s. 9(4) of the Theft Act 1968 states that 'building' shall also apply to an inhabited vehicle or vessel, and also at times when the person having a habitation in it is not there as well as at times when he is. Thus Alf's dormobile is a building and Bert will be guilty of burglary.

Lastly, Alf may also face a charge of going equipped under s. 25(1) of the Theft Act 1968: 'A person shall be guilty of an offence if, when not at his place of abode, he has with him any article for use in the course of or in connection with any burglary, theft or cheat.' However, Alf would be able to argue that his dormobile constitutes his place of abode. This was unsuccessfully argued in *R v Bundy* [1977] 2 All ER 382, where the accused was actually driving around in his car (which he claimed to be his place of abode) when arrested for the offence. Nevertheless, the Court of Appeal did recognise that a car could be a place of abode if it was on a permanent site, used as a place to live and D was not using another residence. It is submitted that as Alf's dormobile satisfies these conditions he would not be guilty of the offence under s. 25.

Q Question 6

Maysa, a vastly wealthy widow, is a neurotic anorexic with a pathological fear of being without a male partner. She meets Bluey through a dating agency. Bluey, aware of Maysa's wealth, declares his undying love for her, although in reality he is involved in a long-standing relationship with Sara, and is only interested in how much money he can get out of Maysa. Over the course of the next three months Maysa gives a total of £50,000 in cash to Bluey to reward him for his devotion.

Maysa then discovers that Bluey has been living with Sara for many years and asks him to return the money. Bluey, who has taken a number of nude photographs of Maysa with her consent, tells her that if she takes steps to recover the money he will send copies of the photographs to *The Stunna* a lurid national tabloid newspaper.

Maysa hires Ray, a private detective, to retrieve the pictures and negatives from the darkroom in Bluey's house. That night the part of Bluey's house that includes the darkroom is demolished in an explosion caused by a gas leak. No one is hurt in the blast, but the pictures and negatives are among the items destroyed. Ray discovers what has happened when he pulls up outside Bluey's house the following morning.

Advise the Crown Prosecution Service as to the criminal liability of: (i) Ray; (ii) Bluey; and (iii) Maysa.

Commentary

This question combines theft, blackmail, burglary plus some general principles of criminal liability. It is essential that a clear structure is adopted taking each of the incidents in turn. The issues relating to the £50,000 clearly require a good understanding of *R v Hinks*. Be prepared, however, to acknowledge situations where there may not be any criminal liability. Hence Bluey may not have deceived Maysa, or he may not have been dishonest. His demands may not be unwarranted. Where there are issues about accessorial liability, establish the liability of the principal offender before dealing with the liability of the accomplice. Note the difficult issue of impossibility arises because of the destruction of the pictures and negatives.

- Obtaining the money by deception

- Theft of the money

- Problems with appropriation — *R v Hinks*

- *mens rea* for theft

- Blackmail — whether demands warranted

- Attempted burglary — whether steps more than merely preparatory

- Whether any ulterior intent

- Maysa's liability as an accomplice

- Maysa's liability for conspiracy and incitement

:Ọ: Suggested answer

(a) Obtaining the money by deception

As a general rule, where the facts indicate that there may be liability for deception or theft the prosecution would be advised to consider deception first. Does Bluey obtain the £50,000 from Maysa by deception? The money is property belonging to another for the purposes of s. 15 Theft Act 1968 (see s. 4(1) and s. 5(1) of the 1968 Act). Bluey clearly obtains the money. Is there a deception? Bluey's declaration of love could be a deception by words — s. 15(4) includes a deception as to the present intentions of the party using the deception — but this could be too vague. The facts indicate that he was involved in a long-standing relationship with Sara, and was only interested in how much money he could get out of Maysa; but unless he confesses, how would the prosecution ever prove that he did not really love Maysa? If a deception can be shown, perhaps on the basis of the evidence given by Maysa, the prosecution would have to prove that it was operative. But for the deception would Maysa have given Bluey the money? Presumably not.

If the *actus reus* of s. 15 could be established, did Bluey have the *mens rea*? He clearly intended to deceive, and he intended to permanently deprive Maysa of the money. A jury might well regard him as dishonest following a direction based on *R* v *Ghosh* [1982] 2 All ER 689. The jury would have to consider two questions:

(a) Were Bluey's actions dishonest according to the ordinary standards of reasonable and honest people? If not, Bluey is not guilty.

(b) If they were, did Bluey realise that reasonable and honest people would regard what he did as dishonest? If so, he is guilty; if not, he is not guilty.

On the facts, the problem of proving a deception may well prove to be insurmountable, thus a s. 15 charge seems unlikely.

(b) Theft of the money

As an alternative the prosecution may decide to proceed with a theft charge under s. 1(1) of the Theft Act 1968. The money is clearly property, but whose money is it? If the property in the cash passes to Bluey, it would be difficult to show that he has appropriated property belong to another. Earlier cases such as *R* v *Mazo* [1996] Crim LR 435, proceeded on the basis that the receiver of a valid *inter vivos* gift could not be guilty of stealing it. This appeared to amount to a 'gloss' upon *R* v *Gomez* [1993] AC 442, suggesting that the *Gomez* approach to appropriation may only be relevant where there is evidence of fraud on the part of D. In *R* v *Hinks* [2000] 4 All ER 833, the House of Lords held, by a majority of 3–2, that the recipient of a valid gift could still be a thief, provided dishonesty was established.

Lord Steyn expressed the view that *R* v *Gomez* 'unambiguously ruled out' any submission to the effect that appropriation as defined in s. 3(1) of the 1968 Act could not occur where a gift of property was effected on the grounds that the entire proprietary interest would have passed to the recipient (i.e., the defendant). He went on to approve the approach taken in *Gomez* to the effect that 'appropriation' was a neutral word which should be taken to cover 'any assumption by a person of the rights of an owner'. This he felt was wide enough to encompass 'gift' situations.

The problem with the majority viewpoint in *Hinks* is that if one accepts, for the sake of argument, that there can be an appropriation even though the donor validly consents to D having the property, it must still be an appropriation of property *belonging to another*. It is not made clear how the property gifted to D by P remains property belonging to P. As Lord Hobhouse (dissenting) observed, D is not 'assuming the rights of an owner', when he appropriates the property, D has them already.

If the court applies *R* v *Hinks* as it is bound to do, a difficult problem arises whereby Bluey could be convicted of theft (subject to proof of *mens rea*) of the property received as a matter of criminal law, but would be able to resist moves to recover it as a matter of civil law, because in civil law the transfer would be valid and he would have an absolute title to it.

Assuming (for the purposes of criminal law) that the property remains property belonging to Maysa notwithstanding her gift, Bluey appropriates the money when he assumes the rights of the owner in respect of it — he can appropriate even though Maysa consents to his having it — *Gomez*.

Bluey may still escape liability on the basis that he was not dishonest at the time of the alleged appropriation. With reference to s. 2(1)(a) Theft Act 1968, did he appropriate the property belonging to another in the belief that he had in law the right to deprive the other of it? This is at least arguable — it was a valid gift to him. Did he act in the belief that he would have had Maysa's consent if she had known of the appropriation and the circumstances of it — (s. 2(1)(b))? This is less promising — especially if the circumstances include his true feelings. Alternatively Bluey could still escape liability following a *Ghosh* direction — as to which see above in relation to deception. Again Bluey's intention to permanently deprive is self-evident.

(c) Blackmail

Maysa's request for the return of the money does not, *prima facie*, indicate any liability. She does not make any threats about what she might do if the money is not returned.

Bluey may have incurred liability for blackmail contrary to s. 21 of the Theft Act 1968. Arguably he does make a demand — he is indirectly asking her to stop pursuing him for the money. A reasonable person would realise that a demand was being made — see *R* v *Collister and Warhurst* (1955) 39 Cr App R 100. The 'menaces' are evident. On the basis of *R* v *Clear* [1968] 1 QB 670, the threat is such as would influence the mind of an ordinary person of normal stability and courage so as to make them accede unwillingly to the demand.

Bluey's threat could indirectly be made with a view to gain — either keeping the pictures or the money. Under s. 34(2)(a)(i) Theft Act 1968 'gain' and 'loss' are to be construed as extending only to gain or loss in money or other property. The prosecution would have to prove that the demand was unwarranted. For these purposes a demand with menaces is unwarranted unless the person making it does so in the belief — (a) that he has reasonable grounds for making the demand; and (b) that the use of the menaces is a proper means of reinforcing the demand. The test is subjective. Does Bluey believe he has reasonable grounds for the demand?; does he believe that the menaces are a proper way of reinforcing the demand? It is significant that he is not threatening to commit a serious criminal offence if his demand is not met — see by contrast *R* v *Harvey* (1980) 72 Cr App R 139.

(d) Ray's liability

Ray could be charged with attempted burglary contrary to s. 1(1) of the Criminal Attempts Act 1981. The *actus reus* would require proof that he took steps more than merely preparatory to committing an offence contrary to s. 9(1)(a) of the Theft Act 1968 — entry into a building as a trespasser with intent to steal. Whether or not he took steps more than merely preparatory is a question of fact: see *R* v *Gullefer* (1990) 91 Cr App R 356, and *R* v *Geddes* [1996] Crim LR 894. Assuming this is made out, the prosecution would have to prove *mens rea* for the attempt — in this case that Ray intended to enter as a trespasser with intent to steal. There was clearly intention to enter, and it seems safe to assume that Ray would have known that he would have been trespassing had he done so. The uncertainty arises because he may not have had an intention to steal because he was not dishonest. Ray might argue that he was doing the 'right thing' by seeking to retrieve the pictures and negatives. Much would depend on the view of the jury following an *R* v *Ghosh* (above) direction. The impossibility of the enterprise will not afford Ray any defence to a charge of attempt — *R* v *Shivpuri* [1987] AC 1, makes it clear that the Criminal Attempts Act 1981 succeeds in imposing liability on a defendant who took steps that he believed would be more than merely preparatory to the commission of the offence, regardless of whether the commission of the offence was possible. In effect the defendant is judged on the facts as he believed them to be. As a residual offence Ray could be charged with having committed conspiracy to burgle with Maysa, unless it can be argued that the taking of the pictures and negatives would not have constituted theft (see above).

Neither party can raise impossibility as a bar to liability for statutory conspiracy — see the Criminal Law Act 1977 as amended by the Criminal Attempts Act 1981.

(e) Maysa's liability

Maysa could be charged with statutory conspiracy to steal or commit burglary contrary to s. 1(1) of the Criminal law Act 1977 (as amended), even though she does not intend to play any active part in the enterprise. This latter point is made clear by the Court of Appeal decision in *R v Siracusa* (1989) 90 Cr App R 340. Maysa could also be charged with counselling what transpires to be an attempted burglary. This is an unusual charge, but it is possible to be an accomplice to an attempt: see *R v Dunnington* [1984] QB 472. Given the facts, perhaps the most likely charge brought against Maysa would be incitement to commit burglary. Her suggestion reaches the mind of the incitee (Ray) and he knows that what is being incited would be a criminal offence (subject to the dishonesty issue). Maysa intends that he should carry out the suggestion.

The remaining query would be as to whether or not she could raise the defence of impossibility. When she made the suggestion the pictures and negatives were capable of being stolen. When Ray actually tries to retrieve them they have been destroyed. *R v Fitzmaurice* [1983] 1 All ER 189, suggests that where what is incited is impossible, in the sense that it could never be achieved, impossibility might afford a defence. (*Fitzmaurice* was seeking to give effect to a distinction identified by Lord Scarman in *DPP v Nock* (1978) AC 979.) As regards common law conspiracy, if there was an agreement to commit a crime capable of being committed in the way agreed upon, but frustrated by a supervening event making its completion impossible, impossibility would not afford a defence. Where, however, there was an agreement upon a course of conduct which could not in any circumstances result in the commission of the offence alleged, impossibility would be a defence. Applying that reasoning to Maysa's case, she should be advised that impossibility would not afford her a defence to a charge of incitement at common law. At the time of the incitement what Maysa suggested was not impossible to carry out. Supervening events made it impossible.

Further reading

Ormerod, D., 'A Bit of a Con?' [1999] Crim LR 789.

Smith, J.C., 'Obtaining Cheques by Deception or Theft' [1997] Crim LR 382.

Mixed questions

Introduction

The styles adopted for criminal law examination questions can vary enormously. Some examiners will set problem questions that focus largely on one area. Others will set mixed questions that cut right across the syllabus, perhaps in the hope that this will wrong-foot students who 'question spot'. A mixed question will, therefore, require knowledge of a wide variety of topics from different parts of the syllabus. Quite often these topics are unrelated, so you could have to deal with criminal damage, manslaughter, theft, conspiracy and duress in the same answer. Mixed questions will generally be of two types: (1) where you have to cover a vast number of issues briefly; (2) where you need to cover some issues briefly, but others in some depth. Type two questions are obviously the more difficult, as you have to decide which are the points requiring detailed discussion. However, this should be fairly obvious for the well-prepared student.

Because a mixed question may cover so many diverse points, it will often yield comparatively high marks. This is sometimes because a student who does not cover one particular point will not lose so many marks, as the student may do when tackling a question with only three or four major points to cover. So don't be intimidated!

In this chapter there are four typical mixed questions which have generally been answered well by exam students.

Q Question 1

Gerry is a member of the Animal Freedom Society, an organisation committed to total freedom for animals. He visits a local zoo and is so appalled by the conditions in the lions' cage that he saws through the iron bars thereby enabling a lion to escape. The marauding lion attacks and badly injures Sally, a passer-by. A police marksman, Bill, is summoned, but in trying to shoot the lion he negligently shoots Karen, a lion tamer, causing her to break her leg.

Discuss the criminal liability of Gerry and Bill.

Commentary

After quickly covering the relevant offences of theft and criminal damage, your answer must analyse in detail the possible offences against the person. The most obvious offences to consider are s. 18 and s. 20 of the Offences Against the Person Act 1861, but there is also s. 1(2) of the Criminal Damage Act to analyse. This is an odd offence, but one that the prosecution can more easily establish than s. 18 or s. 20, because of the applicable objective definition of recklessness.

The other major topic to consider is causation, as no doubt Gerry would argue that he is not responsible for any of the consequences of his actions. However, *R v Pagett* (1983) 76 Cr App R 279, if applied, could mean that he is deemed responsible for all of them. Bill, on the other hand, could not be guilty of any non-fatal offences against the person if he has only been negligent.

- **Criminal damage** — s. 1(1), Criminal Damage Act 1971

- **Theft** — s. 1, Theft Act 1968
    - dishonesty — *Ghosh* [1982]
- **Aggravated assault**
    - *Savage and Parmenter* [1991]
- **Causation**
    - *Pagett* [1983]
- **Aggravated criminal damage** — s. 1(2), Criminal Damage Act 1971
    - *R v G* [2003]
    - *Steer* [1987]

⚗ Suggested answer

Gerry's initial action in allowing the lion to escape could give rise to offences under the Criminal Damage Act 1971 and the Theft Act 1968. His possession of a saw could constitute an offence under s. 3 of the 1971 Act, i.e., being in possession of an article with intent to cause criminal damage, and when he cuts through the bars of the cage this would constitute criminal damage under s. 1(1) of the 1971 Act.

Because the lion has escaped, Gerry could be charged with theft under s. 1 of the Theft Act 1968, i.e., dishonestly appropriating property belonging to another with the intention of permanently depriving the other of it. He has committed an appropriation by assuming the rights of an owner (s. 3) and, although the lion is a wild creature, it is ordinarily kept in captivity and would be regarded as property belonging to another under s. 4(4) and s. 5(1). Gerry could argue that he was not dishonest as he believed it was wrong to keep lions in captivity. His arguments do not engage any of the negative definitions of dishonesty under s. 2(1)(a)–(c) of the 1968 Act, hence it would be a matter for the jury to resolve. Following the model direction suggested in *R v Ghosh* [1982] 2 All ER 689 they would consider the following questions:

(a) Was what was done dishonest according to the ordinary standards of reasonable and honest people? If not, D is not guilty.

(b) If it was, did the defendant realise that reasonable and honest people regard what he did as dishonest? If so, he is guilty; if not, he is not guilty.

Therefore, it will not be sufficient if Gerry thought he was not acting dishonestly, or that his fellow members of the organisation thought the same; he must believe that reasonable and honest people would so believe. This is certainly Gerry's best hope of avoiding a conviction for theft, as it is submitted that he could not claim he believed he had a right in law to the property (and was therefore not dishonest under s. 2(1)(a)) or that he had no intention permanently to deprive as s. 6 includes treating 'the thing as his own to dispose of regardless of other's rights'.

However, the more serious charges will arise out of the injuries sustained by Sally. As she is badly injured it is probable that Gerry would be charged under s. 18 of the Offences Against the Person Act 1861 with wounding or causing grievous bodily harm with intent. The prosecution must prove that Gerry had the necessary intention, and although this is a question of fact upon which the jury would generally require little or no guidance following *R v Moloney* [1985] 1 All ER 1025, it is submitted that on the facts this could present the prosecution with difficulties. They may therefore decide to prosecute under s. 20 of the 1861 Act, i.e., malicious wounding or inflicting grievous bodily harm.

At one time it was thought that the prosecution must prove that an assault took place before there could be a conviction under s. 20 (*R v Clarence* (1888) 22 QBD 23). However it has since been made clear by the House of Lords in *R v Wilson* [1983] 3 All ER 448 that this is not necessary.

Gerry could also argue that he did not cause Sally's injuries and is therefore not criminally responsible. However, the prosecution need only show that Gerry's action was a significantly contributing cause, not the main cause (*R v Cheshire* [1991] 3 All ER 670), and a jury directed to apply the 'but for' test would surely decide that Gerry had in law caused this consequence. On authority of *R v Pagett* it is also probable that Gerry would be held to have caused Karen's injuries. In this case the accused kidnapped his pregnant girlfriend and used her as a human shield when shooting at the police. A police marksman returned fire and one of his shots killed the girlfriend. Nevertheless the Court of Appeal upheld Pagett's conviction for manslaughter, holding that the return fire was a foreseeable act of self-defence and therefore could not constitute a *novus actus interveniens* breaking the chain of causation.

Turning to *mens rea*, s. 20 uses the word 'maliciously', and after much judicial debate the House of Lords decided in *R v Savage and Parmenter* [1991] 4 All ER 698 (following *R v Mowatt* [1967] 3 All ER 47) that it is sufficient that the accused intended or foresaw the risk of some physical harm. Although wounding or grievous bodily harm is required for the *actus reus*, only intention or foresight of some physical harm is necessary for the *mens rea* — another example of the criminal law's use of constructive crime.

Gerry might argue that he was so concerned about the plight of the lion that he did not even consider the risk of some harm; and although the prosecution could maintain that this was an obvious risk to the reasonable man, this state of mind would not be sufficient as subjective recklessness (i.e., conscious risk-taking) is required for s. 20. Even if the charge was only assault occasioning actual bodily harm under s. 47 of the 1861 Act, the prosecution would still have to prove intent or foresight on Gerry's behalf, albeit only for common assault (*R v Savage and Parmenter*).

As Bill is only negligent, he cannot be guilty of common assault or aggravated assault as he lacks *mens rea*. It is therefore just for Gerry to be held responsible for Karen's injuries, although whether he would be convicted of any of the above offences again depends on the prosecution being able to establish *mens rea*.

Because of these difficulties the prosecution would probably also charge Gerry under s. 1(2) of the Criminal Damage Act 1971 with intentionally or recklessly causing criminal damage being reckless as to whether life would be thereby endangered. The recklessness involved is subjective. *Metropolitan Police Commissioner v Caldwell* [1981] 1 All ER 961 is no longer to be followed, given the more recent decision in *R v G* [2003] 4 All ER 765. (In *Caldwell* Lord Diplock had stated that a person was reckless if he did an act which created an obvious risk of that consequence and had not given any thought to the possibility of there being such risk.) Unless Gerry was aware of the risk that life would be endangered, no liability can be imposed. A further difficulty for the prosecution is the condition that the danger to life must have resulted from the damage to property. Thus in *R v Steer* [1987] 2 All ER 833, the House of Lords upheld the Court of Appeal's decision to quash a conviction under s. 1(2) where the accused had fired a bullet, breaking a window and narrowly missing the victim, on the basis that it was not sufficient that the endangerment to life resulted from the accused's act which caused the damage to property. Although in *R v Webster and Warwick* [1995] 2 All ER 168 convictions were upheld under s. 1(2) when Webster damaged a train roof by throwing a coping stone on it, passengers being showered with debris, and Warwick broke a car windscreen with glass shattering over the driver, it is submitted that Gerry's case is covered by *Steer*. The prosecution might therefore fail on a charge under s. 1(2).

In conclusion, Gerry would definitely be guilty of offences under s. 1(1) and s. 3 of the Criminal Damage Act 1971, but there are many difficulties for the prosecution if seeking convictions for the more serious offences.

Q Question 2

Des parks his lorry in a suburban street and opens the driver's door without checking his mirror first. He is in a hurry as he is late for an interview for a job working as a deliveryman with Tardyco Ltd. Adrian is cycling down the road and is hit by the door of Des' lorry. He falls to the ground suffering lacerations to the head. Des notices what has happened to Adrian, offers his apologies, but rushes off without helping.

At the interview Des is asked about his previous work experience and whether he is suitable to work in a position of trust where he will be handling cash on behalf of his employer. He describes the jobs he has done, but remains silent about the fact that he was sacked from his last job for stealing goods from his employer. At the end of the interview Des is offered the job with Tardyco which he accepts there and then.

On his way back to his lorry Des finds a Tardyco staff discount card in the street. The card has been issued to an employee named Bert Figgis. The card entitles the holder to a 25 per cent discount on tyres at a local company called Ropey Remoulds. Des visits Ropey Remoulds and uses the discount card to save money on a new set of tyres for his lorry by producing the card when ordering the tyres. On returning home to his rented flat that evening Des finds a credit card statement showing that he owes £1,000 on his credit card. He writes 'addressee gone away — return to sender' on the envelope and sends the statement back to the credit card company. A week later Des moves to a new address without leaving any forwarding details.

Advise the Crown Prosecution Service as to the possible criminal liability of Des.

Commentary

This question features a mixture of assault and deception issues that should be dealt with largely in the order in which they arise. As with any assault questions it makes sense to start by looking at the harm done and then moving through the possible offences from the most serious down to the least serious. A particular point to note in relation to the deception at the job interview is the effect of silence as a deception. This is a tricky point that is popular with examiners. Most problem questions dealing with deception issues are straightforward in terms of the law to be applied. The test for candidates is in fact management. Look carefully at the order in which things happen — for example ensure that the deception precedes the obtaining. Do not make rash assumptions about deceptions being operative — apply the 'but for' test to determine whether the deception has really had any effect.

- Injuries to Adrian

- Possible s. 18 or s. 20, Offences Against the Person Act 1861

- Actual bodily harm as a residual offence

- Failure to act not causative — *R* v *Miller*

- Obtaining a pecuniary advantage by deception at the interview
  - query silence as a deception
  - query dishonesty
- Use of the discount card
  - obtaining exemption from a liability
- Avoiding debtors
  - making a creditor wait for payment
  - whether any intent to make permanent default

:Q: **Suggested answer**

(a) Injuries to Adrian

Adrian suffers lacerations to his head. The harm done could constitute a wound if the surface of the skin has been broken — see *JCC* v *Eisenhower* [1983] 3 WLR 537. There would appear to be no causation issues. Des causes the harm (however classified) in fact and there is no *novus actus interveniens*. If wounding is established Des could be charged under s. 18 of the Offences Against the Person Act 1861 — that he caused a wound with intention to do some grievous bodily harm. The problem with a s. 18 charge would be *mens rea*. The offence requires proof of intent to do some grievous bodily harm. *R* v *Woollin* [1998] 4 All ER 103, suggests this would involve Des fore-seeing grievous bodily harm as a virtually certain consequence of his actions. The facts do not suggest this. A less serious charge based around wounding would be malicious wounding contrary to s. 20 of the Offences Against the Person Act 1861. The mental element here requires proof that Des foresaw the possibility of some physical harm, albeit slight: see Diplock LJ in *R* v *Mowatt* [1967] 3 All ER 47.

On the facts it is possible that Des did not foresee any harm — especially if he was unaware of any other road user coming up alongside his lorry as he opened the door. Failing a s. 20 charge the prosecution may have to resort to s. 47 of the Offences Against the Person Act 1861. The charge would be that Des assaulted Adrian and thereby occasioned actual bodily harm. The prosecution might also be reduced to relying on s. 47 if wounding as described above cannot be established. Lacerations would certainly amount to the actual bodily harm: see *R* v *Miller* [1954] 2 QB 282, citing *Archbold* — actual bodily harm constitutes 'any hurt or injury calculated to interfere with the health or comfort of the [victim]'. The *mens rea* for s. 47 might yet prove problematic. *R* v *Savage*; *R* v *Parmenter* [1992] 1 AC 699, makes clear that Des only needs to have *mens rea* for the assault on Adrian; he need not have foreseen the actual bodily harm. Even so, Des must have intended the assault or be shown to have been reckless as to whether or not it occurred. The recklessness here is subjective — Des must have been aware of the risk. The problem for the prosecution is that Des might simply have failed to think about the risk of harm. The offence under s. 47 clearly requires subjective recklessness — there must be some evidence that Des was aware of the risk. There is the possibility, therefore, that Des may incur no liability at all in relation to the injuries he causes Adrian to suffer.

The fact that Des fails to help Adrian once he realises what he has done is suggestive of a culpable omission. To paraphrase the explanation given by Lord Diplock in *R* v *Miller* [1983] 1 All ER 978, a defendant's failure to act is capable of giving rise to criminal liability where he fails to take measures that lie within his powers and where those measures could counteract a danger that he has himself created. It is essential that, at this moment of awareness, it lies within his power to take steps, either himself or by calling for the assistance of others, to prevent or minimise the harm in question. On the facts, however, there is no evidence to suggest that the failure to help Adrian actually makes the injuries any worse. Unless the omission can be shown to be causative of further harm it cannot be the basis of liability.

(b) Deception at the interview

The most appropriate offence in relation to Des' behaviour at the interview is obtaining a pecuniary advantage by deception, contrary to s. 16 of the Theft Act 1968. The job in question is clearly a pecuniary advantage as defined by s. 16(2) of the 1968 Act — it is an opportunity to earn remuneration. The problem for the prosecution lies in establishing a deception on the part of Des. He does not make a statement of fact that he knows to be untrue. The deception lies in his failure to bring to the attention of the panel the circumstances in which he lost his previous job.

There are authorities that provide that silence can be a deception — see *DPP* v *Ray* [1974] AC 370 and *R* v *Rai* [2000] 1 Cr App R 242, but these are both 'changed circumstances' cases where the defendant fails to advise another party of circumstances that have changed since a decision in his favour was made. Des is not directly asked about the reasons for leaving his previous job and as a consequence does not provide them. It could be argued that unless he was under a positive legal duty to reveal the information he cannot incur criminal liability for omitting to reveal the information. On the other hand the prosecution will argue that, had Tardyco known the truth they would not have employed Des. Whether or not there is a deception here is, therefore, a moot point.

Even if deception is established Des may argue that he was not dishonest in failing to reveal why he lost his previous job. The test here will be based on the direction in

R v *Ghosh* [1982] QB 1053 — whether according to the ordinary standards of reasonable and honest people Des acted dishonestly in failing to reveal his past? If 'No' Des must be acquitted. If 'Yes' the question will be whether or not Des must have realised that what he was doing was by those standards dishonest. As ever it is very hard to predict what view a jury might take applying this test. Des might argue that he wants to 'go straight' and knows he would never get another job if he revealed the truth. He might also argue that he believed it was up to Tardyco to obtain references if they wanted to investigate his background, especially as the job he applies for is a position of trust.

(c) Use of the discount card

The use of the discount card by Des would be most appropriately charged as an offence contrary to s. 2(1)(c) of the Theft Act 1978 — that he, by deception, dishonestly obtained an exemption from a liability to make a payment. This offence is appropriate because at the time he used the card he had no existing liability to pay for the tyres. The card is used before the contract is entered into. The deception arises from Des purporting to be the cardholder. It is operative because, it is presumed, Ropey Remoulds would not have accepted the card if they had known Des was not entitled to use it. The deception comes before the acceptance that Des is entitled to a discount. A jury would be likely to regard Des as dishonest when directed in accordance with *Ghosh* as outlined above. The only argument Des could raise is that he had just been given a job with Tardyco and hence was entitled to an employee discount card. It is impossible to say if this would be enough to sway a jury in his favour.

In theory, following *R* v *Hinks* [2000] 4 All ER 833, Des could be charged with theft of the tyres even though he purchased them. In *R* v *Hinks* the House of Lords held (3 : 2) that a defendant could be guilty of theft even though he acquired an indefeasible title to property if the circumstances of his doing so indicated that he had been dishonest. It is submitted that proving dishonesty would be difficult and that in any event resort to tortuous reasoning based on bloated concepts of appropriation is unnecessary where there are perfectly adequate deception charges that can be brought.

(d) Non-payment of the credit card bill

By returning the credit card statement in the manner described Des may have committed an offence contrary to s. 2(1)(b) of the Theft Act 1978 — namely, by deception, and with intent to make permanent default in whole or in part on any existing liability to make a payment, he dishonestly induces the credit card company to wait for payment or forgo payment. The bill is the existing liability. The comments on the statement would be the deception. There are difficulties however. Is the statement untrue? Des is moving away, but at the time he writes the comments he clearly has not gone away — hence this could be the deception, an untrue statement of fact. What is the effect of these words? If it takes longer for the credit card company to receive payment then it will have been induced to wait for payment as required by the offence. Dishonesty seems evident, the only live issue therefore being whether or not Des intended to make permanent default. Is he simply trying to buy some time or is he trying to shake off his creditors completely? This is a question of fact that would have to be determined by the courts.

Q Question 3

Joy is hosting a fireworks party in her garden. She drinks a large quantity of alcohol and becomes very drunk. Fiona, a guest at the party who has not been drinking, encourages Joy to throw a large firework over the hedge into the next door neighbour's (Leonora's) garden. The firework hits Leonora who is badly burnt. Leonora's partner Sanjeet decides to exact revenge on Joy. The next morning, when Joy's milk is delivered, Sanjeet hides the bottles in the bushes in her garden. When she eventually finds them the milk has gone sour. Sanjeet also lets the air out of the tyres on Joy's car causing them to go flat.

A few days later Sanjeet persuades Allan to make a series of threatening and abusive telephone calls to Joy. Allan agrees to do this but, unknown to him, he repeatedly dials the wrong number leaving his threatening messages on the answer-phone of Pauline, a frail elderly woman who lives alone. Pauline is terrified by these calls, becomes depressed, and has to receive psychiatric help for the resultant neuroses.

Advise the Crown Prosecution Service as to the possible criminal liability of Joy, Fiona, Sanjeet and Allan.

You should ignore, for the purposes of this question, offences under the Protection from Harassment Act 1997, and offences relating to explosives and the misuse of public telephone systems.

Commentary

A question that brings in so many issues, any candidate would be hard pressed to provide much more than a cursory examination of each point in the time allowed in most examinations. If this were set as a course work question with a reasonable word limit rather more could be achieved. The more issues there are, the more important it becomes for candidates to isolate them clearly and deal with them in a logical order — the use of sub-headings is generally to be welcomed. Most of the criminal damage issues are very straightforward, as is the theft — but do not make the mistake of dwelling at length on non-contentious points. The main issue there is intention to permanently deprive. The accessorial liability issues raise some tricky points. Many exam questions deal with a deliberate departure from the common design, but candidates should also be aware of the rules on accidental departure from the common design. As this question demonstrates, general issues such as intoxication and transferred malice can be inserted just about anywhere by an examiner.

- Joy — s. 18/s. 20, Offences Against the Person Act 1861 — *mens rea* and intoxication
- Section 47 as a residual offence
- Fiona — accomplice — accidental consequences of the common design
- Sanjeet — theft of milk — intention to permanently deprive
- Sanjeet — criminal damage to milk and tyres — note *R* v *G*
- Allan — psychological injury — transferred malice
- Sanjeet — accomplice — different victim — deliberate or accidental?

:Q: Suggested answer

(a) Joy's liability for the injuries to Alison

An examination of Joy's liability in respect of the harm caused to Alison must start by considering the harm done. The expression 'badly burnt' is suggestive of grievous bodily harm, thus opening up the possibility of offences contrary to both s. 18 and s. 20 of the Offences Against the Person Act 1861. Under s. 18 there would have to be proof that Joy had caused grievous bodily harm — which for these purposes would be satisfied by evidence that the burns constituted serious harm: see *R* v *Saunders* [1985] Crim LR 230. There are no causation issues. The throwing of the firework causes the harm in fact and there is no evidence of any *novus actus interveniens*.

The problem for the prosecution would be as regards the *mens rea*. Did Joy intend to cause grievous bodily harm to any person? Unless there is evidence that Joy foresaw such harm as virtually certain (see *R* v *Woollin* [1998] 4 All ER 103) there will be no basis for a s. 18 charge. Proof of such foresight seems unlikely, especially if the throwing of the firework was meant as a prank. Further problems would arise under s. 18 in respect of Joy's alcohol consumption. The offence is one of specific intent — hence if Joy was intoxicated i.e., she could not and did not form the specific intent because of her self-induced intoxication — she cannot be guilty of the s. 18 offence: see *DPP* v *Majewski* [1976] 2 All ER 142. Whether or not Joy was so intoxicated will be a question of fact for the jury.

Bearing these points in mind a charge under s. 20 of the Offences Against the Person Act 1861 would seem more promising. The prosecution will have to prove that Joy maliciously inflicted grievous bodily harm on Alison. The harm will be made out as discussed above in the context of s. 18. For all practical purposes the term 'inflicting' can be regarded as synonymous with 'causing' see *R* v *Burstow*; *R* v *Ireland* [1998] AC 147. The mental element here requires proof that Joy foresaw the possibility of some physical harm, albeit slight, occurring to someone as a result of her actions: see *per* Diplock LJ in *R* v *Mowatt* [1967] 3 All ER 47. On the facts it is possible that Joy did not foresee any harm — especially if she gave no thought to the possibility of there being anyone on the other side of the hedge. If Joy was intoxicated, she could still incur liability under s. 20 (a basic intent crime) if there is evidence that she was reckless in becoming intoxicated and, as a result, was unaware of a risk of physical harm being caused that she would have been aware of had she been sober: see *DPP* v *Majewski* (above), and subsequent decisions such as *R* v *Richardson and Irwin* [1999] Crim LR 494 and *R* v *Hardie* [1984] 3 All ER 848.

If the harm done does not amount to grievous bodily harm, or the *mens rea* for s. 20 cannot be established, Joy may be charged under s. 47 of the Offences Against the Person Act 1861 — that she assaulted Alison (i.e., assaulted and/or battered) and thereby occasioned actual bodily harm. The burns would undoubtedly satisfy the definition of actual bodily harm: see *R* v *Miller* [1954] 2 QB 282. The only *mens rea* required would be the intention to assault or recklessness, but it is subjective recklessness: see *R* v *Cunningham* [1957] 2 QB 396. Joy must have been aware of the risk that another person might be assaulted or battered by her actions. There would be no need to show that she foresaw any actual bodily harm: *R* v *Savage*; *R* v *Parmenter* [1992] 1 AC 699. Again s. 47 is a basic intent crime — hence the comments above regarding the significance of intoxication in relation to s. 20 apply here.

(b) Fiona's liability as an accomplice to Joy

Fiona encourages Joy to throw the firework and can thus be described as someone who abetted the offence by Joy — i.e., Fiona was at the scene of the crime and spurred Joy on. Fiona will argue that she did not think that anyone would be hurt, but this will not avail her. An accomplice will be a party to all the unforeseen or accidental consequence of the agreed course of conduct carried out by the principal offender. In the present case Joy does precisely what Fiona suggests she should do, hence Fiona will be a party to the resulting offences: see *R* v *Betts and Ridley* (1930) 22 Cr A-p R 148 and *R* v *Baldessare* (1930) 22 Cr App R 70. It is possible that Fiona, as an accomplice, may be charged with and found guilty of a more serious offence than that which Joy is charged with. Note that Fiona is sober — hence she may be capable of greater foresight of harm occurring to another. There is nothing in principle to prevent Fiona being charged with a more serious offence than that charged against Joy.

(c) Sanjeet's liability regarding the milk

Sanjeet may be guilty of theft of the milk. It is clearly property belonging to another: see s. 4(1) and s. 5(1) of the Theft Act 1968. He appropriates the milk by hiding it: see

s. 3(1) of the 1968 Act. Any assumption of any right of the owner can amount to an appropriation of property. It is hard to see any argument by which he could claim not to be dishonest. The only issue here is intention to permanently deprive. Sanjeet will argue that he had no such intention, but s. 6(1) of the Theft Act 1968 provides that even if he did not actually intend Joy to permanently lose the milk, his dealing with it can be *regarded* as evidence of his having the intention of permanently depriving her of it, because he chose to treat the milk as his own to dispose of regardless of Joy's rights. *R* v *Cahill* [1993] Crim LR 141, suggests that removing another's property to another place as a prank falls outside s. 6(1) but the courts are likely to follow *DPP* v *Lavender* [1993] Crim LR 297, which suggests that such action can be theft. The perishable nature of the commodity will strengthen the prosecution case on this point.

In the event that intention to permanently deprive poses a problem, note that the damage to the milk could also provide the basis for a criminal damage charge contrary to s. 1(1) of the Criminal Damage Act 1971.

(d) Sanjeet's liability regarding the deflated tyres

Deliberately deflating the tyres could be criminal damage contrary to s. 1(1) of the Criminal Damage Act 1971 — the point to note here is that the tyres can be 'damaged' simply by being altered. The *mens rea* is evident. A charge of aggravated criminal damage contrary to s. 1(2) might also be considered, but if the car cannot be driven because the tyres are flat it would be difficult for the prosecution to prove that Sanjeet intended to endanger life or was reckless as to whether his action would have that effect. Tampering with the brakes, by contrast, would support a s. 1(2) offence. It should be noted that, following *R* v *G* [2003] 4 All ER 765, the recklessness involved in the offence of criminal damage is subjective — hence Sanjeet would have to be aware of the risk of damage to the property, or that life would be endangered thereby.

(e) Allan's liability regarding the telephone calls

Lord Steyn in *R* v *Burstow*; *R* v *Ireland* [1998] AC 147, held that both grievous bodily harm and actual bodily harm could take the form of neurotic disorders induced by a defendant's conduct. It was also accepted in that case that such harm could be caused without any direct assault on the victim by the defendant. Whether a case involved grievous bodily harm or actual bodily harm would simply be a matter of degree. The House of Lords also held in that case that although in s. 47 actual bodily harm cases an assault had to be proven, it could be committed by the use of words alone, by a telephone call, even by a silent telephone call. The prosecution would have to prove, however, that the victim apprehended *immediate* physical violence as a result of the telephone calls. On this basis Allan could be charged under s. 20 or s. 47 in respect of the harm he causes to Pauline. There is no problem in relation to causation. As to *mens rea*, the fact that he telephones the wrong victim by accident is irrelevant — the principles of transferred malice would apply, the identity of the victim being irrelevant: see *R v Latimer* (1886) 17 QBD 359. Problems might arise under s. 20 in establishing that Allan acted maliciously: see *R v Mowatt* (above). He might not have foreseen the risk of any physical harm occurring to anyone. On this basis a s. 47 charge seems more likely. The only *mens rea* requirement would be evidence that Allan foresaw the risk of another person apprehending immediate physical violence as a result of his telephone calls. Whether or not this could be established would depend to a large extent on the evidence of what he said when making the calls. The statement 'I am coming to fire bomb your house in two minutes' would be an example of a threat where the required intent would probably be made out.

(f) Sanjeet's liability as an accomplice to Allan

Sanjeet counsels Allan in the commission of the offences against Pauline in the sense that he persuades him to make the calls — there is a connection between Sanjeet's requests and the actions of Allan. Allan acted within the scope of the authority given by Sanjeet: see *R v Calhaem* [1985] 2 All ER 266. That Allan hurts Pauline, not Joy, is irrelevant. Only if Allan had deliberately chosen a different victim would Sanjeet have escaped liability as an accomplice; see *R v Saunders and Archer* (1573) 2 Plowd 473, as applied in *R v Leahy* [1985] Crim LR 99. Sanjeet contemplates the actions of Allan that cause the harm to Pauline, hence Sanjeet has the *mens rea* to be an accomplice. There is no deliberate departure from the common design by Allan.

Q Question 4

Marvin owes £5,000 to Paul, a drug dealer with a formidable reputation for resorting to violence against those who cross him. Paul tells Marvin that he must get the money he owes or he will have Marvin tortured and killed.

Marvin decides to burgle Harriet's house. Hoping to avoid any trouble Marvin watches the house to see when it might be unoccupied. Having called at the house to check that there is no one in, Marvin enters via an unlocked ground floor window. Unknown to Marvin, Harriet is at home. She had been fast asleep upstairs when he had earlier knocked on the door. On confronting Marvin, Harriet attacks him with a hammer. Seeking to protect himself Marvin pushes Harriet downstairs. She suffers a fractured skull when her head hits the stone floor.

Advise the Crown Prosecution Service as to the possible criminal liability of Marvin and Paul. You are not required to consider Harriet's liability.

How, if at all, would your answer differ if:

(a) Marvin had taken a large quantity of cocaine prior to the burglary in order to give himself the courage to carry it out?;

(b) Paul had told Marvin to burgle Harriet's house?

Commentary

This question explores issues such as burglary, assault, self-defence, duress and accessorial liability. Given the debate regarding the right of householders to defend themselves against burglars, examiners will quite commonly use a question like this — and as will be seen it is not free from difficulty.

It is important to read the instructions carefully. Two very common errors with questions such as this are: first to advise on Harriet's liability despite the clear statement in the question instructing candidates not to do this; secondly, to assume that Harriet has died, thus necessitating advice on liability for homicide. Saving (one hopes) rare cases where an examiner has been sloppy in drafting a question, candidates should assume that a victim has not been killed unless the facts of the question make this explicit.

This question also provides a warning about the way in which duress issues might arise — note the distinction between duress *per minas* and duress of circumstances.

Finally, there are some tricky issues here regarding the extent to which an accomplice can be held responsible for the actions of a principal offender. Candidates should distinguish clearly between issues of law, upon which they can be expected to advise, and issues of fact that should be left to the jury to determine.

- Marvin — burglary — s. 9(1)(a), Theft Act 1968 — conditional intent

- Section 18 and s. 20, Offences Against the Person Act 1861, against Harriet — availability of self-defence where D is 'in the wrong'

- Duress *per minas* — no crime nominated

- Duress of circumstances — policy limitations where self-induced

- Paul's liability — not accessorial — blackmail — assault by words

- Marvin's liability if intoxicated — specific/basic intent dichotomy — *DPP* v *Majewski*

- Paul specifies burglary — Marvin has duress *per minas* — Paul as a counsellor

- Query extent of Paul's accessorial liability

⚙ Suggested answer

(a) Marvin burgles Harriet's house

Marvin clearly enters a dwelling as a trespasser and with intent to steal: see s. 9(1)(a) of the Theft Act 1968. The fact that he does not have a specific item in mind that he wants to steal does not prevent him from having a present intention to steal:

see *Attorney-General Refs (Nos. 1 and 2 of 1979)* [1980] QB 180. This rather liberal reading of the 1968 Act reflects the reality that most burglars enter a property hoping that there will be something worth stealing — whether there is or not has no bearing on the burglar's state of mind at the point of entry. If it can be shown that Marvin entered prepared to use force if necessary he may also be said to have entered with intent to do some grievous bodily harm. His careful planning to avoid confrontation would militate against this, however. The *mens rea* for theft seems evident.

(b) The injuries to Harriet

Harriet's fractured skull would be grievous bodily harm — i.e., serious harm: *R v Saunders* [1985] Crim LR 230. Marvin has caused this harm — there is no suggestion of a *novus actus interveniens*. Whether Marvin had the intent necessary for the offence under s. 18 of the Offences Against the Person Act 1861 will depend on whether there is evidence that he foresaw grievous bodily harm as virtually certain to result from his actions: applying *R v Woollin* [1998] 4 All ER 103. It is submitted that unless such foresight can be shown the jury would not be entitled to infer the intent required by s. 18. The facts suggest this may be doubtful. An alternative charge under s. 20 of the Offences Against the Person Act 1861 would be maliciously inflicting grievous bodily harm. Marvin must be shown to have foreseen at least the possibility of physical harm occurring to Harriet: see *R v Mowatt* [1967] 3 All ER 47. An intention merely to frighten her would not suffice: see *R v Sullivan* [1981] Crim LR 46. These decisions were confirmed by the House of Lords in *R v Savage; R v Parmenter* [1992] 1 AC 699. On the facts the *mens rea* for s. 20 would seem to be beyond doubt, hence a s. 20 charge would be appropriate.

Marvin could raise the defence of self-defence, although the jury is likely to look askance at any burglar who seeks to rely on this. Marvin will argue that Harriet's actions were excessive and thus unlawful. He was therefore attempting to prevent harm to himself arising from an unlawful attack. On the basis of *R v Julien* [1969] 1 WLR 839, he will have to provide evidence that he did not want to fight and that he was prepared to 'temporise and disengage' — even run away — although *R v McInnes* [1971] 3 All ER 295 suggests that a failure to retreat is only one element of the various considerations upon which the reasonableness of an accused's conduct is to be judged. Ultimately it will be a question for the jury to consider whether the force used by Marvin was excessive. It is the force that should be considered, not the fact that Harriet suffered a fractured skull in the fall down stairs: see further *Shaw (Norman) v R* [2002] Crim LR 140.

(c) Duress

Marvin may try to argue that he was forced to commit the crimes by Paul and thus acted under duress. The courts will reject this, however. Paul threatened to kill Marvin if he failed to pay his debt. He did not threaten to kill him if he refused to commit a crime: see *R* v *Cole* [1994] Crim LR 582. Whilst this would rule out the defence of duress *per minas* — i.e., duress based on threats, Marvin may nevertheless try to argue that he is entitled to raise the defence of duress of circumstances: see *R* v *Martin* [1989] 1 All ER 652. The defence is available only if, from an objective standpoint, the accused can be said to be acting reasonably and proportionately in order to avoid a threat of death or serious injury. The jury should be directed to determine two questions: (i) was the accused, or may he have been, impelled to act as he did because as a result of what he reasonably believed to be the situation he had good cause to fear that otherwise death or serious physical injury would result? (ii) if so, might a sober person of reasonable firmness, sharing the characteristics of the accused, have responded to that situation by acting as the accused acted? Both questions would have to be answered in the affirmative for the defence to be made out.

Even if the trial judge allows the defence of duress of circumstances to go to the jury, the decision in *R* v *Harmer* [2002] Crim LR 401, presents a formidable obstacle to Marvin. The Court of Appeal held that the defence of duress was not available where a defendant voluntarily became involved with others and he could foresee that they might threaten him with unlawful violence. For this policy limitation on the availability of duress to arise there is no need for the prosecution to show that the defendant had foreseen that he would be forced to commit particular crimes. The decision follows the earlier Court of Appeal ruling in *R* v *Heath* (1999), *The Times*, 15 October.

(d) Paul's liability

At this stage Paul is not an accomplice to Marvin's offences, as he does not tell him that he must commit any crimes (see below). Paul did not order Marvin to commit a crime; neither did he encourage him to do so. In *DPP for Northern Ireland* v *Maxwell* [1978] 3 All ER 1140, Lord Scarman observed that an accomplice who leaves it to the principal offender to choose the offence to be committed will incur accessorial liability, but only where the choice is made from the range of offences from which the accomplice contemplates the choice will be made. Paul, if he has any sense, will presumably contend that he contemplated Marvin arranging a loan in order to repay the debt.

Paul may, however, be guilty of blackmailing Marvin. With reference to s. 21 of the Theft Act 1968, Paul makes a demand that is clearly supported by menaces. It is with a view to gain, as this encompasses the situation where a defendant makes threats in order to recover debts — see s. 34(2) Theft Act 1968 — and gain is to be construed as extending to keeping what one has.

To secure a conviction the prosecution will have to show that Paul's demand was unwarranted — i.e., that he did not believe he had reasonable grounds for making the demand; and he did not believe that the use of the menaces was a proper means of reinforcing the demand. As a violent criminal Paul may think death threats are a reasonable way of forcing indebted addicts to pay up, but *R v Harvey* (1980) 72 Cr A-p R 139, makes it clear that such demands can never be warranted. As Bingham J explained, no act, which was not believed to be lawful, could be believed to be proper within the meaning of the subsection: 'Where . . . the threats were to do acts which any sane man knows to be against the laws of every civilised country no jury would hesitate long before dismissing the contention that the defendant genuinely believed the threats to be a proper means of reinforcing even a legitimate demand.'

Paul will, therefore, be guilty of blackmail.

A further possible charge against Paul would be common assault. His words may have had the effect of causing Marvin to apprehend immediate physical violence. That an assault can be committed by words alone has been established by the House of Lords' decision in *R v Burstow*; *R v Ireland* [1998] AC 147. The *mens rea* required is intention or at least recklessness as to whether or not Marvin would apprehend immediate physical violence. Given that the threat is made in circumstances where Marvin is given the opportunity to go away and obtain the money it is hard to see how the element of immediacy can be satisfied on these facts. It is a moot point as to whether or not Paul could also be charged as an accomplice to the attack on Harriet. On the one hand he does specify that it is Harriet's house that should be burgled; on the other hand there is no evidence that he knows that Harriet is an elderly lady, or that he contemplates any violence being inflicted by Marvin. As a simple question of fact the jury can be asked to consider, using the *R v Bainbridge* [1959] 3 All ER 200, direction, whether or not Paul contemplated any offences of violence being committed. If he did not, Paul will argue that the use of force was a deliberate departure from what was counselled, and therefore Marvin was acting on his own.

How, if at all, would your answer differ if: (i) Marvin had taken a large quantity of cocaine prior to the burglary in order to give himself the courage to carry it out?

If Marvin was in a state of self-induced intoxication at the time he committed these offences he may be able to plead intoxication as a defence to specific intent crimes. For these purposes that would encompass the burglary offences and s. 18 of the Offences Against the Person Act 1861: see *DPP v Majewski* [1976] 2 All ER 142. There are no lesser-included offences in s. 9(1)(a) of the Theft Act 1968, hence Marvin would have a complete defence. His liability under s. 18 would be reduced to s. 20. It should be noted, however, that the courts have recognised exceptions in those cases where there is evidence that the defendant deliberately got himself intoxicated in order to have the courage to commit the crime: see *Attorney-General for Northern Ireland* v *Gallagher* 1963] AC 349. In such cases intoxication is not allowed even as a defence to crimes of specific intent.

Again Paul would probably avoid any liability as an accomplice as he had not ordered Marvin to commit a crime; neither had he encouraged him to do so.

(ii) Alternatively how, if at all, would your answer differ if Paul had told Marvin to burgle Harriet's house?

As regards Marvin, the defence of duress *per minas* could be available, but see comments above regarding policy limitations on the availability of duress defences where a defendant knowingly puts himself at risk of being threatened with death or grievous bodily harm. Paul could incur liability as an accomplice to the burglary on the basis that he counselled the commission of the offence. In *R v Calhaem* [1985] 2 All ER 266, the Court of Appeal explained that counselling did not require a causal connection between the counselling and the offence, there simply had to be a connection between the counselling and the offence committed by the principal offender. There seems little doubt that the actus reus of counselling is established on these facts. As to *mens rea*, *R v Bainbridge* (above), provides that it is sufficient that the accomplice contemplated the 'type' of crime committed by the principal offender. If the evidence is that Paul specified burglary there would seem to be little doubt about this.

Index